SHAMBHALA DRAGON EDITIONS

The dragon is an age-old symbol of the highest spiritual essence, embodying wisdom, strength, and the divine power of transformation. In this spirit, Shambhala Dragon Editions offers a treasury of readings in the sacred knowledge of Asia. In presenting the works of authors both ancient and modern, we seek to make these teachings accessible to lovers of wisdom everywhere.

The
Buddhist
I Ching

Chih-hsu Ou-i

Translated by Thomas Cleary

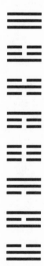

SHAMBHALA · BOSTON & LONDON · 2001

Shambhala Publications, Inc.
Horticultural Hall
300 Massachusetts Avenue
Boston, Massachusetts 02115
www.shambhala.com

9 8 7 6 5 4 3 2 1
Printed in the United States of America
⊗ This edition is printed on acid-free paper that meets the
American National Standards Institute Z39.48 Standard.
Distributed in the United States by Random House, Inc., and in
Canada by Random House of Canada Ltd

Library of Congress Cataloging-in-Publication Data
Chih-hsü, 1599–1655.
   The Buddhist I ching.
   (Shambhala dragon)
   Translation of: Chou i ch'an chieh.
   1. I ching.   I. Cleary, Thomas F., 1949–
II. Title.   III. Series.
PL2464.Z6C5313   1987   299'.51282   86-31460
ISBN 0-87773-408-9 (pbk.)

Contents

Translator's Introduction

This book is a reading of the classic *I Ching* by the noted Chinese Buddhist Chih-hsu Ou-i (1599–1655), an outstanding author of the late Ming dynasty whose work influenced the development of modern Buddhism in China. Ou-i uses the *I Ching* to elucidate issues in social, psychological, and spiritual development.

The *I Ching* is the most ancient Chinese book of wisdom, widely considered a basic guide for conscious living. While it has been extensively expounded by the traditional sociologists and psychologists of the Confucian and Taoist schools, the written records of Chinese Buddhism are nearly silent on the *I Ching*. Of course, several key phrases and signs were adopted into the commentaries of the Ch'an (Zen), Hua-yen, and other Buddhist schools, but no extensive explanation of the *I Ching* seems to have been written by a Buddhist until Chih-hsu Ou-i composed the present work in the seventeenth century.

When Buddhism came into China, it picked up certain key phrases from the Chinese classics to put forth its message in the local idiom. Among the classics Buddhists drew from was, naturally, the *I Ching*. Eleventh-century Ch'an Buddhists used well-known lines referring to effective adaptation, an axial Buddhist theme. Taoist reading of the *I Ching* is especially marked in the Ch'an-like *Treatise on the Avatamsaka Sūtra* by the lay adept Li T'ung-hsuan. The celebrated "Five Ranks" device of the ninth-century Ts'ao Tung (Sōtō) school of Ch'an was in some texts illustrated by trigrams and hexagrams from the *I Ching*, and this association was much elaborated by the Sōtō Zen monks of the seventeenth and eighteenth centuries.

I am not aware, however, of any text, before or since this one by Ou-i, that treats the *I Ching* in a systematic way from the point of view of Buddhist teaching and practice. Ch'an masters of the classic era seldom did systematic explanations of any text, but in the postclassical periods of Ch'an in China and other East Asian nations, there were people who combined scholarship with meditation and used their experience to elucidate not only Buddhist texts of all schools, but also classics of Confucianism and Taoism.

This sort of activity always seems to be heightened in pitch during times of degradation in the general tone of the civilization's consciousness, perhaps coinciding with relaxation or with crisis. Generally, the later teachers wrote much more than the earlier teachers. We usually have only hints of the colossal inner and outer learning of the ancients; of the learning of the later teachers, who also had more to study, we have evidence of intellectual effort that would be staggering by standards common today. In the case of Ou-i, as with other great Buddhists who took up scholarship, this was done as a part of religious practice, linking personal efforts with needs of the contemporary society.

The Ming dynasty was one such time of stress in China. The dynasty had started in the fourteenth century as a revolt against the Mongolian Yuan dynasty and ended in total overthrow by the Manchu Ch'ing dynasty in the mid-seventeenth century. During that time there were many civil wars, including numerous revolts led by Buddhist societies. There seem to have been very few creative, progressive leaders in the secular world, and intellectual growth was threatened by the imposition of institutionalized orthodoxy.

Though the upstart founder of the Ming dynasty had himself been a Buddhist monk, as he gained support among established sectors of society, he began to withdraw from his associations with the Buddhist order, particularly the *yao-seng*, or charismatic monks, who had considerable influence on a popular level and often brandished revolutionary visions. Attempts to control the clergy, particularly to control contact between the clergy and the populace, played an important role in the development of the forms of institutionalized Buddhism in this transition period between the postclassical and modern eras of Chinese Buddhism.

The face of religion was changing, it seemed, or different phases of religion were becoming visible. The Chinese Buddhists accepted Tibetan tantrism, and the powerful Complete Reality Taoists seemed to take up some of the ancient ways of Taoist tantrism. When the great T'ang dynasty was flourishing centuries before the Ming, tantric texts giving formulae for killing unjust kings were suppressed or changed, but in the Ming dynasty civilian armies rallied their personal attention and group solidarity around religious ideals, such as the coming of Maitreya, the future Buddha, as they fought to overthrow what they perceived as corrupt and oppressive "government."

A similar phenomenon occurred in Japan about this time, with the well-organized Pure Land and Sun Lotus Buddhist movements in the midst of the Warring States period of medieval Japan assuming both temporal and spiritual functions. In the Near East, the military organization known as the Janissaries was established, it is said, with the blessing of Sufi Hajji Bektash, revered as a saint by both Christians and Muslims. In Central Asia, the great conqueror Tamerlane, who like the Ming Chinese took up after the Jinggisid Mongols, was at once a relentless warrior and reveler, and a great patron of arts, sciences, and religions. He is said to have known Nasruddin, the Sufi counterpart of Ikkyu, the medieval Japanese Zen master who had at least three or four careers, and like Nasruddin knew the local conqueror of his time, one of the Ashikaga shoguns.

It would seem that one of the concerns of the time, therefore, was the "deposit" of knowledge that would allow humankind to survive in the future. Geniuses everywhere from Europe to East Asia seem to have deposited part of that knowledge right in the infrastructures of conflict (such as the martial arts), and then moved to balance this by developing culture to a high pitch. Thus we find great developments in liturgy, music, art, scholarship, and literature, often carried out by the same person or group. This whole process itself illustrates a principle of the *I Ching*, whereby waxing and waning balance each other.

There seems to be a general consensus among Buddhist writers that institutional Buddhism was in a severe decline in the Ming dynasty. Ou-i himself, commenting on the typical forms of degeneration among the various branches of Buddhist study, cites widespread ignorance, hypocrisy, and empty imitation as characteristic flaws of contemporary Buddhist clergy. This situation naturally created problems for those who sincerely tried to pursue Buddhist studies in a monastic context, but on the other hand it seems to have further stimulated Buddhist thinkers from a cloistered environment to reach out into secular life, continuing a trend strongly marked in the earlier Sung and Yuan dynasties.

The story of Qu-i's own life appears to be one of great struggle and effort, plagued by the difficulties of finding good teachers and companions in the Buddhist world. He wrote of himself that he did not have a fixed teacher, but tried to learn from everyone; eventually he read through the entire Buddhist canon, like others in similar positions, and attempted to extract the essence from all of the Buddhist teachings. Though he had no such institutional affiliation, Ou-i is commonly thought of as an outstanding latter-day exponent of T'ien-t'ai Buddhism, the great syncretic school of Chinese Buddhism combining study and exercise.

Ou-i's early exposure to Buddhism was, of course, through his cultural and family environment. Like most literate Chinese men, however, he devoted his early studies to Confucianism, in preparation for possible advancement through the civil service examination system. At the age of twelve he was already writing anti-Buddhist essays, a Confucian fashion that he seems later to have regretted very deeply.

A climax to Ou-i's Confucian studies was reached when he was twenty years old, while he was writing a commentary on the *Lun-yu* or *Analects of Confucius*, one of the basic classics. According to his own account, he became stuck on the expression "The whole world takes to benevolence" and was unable to think of anything else for three days and nights. Finally he experienced a mental opening and suddenly "understood the psychology of Confucius."

At that time, the orthodox school of Confucianism was the Ch'eng-chu school, a relic of the Sung dynasty, and like everyone aiming for a career in civil service through the official examination system, Ou-i began his studies in this school. Eventually, however, he came to prefer the new school of Wang Yang-ming (1472–1528), whose doctrines and methods were strongly influenced by Buddhism. After his awakening to the psychology of Confucius and following his interest in Wang Yang-ming's psychological Confucianism, Ou-i now began to practice Ch'an Buddhist meditation.

Ou-i's early attempts at meditation were not fruitful, and he consequently began to think that he would have to become a renunciate in order to succeed in his new spiritual endeavor. He thus became a Buddhist monk in his early twenties and once again set himself to the practice of meditation, using the *Śūraṅgama Sūtra* as a guide to handling the mental states that may arise during concentrated meditation.

This time Ou-i obtained dramatic results from meditation. In his autobiographical notes he records that he felt that his "body, mind, and world all disappeared." Subsequently, he continues, all the scriptures and *kung-an* (Ch'an Buddhist teaching stories) became obvious to him. Nevertheless, he says, he did not consider this the "enlightenment of sages," and did not tell anyone about it.

Several years later, at the age of twenty-eight, Ou-i fell seriously ill and in the midst of his life-and-death crisis found that his early realization was of no practical use to him. He then added the Buddha-name recitation practice of the T'ien-t'ai and Pure Land schools to his Ch'an meditation practice. He had been interested in Buddha-name recitation since his early twenties, and it was also fashionable in his time to combine silent and incantational meditation.

Still later, at the age of thirty-one, Ou-i met the distinguished Ch'an master Po-shan Yuan-lai (1575–1630). Yuan-lai explained to him the various characteristics of the progressive deterioration of Ch'an practice in their time, and this prompted Ou-i to give up Ch'an altogether. Now he began to concentrate intensely on Pure Land practice, restoration of the *vinaya* (monastic orders), and exposition of classic Buddhist scriptures and treatises.

During his thirties, Ou-i took up the practice of *mantrayāna*, the vehicle of mystic spells. Among the various spells he is known to have recited, the one to which he devoted the most effort was the spell of Kṣitigarbha, the bodhisattva associated with the salvation of those in hell. This spell is particularly focused on absolution, and Ou-i notes that he recited it approximately forty million times over a period of ten years.

It is recorded in Buddhist lore that mantrayanic practice is often associated with the development of extraordinary linguistic and mnemic skills, and it may have been this decade of intense spell concentration that enabled Ou-i to perform the tremendous feats of scholarship that he subsequently accomplished. Be that as it may, when Ou-i subsequently began to study esoteric tantric Buddhism in earnest and learned of the strict requirements of *mantrayāna* (to prevent the strengthening of bad qualities as well as good ones), he ceased to practice or encourage incantation, save incantation of the name of the Buddha of Compassion.

Also during his thirties, Ou-i suffered the final failure of his attempt to revive orthodox *vinaya* practice in China and at length even renounced his ordination, regarding it as technically illegitimate. He turned his attention to the Mahayāna *vinaya* in the *Brahmajāla Sūtra,* and, at the age of thirty-nine, while lecturing on this *sūtra,* he experienced another great realization. According to his account, he now saw that all the doctrinal differences among Buddhism, Confucianism, and Taoism were due to the fact that these teachings were nothing more than temporary means.

Finally, at the age of forty-six, under the impact of another serious illness, Ou-i again reevaluated his Buddhist practice and decided to devote himself to Pure Land Buddhism. An outstanding characteristic of Pure Land Buddhism is that it promises salvation through the simple invocation of a Buddha-name, regardless of other conditions. For Ou-i, intensely aware of both the temporal and the spiritual malaise of his time, personally burdened with a sense of guilt for his early repudiation of Buddhism, chronically unhealthy and often ill, and moreover regretful at having lost opportunities for personal cultivation because of his scholarly activities, to enter into Pure Land devotion would seem to be almost a matter of course. Ten years later he passed away, leaving a rarely matched legacy of Buddhist scholarship.

Considering the fact that Ou-i was in poor health almost all of his life, and was sometimes very ill for extended periods of time, his enormous literary output appears all the more incredible. In his teen years, when he began to write anti-Buddhist essays and Confucian commentaries, he is said to have composed over two thousand tracts, so his literary talents were apparently quite considerable even at this early age. He later burned all of these essays, so we have no idea of the state of mind of the young Ou-i, but his later work clearly demonstrates a formidable knowledge of Confucianism.

Aside from some miscellaneous works—letters, prayers, essays on Ch'an—he did not begin his Buddhist writings in earnest until he was nearly forty years old. By the end of his life—which was short in comparison with many other noted Buddhist teachers—he had composed over seventy-five works in some two hundred and fifty volumes.

About fifty of these works still exist, including a comprehensive guide to the Buddhist canon, useful compendia of major Buddhist systems, commentaries on Buddhist *sūtras* and *śāstras*, and interpretations of several native Chinese classics, including this work on the *I Ching.*

Chinese Buddhism in the Ming dynasty inherited a twofold tradition: there were the Chinese schools that had arisen between the fourth and eighth centuries, and the Tibetan schools that entered under the Yuan dynasty Mongolian rule during the thirteenth and fourteenth centuries. The old schools of Chinese Buddhism had more or less amalgamated by the Ming dynasty, depending on the type of practitioner—there were *vinaya* specialists, *sūtra* and *śāstra* specialists, and Yoga specialists, the latter including those reputed to have various kinds of ordinary and occult knowledge, generally working among the people.

The newer Tibetan schools apparently began to influence the Chinese when Tibet and China were both absorbed into the Mongolian Empire. The Ming dynasty was a native Chinese breakaway from Mongol rule, which maintained its own diplomatic relations with other nations, as many as thirty-three under the famous Yung-lo Emperor Ch'eng-tsu (r. 1403–1424), who was in contact with the Karmapa, a high incarnate lama of Tibet.

Under the native Chinese Ming dynasty, therefore, the connection between Tibetan and Chinese schools of Buddhism continued, marked by an increasing emphasis on ritual, prostration, and incantation practices. While the general form of Chinese Buddhist practice showed Tibetan influence, however, the contents of its rituals were taken not from the Indian esoteric tradition through the Tibetan or even the Chinese esoteric canon, but mainly from the liturgy of the T'ien-t'ai school, which had been formulated for the Chinese from Buddhist scriptures centuries before, in the Sui, T'ang, and Sung dynasties, from the late sixth to early eleventh century.

Ou-i was therefore very unusual among native Chinese Buddhists in having actually read the esoteric canon existing in the Chinese language. Nevertheless, he finally concluded that the living tradition of Tantra was no longer available in China (travel was difficult and limited in Ou-i's time, due to civil and international unrest in many areas) and this led to his decision to abandon Mantrayāna, except for the name of Amitabha Buddha, the Buddha of Infinite Light, the embodiment of compassion. The practice of reciting this name had been openly offered in *sūtra*s and *śāstra*s since time immemorial, and because it was associated with pure compassion, it could be considered the least dangerous of all *mantras*. This was the *mantra*, in fact, of the first native Chinese school, the Pure Land school founded by the great scholar and visionary Hui-yuan (334–416), originator of the first Lotus Society.

Furthermore, Ou-i found an esoteric plane in the work of the great Sung dynasty T'ian-t'ai writer Ssu-ming (960–1028), who revived the school eight generations after the last great master, Chan-jan (711–782). Ou-i made Ssu-ming's work one of his main sources on liturgy and ritual, and he also commonly used T'ien-t'ai terminology in dealing with other forms of meditation and other Buddhist practices as well.

This is certainly true of his commentary on the *I Ching*, translated in the present volume, and it is therefore useful to note certain recurring key terms. A general outline can first be glimpsed in Ou-i's own explanation of the overall structure of the *I Ching*:

The upper course of the *I Ching* starts with The Creative and The Receptive, and ends with Water (Multiple Danger) and Fire. These are symbols of heaven, earth, sun, and moon. They also represent the qualities of calm and awareness, concentration and insight. This course deals with the beginning and end of inherent qualities.

The lower course starts with Sensing and Constancy, and ends with Settled and Unsettled. These are symbols of sensing and response, getting through impasses. They are also symbols of potential and teaching calling on one another, benefiting people in all times. This deals with the beginning and end of cultivated qualities.

Also, the upper course begins with the inherent qualities of Creativity and Receptivity, and ends with the cultivated qualities of Water and Fire. This is the fulfillment of cause and result of one's own practice.

The lower course begins with the potential and teaching of Sensing and Constancy, and ends with the endlessness of being Settled and Unsettled. This is the fulfillment of the subject and object involved in education and enlightenment of others.

This is the general point of the two parts of the *I Ching*.

The inherent qualities Ou-i speaks of are the natural qualities of buddha-nature, the complete potential of awareness; cultivated qualities are developments of the various facets of inherent qualities, bringing them to full maturity and putting them to appropriate use. Thus inherent qualities and cultivated qualities are the same in essence but distinct in practice.

In T'ien-t'ai Buddhist terms, this is the unity and distinction of fundamental enlightenment and initial enlightenment. This is the teaching that all beings have the buddha-nature, or potential for awakening to reality, but it usually cannot be fully expressed or used without deliberate cultivation.

A refinement of this idea is the doctrine of successive stages coexisting with an underlying unity or continuity. Using the T'ien-t'ai model, Ou-i provisionally distinguishes six stages of initial enlightenment into fundamental enlightenment.

The first stage might be termed ideal enlightenment, where *ideal* means something that is so in principle or in ultimate truth, but not yet in manifest fact.

The second stage might be called intellectual enlightenment. This is the stage of intellectual awareness of this ideal or ultimate potential of buddhahood. At this stage the intellectual awareness comes through concepts, through reading, hearing, and thinking.

The third stage is that of contemplative practice, an intensification and purification of the thinking process, also including transcendence of thought itself. As is well known, there are countless methods of contemplative practice in Buddhism, and according to Buddhist teaching principles there is a great deal of individual difference in what methods are effective when and for whom. In this reading of the *I Ching*, Ou-i is concerned not so much with specific techniques as with their generic types and their place in the overall pattern of the practitioner's life.

The fourth stage can be called the stage of conformity or resemblance and represents a development of contemplative practices to a point where they become, as it were, second nature. It is traditionally defined as the stage where the six senses are purified. This stage might be called the clearing of the channels for the next stages.

The fifth stage is that of partial realization, when the purification of the senses accomplished in the preceding stage allows the buddha-nature, the enlightenment potential, to begin penetrating the veil of illusion and reveal new perspectives and possibilities.

The sixth stage is that of ultimate realization, representing the full expression of the inherent essence of conscious being, with all of its faculties being continually developed and tuned to an infinite and ever expanding reality.

Two of the most important terms Ou-i uses in the context of Buddhist interpretation are *concentration* and *insight*. As practices, these properly belong to the third of the sixth stages mentioned above, but according to T'ien-t'ai theory, they are also natural qualities of consciousness that can be restored and maintained by cultivation. Furthermore, a proper understanding of concentration and insight is also considered important, to assist in the all-important balancing of these two fundamental aspects of Buddhist use of mind.

Concentration and insight may be thought of in association with calmness and contemplation. The concentration and calmness empower the contemplation and insight, while the contemplation and insight make the concentration and calmness meaningful. Thus it is said that both concentration and insight may be right, wrong, or unstable; and a critical element in that question is measure and proportion. This seems to be the primary function of the *I Ching* as presented by Ou-i for evaluating Buddhist practice.

Concentration and insight are not, of course, simply items of "Buddhist practice." Whatever people may do, the degree and quality of concentration and insight they bring to bear in their thoughts and acts directly affect the results. Put simply, concentration without insight leads to persistent blundering, while insight without concentration leads to lack of will. And when insight is partial or biased, and concentration shades off into obsession and fanaticism, the results are correspondingly distorted. So it seems only natural that Ou-i would find the basic *I Ching* desirables of centeredness, balance, and correctness to be in perfect accord with the Middle Way teaching of T'ien-t'ai Buddhism.

Finally, in speaking of realms of experience from a T'ien-t'ai Buddhist point of view, Ou-i uses the concept of four lands. These four lands always interpenetrate one another in some way, but they are not necessarily visible or accessible to one another at all times.

The first, "lowest" land is that land of common presence, the world of ordinary experience, where both the enlightened and the unenlightened live together. Next is the land of expedient liberation, the realm of release from worldly cares. Though taken by some as a life-long refuge, it is more widely visited as an expedient curative, to enable people to work more efficiently in the world of common presence.

The land of expedient liberation is only hearsay for most in the land of common presence, but elements from the land of common presence are also present to greater and lesser degrees in the land of expedient liberation.

Beyond the land of expedient release is the land of true reward, the purified vision and knowledge of the enlightened in any world. In Buddhist terms, this is the revelation of the matrix, or mine, of awareness of being as is.

According to one way of looking at Buddhism, the land of expedient liberation is the ultimate goal of the so-called Hinayāna, or Small Vehicle practice, while the land of true reward is the proximate goal of the so-called Mahāyāna, or Great Vehicle practice.

Scripture suggests that those in the land of expedient release may or may not hear of the land of true reward, and if they hear of it, they may or may not believe in it or seek it. On the other hand, the land of expedient release is seen as a sort of border territory by those in the land of true reward, a purifying but beguiling region inwardly passed through on the way to the so-called land of treasure, the realm of full awareness.

Finally, originally and always, there is said to be a land of eternal silent light, perhaps the essence of consciousness itself, always peaceful, always aware, forever quietly penetrating all the worlds in the other three lands. Glimpses of this are said to appear in all realms, and while beings are thought to enter into it completely only after death, it is paradoxically by cultivating contact with this subtle plane that, it is believed, beings can transcend death in some way.

The theme of progress through stages of enlightenment and realms of experience to final remergence with eternal silent light may be taken to represent a kind of life cycle from a certain point of view. Again using the concepts of inherent and cultivated qualities, this cycle begins and ends in inherent qualities, through the medium of cultivated qualities. In the first half of Ou-i's commentary on the *I Ching*, he gives sociopolitical, Buddhist, and meditational readings, according to the situation; in the second half, dealing with themes of cultivated qualities and public education, he generally uses structural concepts of native *I Ching* tradition to explain human development through interaction.

As is well known, the *I Ching* is based on sixty-four hexagrams, or six-line signs, each one representing a specific configuration of relationships. These designs have been used for thousands of years to analyze all sorts of situations and project the results of particular attitudes and behaviors in response to given conditions.

The fundamental terms of relationship in the *I Ching* system, yin and yang, are so familiar that they may well be considered naturalized English words. In my earlier translation, *The Taoist I Ching* (Boston: Shambhala, 1986), I presented a summary of yin and yang associations. There is such a basic kinship between Taoism and Buddhism, plus a close historical relationship over nearly two millennia, that there is considerable confluence even of terminology, much more of meaning underlying terminology.

In *The Buddhist I Ching*, yin and yang commonly stand for concentration and insight, thought-stopping and thought-cultivating exercises, but they can also mean weakness and strength, ignorance and knowledge, inaction and action, and similar qualities that interact in opposition and complementarity.

The relations among and between the yin and yang elements of a situational process may be perceived variously by readers. They may be indicated by the proximity of one line to another, the position of one line in the whole hexagram, or the correspondence between two lines in the same relative position in their respective trigrams.

Proximity usually means relations with immediate neighbors. Position may be described in reference to the whole hexagram or to the two trigrams that make it up. The first and fourth positions, which correspond to the bottom of the bottom trigram and the bottom of the top trigram, are generally referred to as positions of weakness, lowliness, and beginnings. The third and top lines, corresponding to the top of the bottom trigram and the top of the top trigram, are often referred to as positions of strength, excess, and culmination. The second and fifth lines have special significance as positions of balance, being in the center of their trigrams; of these, the fifth, in the upper trigram, has the "position of honor," the leadership.

Correspondence refers to the relation of corresponding lines: the first with the fourth, the second with the fifth, the third with the top. Of special importance is the relation between the second and fifth. With but one exception, it is considered best for correspondents to be complementary opposites.

Correspondence is not, moreover, on an equal basis. Thinking in terms of an organization or a society, the upper and lower trigrams in a hexagram represent the upper and lower echelons. Nevertheless, position is always relative, so the second position can represent the highest administrative rank, subordinate only to the leader in the fifth place.

Different patterns of analysis from among the many available may be invoked by different readers at the same time, or by the same reader at different times; and this is one of the reasons for the richness of the secondary and tertiary literature on the *I Ching*.

Such is the importance of the reader in the *I Ching* consultation, and the choice of specific procedures and analytic designs, that this influence carries all the way back to the original text. The core text of the *I Ching* is so old, the language so archaic, that it admits of often widely divergent readings. At times a character may even be read not merely in multiple meanings, but as one character or another, each with its own meanings.

This difference naturally affects any translation, and the present text is no exception. Not only is the text and commentary different from my earlier *Taoist I Ching,* but the translation of certain portions of the common text are also necessarily different. Ou-i's text includes the early Confucian commentaries, here labeled "Overall Judgment" and "Image." The Confucian appendices are also included in Ou-i's text, along with his commentary, but I have omitted them from this already lengthy volume, as they present a separate study.

Since the publication of *The Taoist I Ching,* numbers of people have conveyed to me news of the usefulness of that reading. Thanks in that case are due to Liu I-ming, the reader, and his teachers. Here I express the hope that *The Buddhist I Ching,* by another extraordinary reader, will also be of use to other readers.

In the future I plan to complete this series with a simplified translation of the reading of Ch'eng I, the eleventh-century Neo-Confucian who helped to revive social studies in his time by incorporating elements of Buddhism and Taoism and using their educational methods in studying history. Put simply, this reading is on the Tao of organization and applies to groups, whether they be companies or countries.

The final volume will be a manual on the diagrammatic explanations of the *I Ching,* which seems to have appeared in public among the Taoists in the Sung dynasty (960–1276). Said to have been secretly transmitted since the time of the Magicians of the Han dynasty, in the time of the Roman Caesars, it presents a number of *I Ching* reading systems that can be used for a number of purposes. It is my hope that these readings and diagrams will enhance the use and enjoyment of all the translations and adaptations of the *I Ching* available in English today, as all of them bring something more from this inexhaustible classic of ancient China.

Using *The Buddhist I Ching*

The Buddhist I Ching has a number of uses. It links spiritual life with social life, and it describes inner dynamics of both spiritual life and social life.

Thus it could be used to understand something about Buddhism. It could be used to understand how particular conditions or situations might be understood and dealt with in a Buddhist light.

In terms of this commentary, it has to do with the cultivation of inherent qualities that enable the human being to realize maximum potential, so it is not always necessary to talk about Buddhism or enlightenment.

One description of this commentary is that it is designed to lead sociologists into an understanding of meditation, and lead meditators into an understanding of society.

In Buddhist terms, this commentary uses several sets of six to associate with the lines of the hexagrams. Consider these sets:

First line: Ideal, potential

2: Intellectual understanding of ideal or potential

3: Meditation on ideal or potential, initiation of actions

4: Intimations of awakening, effects of practices

5: Realizations

Top line: Ultimate realization, not remaining static

First line: Beginning of worldliness

2: Meditation in the world yet pure, seeing reality

3: Meditation in the world and beyond the world

4: Meditation beyond the world

5: Meditation neither in nor beyond the world

Top line: End of tasting meditation

First line: Generosity

2: Self-discipline

3: Tolerance

4: Energy

5: Meditation

Top line: Wisdom

Now, as you read the text, do not pause over doubts and questions, but note the various meanings of yin and yang: concentration and insight, softness and hardness, flexibility and firmness, restraint and action, receptivity and creativity, withdrawing and advancing, yielding and proceeding, essence and function, and so on. Read the whole text as many times as necessary to get a general idea of the system. Note that there will be many lists like the above. Pay special attention to the text and commentaries of the first two hexagrams, as they are the parents of all the hexagrams.

After obtaining some familiarity with the imagery and terminology of the text, readers may use these associations of yin and yang in relative positions as models to analyze an individual, a group, a practice, a situation, an event. Try choosing the model that seems most fitting; note the values of yin and yang you use. Then observe the changes as you look up the hexagrams formed by your choices and compare one possibility with another. Note those lines that fit into your scheme and those that do not on an impartial basis, because both contain valuable material. Since yin and yang are interdependent, it is also useful to consult the antithesis of any hexagram you generate, and to consult the hexagram generated by substituting the antithesis of any line of particular interest.

For traditional programs designed to facilitate sophisticated in-depth analysis using the *I Ching* and to guide study for *I Ching* expertise, see my forthcoming rendering of *I Ching* mandalas, to be published by Shambhala Publications. These mandalas can be used with any tradition and any translation of the *I Ching*, including this *Buddhist I Ching*.

How to Consult the *I Ching*

A simple method of consulting the *I Ching* entails the use of three U.S. pennies. This is the method described here. Readers wishing to follow the more traditional methods using yarrow sticks or Chinese coins are referred to the Wilhelm/Baynes translation of the *I Ching*, published by Princeton University Press (Bollingen Series).

After formulating your question, toss the three pennies on a flat surface. Notate the tosses according to the following system, in which tails has a value of 2 and heads a value of 3:

2 tails, 1 heads	=	7	——	yang (solid line)
2 heads, 1 tails	=	8	— —	yin (broken line)
3 tails	=	6	—x—	yin (moving line)
3 heads	=	9	—o—	yang (moving line)

Cast the pennies six times in all, and write your notations in a column. Your first toss will be the first line, starting from the bottom. For example:

top line (last toss): 3 heads	=	9	—o—	
fifth line: 2 tails, 1 heads	=	7	——	upper trigram
fourth line: 3 tails	=	6	—x—	
third line: 3 tails	=	6	—x—	
second line: 2 heads, 1 tails	=	8	— —	lower trigram
first line: 2 heads, 1 tails	=	8	— —	

Identify the hexagram by consulting the key at the back of this book. In this case, we have received Hexagram 20, *Observing*.

The next step is to read the text for your hexagram, up until the section covering the numbered lines. If your hexagram contains only 7's and 8's, you do not read any further. If it contains any moving lines—6's and 9's—you also read the text pertaining to those particular lines. Thus, in our example, we would read the text for the third, fourth, and top lines.

When your hexagram contains moving lines, you can then receive a new hexagram—one in which each of the moving lines of your original hexagram has changed into its opposite. That is, the 6's (yin lines) become 9's (yang lines), and the 9's become 6's. Thus, in our example:

Original Hexagram			New Hexagram		
20. *Observing*			31. *Sensing*		
9	—o—		6	— —	
7	———		7	———	
6	—x—	⟶	9	———	
6	—x—		9	———	
8	— —		8	— —	
8	— —		8	— —	

This new hexagram represents a further development or amplification of the situation about which you are consulting the *I Ching*. For your second hexagram, you would consult the main text only, not the lines.

The Buddhist I Ching

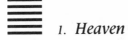

1. Heaven

heaven below, *heaven* above

The creative is successful; this is beneficial if correct.

Heaven is strength. In the sky it is the sun; in the earth it is firmness. In people it is knowledge and duty. In the essence of mind it is awareness. In spiritual practice it is observation.

Also, in the material world it is what covers. In the physical body it is the head, the higher ruler. In the family it is the head of the household. In a country it is the king; in an empire it is the emperor.

Some interpret this in terms of the Tao of nature, some in terms of the Tao of government. Either way is biased, for it only brings out one aspect.

When strong, acts are uninhibited, so "the creative is successful." But it is necessary to see what it is that is made strong; this warning, that it is beneficial only if correct, is considered by sages very important to learning. It tells about practicing the Tao.

Strength in doing evil results in hellish, animalistic, or ghostlike existence. Strength in doing good results in power, social order, or heavenly states of mind. When cultivation of meditation is added to strength in the best ways of doing good, this results in existence on the plane of pure form, or even formlessness.

Strength in the best ways of doing good, added to understanding of human suffering and the process of conditioning, plus action to free oneself from bondage, results in personal liberation.

Those who are strong in the highest virtues, and are able to liberate others as well as themselves, are called enlightening beings.

Those who are strong in the highest virtues, and realize that virtues are identical with the realm of reality and buddhahood, will complete unsurpassed enlightenment.

Thus all realms of existence are results of the success of creation. Some are bad, some are good. Even some good states are still contaminated; only the liberated are uncontaminated. But even the personally liberated are wrong if they become complacent.

When it comes to helping others and self together, expedient means dealing with either affirmation or negation are not ultimately correct, but should give way to the perfect central balance of the realm of the enlightened.

Yet to define center and extremes as disparate is still not correct. One should realize that everything is poised between being and nonbeing.

This is why the admonition "beneficial if correct" should be given to people who act with strength.

- *First yang:* **The hidden dragon is not to be employed.**

A dragon can be great or small, can shrink or expand. Therefore it is used to symbolize a quality of *Heaven*. In the beginning it is a dragon, to be sure, but because it is at the bottom, it is best to conceal it and not employ it. This refers to discovering great potential, yet working quietly and unassumingly to develop it inwardly.

- *2 yang:* **Seeing the dragon in the field; it is beneficial to see a great person.**

At first it was like an abyss, here it is like a field—one's position at a particular time may be different, but the dragon is not different. Here the text speaks of a great person, and in the next stage it speaks of a leader; these are people who can be like a dragon.

- *3 yang:* **A leader works all day and is wary at night. There is danger, but no error.**

This is a dangerous position, in which there is strength but great responsibility. Therefore one must work all day and still remain wary at night. This means not forgetting danger when secure, like one in command who nevertheless is humble and circumspect.

- *4 yang:* **One may leap in the abyss. No error.**

In the beginning, where action is proscribed, the dragon is in a deep abyss. Now, at the fourth stage, it is again in the abyss. Why? In the beginning it hid; now it leaps. The forces of the times are not the same, but the appearances are temporarily the same. This is like a ruler abdicating, or an official being lenient; it means retreating in order to advance.

- *5 yang:* **The flying dragon is in the sky. It is beneficial to see great people.**

What flies is what had leaped, what had been wary, what had become visible, what had hidden. Unless you are like this, you can hardly be called a great person. If you are a great person, all you see are great people. This is like the noninvasive government of enlightened leaders.

- *Top yang:* **At the peak, the dragon has regret.**

The peak is the culmination of the configuration of power of a time. "Regret" is the way to deal with arrogance. This is like when an ancient sage leader won over an unruly tribe by performing dances representing warfare and civilization. Unless they regretted arrogance, few people in positions of power would avoid becoming tyrants and aggressors.

Interpreting the six lines of *Heaven* in terms of Buddhism, a dragon is something that has spiritual capacity and adaptive creativity—a metaphor for the buddha-nature.

In the stage where buddhahood is an abstract ideal, an inherent possibility but not yet an actualized fact, the buddha-nature is covered by personal problems, so it "is not to be employed"—it cannot be used.

In the stage of intellectual understanding of this ideal essence, one should go to see teachers; therefore "it is beneficial to see a great person."

In the stage where one practices meditations to actualize the buddha-nature, one should continuously direct one's vitality to advancing in this exercise, so one "works by day and is wary at night."

In the stage where one conforms to buddha-nature, one does not hold religious attachment, an imitative path, and so one "may leap in the abyss."

In the stage of partial realization, one is revealed as an illuminate and benefits all creatures; such a one is beneficial to see.

In the stage of ultimate realization, one does not enter into ultimate liberation, but shares in the flow of all worlds. Therefore it is said that there is regret.

Speaking solely in terms of cultivating inner qualities, yang is the quality of knowledge; this is the practice of insight. The infertile insight of beginners needs concentration to balance it—it should not be used alone.

The second line represents harmonization of concentration and insight, whereby one can see the buddha-nature; therefore it says, "it is beneficial to see a great person."

In the third stage one uses insight to observe all things.

In the fourth stage one uses concentration to nurture potential.

In the fifth stage correct insight into central balance witnesses the design of reality.

At the peak, the characteristics of knowledge and insight cannot be apprehended, cannot be grasped.

Speaking in terms of effectiveness, the bottom line represents shallow insight, not to be used; the top line represents intellect exceeding concentration, also not to be used. The four lines in between all represent subtle insight: the second is like opening up enlightened knowledge and vision, the third is like showing enlightened knowledge and vision, the fourth is like awakening to enlightened knowledge and vision, and the fifth is like penetrating enlightened knowledge and vision.

Using yang, you see a group of headless dragons;
this is auspicious.

In Buddhist terms, this means using flexible insight, not inflexible intellect. When yang moves, it changes to yin; this represents how insight must be accompanied by concentration. *The Flower Ornament Scripture* says, "Knowledge comprehending objects is the same as concentration." Zen Master Ta Hui said, "Once enlightened, you are at peace."

The "group of dragons" means the three contemplations exercised to awaken three kinds of knowledge. These are the three contemplations and three knowledges that everything is interdependent, nothing exists alone; that while nothing therefore exists in and of itself, nevertheless things do exist, conditionally; and that because of this nature of things, everything is always in between being and nonbeing.

Contemplation and knowledge are impossible to define, ontologically or epistemologically; they cannot be found through forms, cannot be discerned by conditioned cognition. This is the meaning of "headless" which is auspicious.

THE OVERALL JUDGMENT: **How great is the creativity of heaven!**
All things originate from it, so it sums up nature.
Clouds move, rain falls, beings form a concrete flow.

This is the judgment attributed to Confucius, interpreting the statement of King Wen on the hexagram. The method of interpreting King Wen's judgments is varied: sometimes Confucius elucidates inner dimensions of King Wen's sayings, sometimes he points out King Wen's unspoken messages; sometimes he borrows King Wen's statements to bring out his own approach and express another subtle meaning.

Now, in the case of the hexagrams *Heaven* and *Earth,* Confucius either brings out his own approach or points out an unspoken message. This passage interprets the two words "creative" and "successful" to illustrate the wonder of the spontaneity of inherent qualities. That is to say, all things come from the realm of realities.

The qualities of *Heaven* cannot be all told, but creativity sums them up. The quality of creativity is indescribable, but it can be witnessed in the origination of all things. The sum of nature means from origination to ending.

The movement of clouds, the disbursal of rain, and the formation of beings into a concrete flow are all functions of the quality of creativity. This refers to the success or development of what originates.

Greatly understanding end and beginning, and how the six
stages are accomplished in the appropriate time, at the right
time one rides the six dragons to direct nature.

This passage illustrates how sages harmonize with the essence of life by
practice, so that their self-development is completed.

Sages see the beginning of things, so they can see the end already in the
beginning. They know that the true nature of beginnings derives from their
ends, and that beginning and end are one pattern, yet because of temporal
conditions there is a division into six stages.

When one attains the six stages, they are all one pattern; so every stage
has "dragon" qualities, whereby it is possible to direct nature.

"Nature" means intrinsic qualities; only with accomplishment in cultivating these qualities do intrinsic qualities become apparent. Therefore it is
called directing nature.

The transformations of the path of heaven each correct nature
and life, preserving unity with universal harmony; so it is
beneficial to be correct.

This passage explains the words "beneficial" and "correct," to illustrate how
essential qualities are originally fluid and pervasive. This means that all returns to the realm of realities.

All beings originate from the creativity of *Heaven*, so all are transformations of the path of *Heaven*. Being transformations of the path of *Heaven*,
each has the great function of the whole body of the path of *Heaven*, and is
not just a small portion of the effective capacity of *Heaven*. Therefore they
can each correct nature and life.

Every being contains the totality of the path of *Heaven* and can preserve
unity with universal harmony. Every being contains the function of origination from the creativity of *Heaven*. This is what is referred to by the saying "It
is beneficial to be correct."

With the emergence of true leaders, all nations have peace.

This passage illustrates how the enlightened freely help others after they
have cultivated their own qualities to perfection.

In this whole tradition on the *I Ching*, Confucius borrowed the words
used to interpret the judgments of the lines to elucidate the science of nonduality of essence and practice, nature and culture.

Heaven represents the buddha-nature, the essence of enlightenment, powerful and indomitable. Creativity, success, benefit, and correctness represent
the four inherent qualities of the nature of enlightenment—eternity, happiness, selfhood, and purity.

The nature of enlightenment must be eternal, and the eternal must include the four qualities. It is everywhere throughout time and space, its very being without antithesis. Therefore the text says, "Great is the creative basis."

Look at all the things and beings in the world—what is not constructed from the real eternal awake nature? If there were no awake nature, there would be no manifestation of different realms of consciousness.

Therefore, whenever we mention the eternally present awake nature, the nature of enlightenment, all worlds are included therein, including paradises of worldly rewards, paradises of expedient purification, paradises of true rewards, and the paradise of great nirvana, in which there is nothing but an eternal silent light.

Based on this eternal reality body of the awake nature, there come to be "clouds" (multitudes) of responsive manifestations, with "rains" of teachings presented in various phases and modes, to enable all kinds of people to grow and develop in accord with their own natures.

As for sages, they find out the true character of things, to attain perfect lucidity. The "true character of things" is not beginning or end, but ultimate thorough experiential realization is called the "end," and the basis for this inherent in people is called the "beginning."

So we know that both beginning and end are the awake nature; the only difference between beginning and end is that of temporal conditions of confusion and enlightenment.

So we temporarily set up six stages. Though there are six stages, there is a dragon in each stage, from ideal buddhahood to ultimate realization of buddhahood.

Riding on these cultivated qualities, which are identical yet different, one manifests the inherent qualities, which are different yet identical. Therefore the text speaks of riding six dragons to direct nature.

Though this creative path of the eternal essence of enlightenment spans all time and is unchanging and indestructible, yet it contains within it the function of all changes. Therefore it can enable the various types of people to realize buddha-nature according to their states.

So every stage is of the realm of realities, which encompasses all things, preserving unity with universal harmony.

Thus the enlightened emerge as true leaders, beyond all personal psychological states, and help the multitudes to find permanent peace in the essence of enlightenment.

THE IMAGE: **The action of heaven is strong. People with leadership qualities use it to unceasingly grow strong themselves.**

The overall images of the sixty-four hexagrams transmit a psychological interpretation based on contemplation. This means all comes back to the nature of mind itself. Originally it is because it proceeds ceaselessly from nature that the action of *Heaven* is always strong. To unceasingly grow strong oneself, emulating the strength of *Heaven*, is to unify with nature by means of culture, to use cultivation to become one with essence.

"The hidden dragon is not to be employed," because the positive energy is at a low level.

"Seeing the dragon in the field" means that the exercise of inner qualities affects everything.

"Working all day" is repetition of the path.

"Sometimes leaping, in the abyss" is proceeding impeccably.

"The flying dragon is in the sky" refers to the attainment of human greatness.

"At the peak the dragon has regret" means that fullness cannot last forever.

"Using yang," celestial qualities cannot act as the overt leader.

When the body of reality is involved in other states of being, it is referred to by its personas; so it is a "hidden dragon." This is ideal identity with the body of reality, and cannot yet be used.

Yet it is precisely because people in mental bondage can still think of this inherency, and can sense inexplicably hidden resources within themselves, that there is a chance of actualizing this ideal—for this too is a quality of consciousness. Therefore "the exercise of inner qualities affects everything," as the qualities of our consciousness form our world.

Cultivating the inner qualities of enlightened consciousness by means of the comprehensive exercise of subtle observations is here referred to as "repetition of the path."

One can "proceed impeccably" by not dwelling in religious attachment to pseudo-centeredness.

Fully embodying human enlightenment and liberating many other people and other beings is the work of "human greatness."

The true being in ultimate nirvana with no abode still does not become finally extinct, but always takes part in all states of being; therefore "fullness cannot last forever."

If we relied only on our inherent qualities, we would neglect the cultivation or culture of worthy qualities; so exoteric teachings make the cultivation of worthy qualities their outer door, and natural celestial qualities are not to take the lead overtly.

According to what the writings say, "hidden" does not mean it will emerge in action sometime; it is always hidden even in action. "At a low level" does not mean it will sometimes rise; even at a high level it does not separate from the lower levels.

The written statement says: Creativity is the growth of good, success is the confluence of the dimensions of goodness, benefit is the harmonization of duty and meaning, correctness is the effective accomplishment of what is to be done.

The sixty-four hexagrams are all in the two lines yin and yang. Purity of yin or yang makes the two hexagrams *Heaven* and *Earth;* when the meaning of *Heaven* and *Earth* is understood, then the meanings of all the hexagrams are understood. Therefore a special commentary, "The Written Statement," was composed to expound this. This first passage elucidates inherent qualities.

When leaders fully understand and embody humanity, this gives them the means to develop other people. When the dimensions of goodness combine, this makes it possible to behave impeccably. To accomplish the benefit of other people makes it possible to harmonize duty and meaning. Correct stabilization makes it possible to effectively accomplish what is to be done.

This passage elucidates cultured qualities.

True leaders exercise these four qualities, so it is said, "*Heaven* means the creative is successful, beneficial insofar as it is correct."

This passage sums up, to illustrate using culture to harmonize with nature, cultivating inner potential to bring out the best in humanity. How could it be possible to manifest the fundamental nature of the strength of the creative without the subtle culture that develops humankind?

To give a general discussion of the twin modes of *Heaven* and *Earth,* the creative and the receptive, in terms of nature, they are the body of tranquillity and awareness; in terms of culture, they are the qualities of perceptivity and peacefulness; in terms of cause, they are the accomplishment of calmness and observation; in terms of effect, they are the adornments of stability and wisdom.

Whether we speak in terms of nature or culture, of cause or effect, it is all eternity, happiness, selfhood, and purity. The knowledge of eternity, happiness, selfhood, and purity is called omniscience. Stabilization in eternity, happiness, selfhood, and purity is referred to as the stability to freely enter into and emerge from any state of mind. Therefore both *Heaven* and *Earth* each clarify the four qualities of creativity, successfulness, beneficence, and correctness.

Now, if these four qualities were spoken of in terms of Confucian principles, they would be humanity, justice, courtesy, and knowledge. To align the interpretations, humanity is the quality of eternity, because it essentially does not change; courtesy is the quality of happiness, because of the beauties it contains; justice is the quality of selfhood, insofar as it means autonomous exercise of judgment; knowledge is the quality of purity, in the sense of being unobscured.

Now, to speak of them from the point of view of their mutual inclusiveness, the essences of humanity, courtesy, justice, and knowledge are eternal, so this is the quality of eternity. Humanity, courtesy, justice, and knowledge are useful, so this is the quality of happiness. Humanity, courtesy, justice, and knowledge are fulfilled independently, so this is the quality of selfhood. Humanity, courtesy, justice, and knowledge are unadulterated and undefiled, so this is the quality of purity.

- **The first yang says not to employ the hidden dragon. What does this mean?**

Confucius said, "This refers to those who are like a dragon but are concealed, not changed by society, not making a name for themselves, unknown to the world, untroubled in mind, not opinionated, free from worry, doing what is pleasant, avoiding what brings grief. They certainly cannot be made to work for a ruler—they are hidden dragons."

The interpretation of this passage in terms of the qualities of sages can be understood from the literal meaning. If we interpret in terms of the essential potential for enlightenment, the dragon qualities that are hidden are what are called the mine of enlightenment. Even in ignorance, delusion, error, and confusion, the essential potential is always there; so it is "not changed by society."

Now, at this point the idea of buddha-nature is not obvious, so it "does not make a name."

People use the buddha-nature every day but are not inwardly aware of it; they crazily get into all sorts of trips. Nevertheless, the buddha-nature does not decrease, even though it is in the ordinary. So it is "unknown to the world, untroubled in mind, not opinionated, free from worry."

That which "does what is pleasant" is the buddha-nature, and that which "avoids what brings grief" is also the buddha-nature. It goes along with conditions, but conditions never change it; therefore it "certainly cannot be made to work for a ruler."

■ The yang in the second place says that when seeing the dragon in the field, it is beneficial to see a great person. What does this mean?

Confucius said, "This refers to dragon qualities in correct balance. The trustworthiness of balanced words, the prudence of balanced actions—these stop aberrations and preserve truthfulness and sincerity. They make the world good without killing; their virtues are far-reaching and exert a civilizing influence. This line of the *I Ching* refers to the qualities of true leaders.

This passage is also clear in its obvious meaning. If we interpret in terms of intellectual buddhahood, balanced speech and balanced actions are means of knowing the nature of things; by being unaffected, we can cultivate perfect self-control in all situations. In this way we can get rid of aberrated mental states and preserve the true buddha-nature.

The root of good in a beginner's moment of complete understanding is already beyond the virtues accumulated over aeons of practice of provisional vehicles; yet one does not feel self-satisfied, for this is not yet the real. Therefore even though one's virtues may be far-reaching, still one does not entertain images of far-reaching virtues, because that would produce conceit.

The inspiration and the ultimate state of mind, though two, are not separate. Of these two, the inspiration and the ultimate, the first is the harder. So even beginners in the intellectual stage already have the knowledge of enlightenment and the vision of enlightenment, and these are the qualities of true leaders.

■ Yang in the third place says that a leader works all day and is wary at night; there is danger but no error. What does this mean?

Confucius said, "Leaders develop their inner qualities and do their work. They develop inner qualities through faithfulness and truthfulness. They keep at their work by cultivating their speech and establishing their honesty. Knowing the goal and reaching it, they can see things through; knowing the end and concluding it, they can preserve its meaning. Therefore they are not proud when they are in high positions and do not worry when they are in low positions. Therefore they work

diligently, and by wariness at the proper times they make no
error even in danger."

Faithfulness and truthfulness are essential for preservation of mind and are
proper means of developing inner qualities. Cultivating speech and establishing honesty are methods of promoting practice, and are proper means of
keeping at work. This is the path of uniting the inner and the outer.

To go into action at the appropriate time is to see things through; to stop at
the appropriate time preserves the meaning of the action. When one does
not lose the way whether going forward or withdrawing, it does not matter
whether one is in a high or low position.

To interpret in terms of the six stages of buddhahood, this passage represents the rounded, subtle work in the stage of correct practice of
contemplation.

The direct mind accurately aware of reality as it is—this is called faithfulness and truthfulness. This is the means for developing inner qualities, and
stands for the main practice.

As explanation of truth is pure, knowledge is pure; when guiding people
for their benefit, the effect of one's influence depends on oneself—this is
called cultivating speech and establishing honesty. This is the means for
keeping at work, and stands for auxiliary practice.

Knowing the goal and reaching it is subtle observation; knowing the end
and completing it is subtle tranquilization. When tranquillity and observation are practiced together, stability and wisdom are fulfilled; then one can
meet the buddhas' power of compassion above yet not become proud; meet
the hopes of people below, yet not become worried.

■ **Yang in the fourth place says one may leap in the abyss
without error. What does this mean?**

**Confucius said, "Rising and descending without fixation is not
wrong; advancing and withdrawing without fixation, one does
not separate from the masses. A leader develops inner
qualities and cultivates work so as to meet the needs of the
time; therefore there is no error."**

This passage shows how ancient sage-kings abdicated their thrones in the
same state of mind as when they assumed their thrones.

In Buddhist terms, directly observing the realm of inconceivability is
"rising"; using other realms to assist this is "descending."

The consistent intent to proceed toward the ocean of all knowledge is "advancing"; profoundly observing the six grades of buddhahood and not becoming conceited is "withdrawing."

The desire to meet the needs of the time is the intent to do what is most important in this life. If we are not liberated this life, when will we ever be liberated? Until we enter the true state of completeness and permanence, we have not crossed over the oceans of body and mind death.

- **Yang in the fifth place says the flying dragon is in the sky, it is beneficial to see a great person. What does this mean?**

  Confucius said, "Harmonization—response and attraction of what is alike. Water is wet, fire is hot, clouds follow dragons, wind follows tigers. Sages make, myriad beings watch. Those based in heaven are close to the top; those based on earth are close to the bottom; so each follows kind."

This illustrates how sages govern the world without overt action, without intentional artifice.

To interpret in Buddhist terms, when the enlightened attain true awareness, they see all sentient beings attain true awareness. In the first stage, they leave distinction from other types of beings and enter sameness with other types of beings, to their great happiness and delight.

Then, when they have reached experience of the body of reality, they enter a sort of concentration whereby they are able to adapt their outward manifestations to any situation; in heaven they are the same as gods and goddesses; among humans they are the same as humans.

This is what is called the benefit in seeing a great person; all alike in all realms look up to the enlightened, because they themselves have the same nature within them.

- **The yang at the top says the dragon has regret at the peak. What does this mean?**

  Confucius said, "Noble without rank, high without subjects, the wise are in low positions, and have no helpers; therefore regret accompanies activity."

According to one explainer, up until now Confucius has been saying that a sage does not become arrogant at the peak of exaltation; but when it is viewed from the point of view of fulfillment of practice and effecting self-reduction, Confucius then can be seen to be using "no rank, no subjects, no helpers" to represent this.

This is the spirit of ancient kings who ruled the world but were not impressed with themselves because of it; it does not mean rank is lost, the people rebel, and the wise leave.

The word "activity" is used well here. The most intransigent obstacle in the world is easy for the sage who does not stop and ponder, and has no second thoughts. It only takes action to bring about regret, and it only takes regret to deal with arrogance.

To interpret this in Buddhist terms, the body of reality is not in any category, so it is "noble without rank." Buddhahood goes beyond all realms, so it is "high without subjects." The experience of silent light, the land of the eternal buddhas, is not accessible to those below the stage of enlightenment equal to buddhas, so "sages are in low positions, without helpers."

Therefore, in the ultimate stage it is imperative to turn back and appear in the world in forms consistent with those of the people in various states, to manifest innocence in the midst of the world and deal compassionately with their problems.

"The hidden dragon is not to be employed" means lying low. "Seeing the dragon in the field" means leaving off for the moment. "Working all day" means carrying out tasks. "Sometimes leaping in the abyss" means self-testing. "The flying dragon is in the sky" means the leadership is itself properly governed. "At the peak the dragon has regret" means the calamity of going to extremes. Using yang, positive energy, the creative basis, means the whole world is functioning harmoniously.

This is a reinterpretation of the six lines in terms of the states of times.

"Using the positive energy" as "the creative basis" illustrates the great function of the whole body of the hexagram *Heaven.*

It also illustrates how "hiding, appearing, watching out, leaping, flying, and rising to the peak" are all auspicious if they are not done egotistically.

In Buddhist terms, ideal buddhahood is the ultimate opprobrium, so it is low.

Intellectual buddhahood still lacks work, so it is "leaving off for a time."

Correctly doing the various stages of meditation practice is "carrying out tasks."

The stage of conformity is when you are about to witness reality, so it is "self-testing."

The stage of partial realization is full embodiment of human enlightenment, so it is "the leadership itself properly governed."

The stage of ultimate realization does not abide in extinction, so it illustrates "the calamity of going to extremes."

Using yang, the positive energy, is using culture to conform to nature, cultivating oneself so as to be at one with the essence of human nature. Therefore "the whole world is functioning harmoniously."

"The hidden dragon is not to be employed" means the positive creative energy is hidden in storage.

"Seeing the dragon in the field" means the land is civilized.

"Working all day" means carrying on activities in accord with the time.

"Sometimes leaping in the abyss" means the course of creativity is revolutionized.

"The flying dragon is in the sky" means attainment to higher qualities.

"At the peak the dragon has regrets" means coming to an end with the time.

"Using yang" implies seeing higher law.

This reinterprets the six lines in terms of both qualities and times. Seen from the point of view of the contrast between coming to an end with the time and carrying out activities according to the time, all of this is what is called "taking the opportunity at the right time to direct nature." This is "seeing higher law."

To interpret in Buddhist terms, insofar as the nature of enlightenment is hidden in the body of living beings, it is "hidden in storage."

Once we hear of the nature of enlightenment, we know that mind, buddhas, and beings, while three, are no different. Therefore "the land is civilized."

By constant application of attention to astute observation we "carry on activities in accordance with the time."

On giving up the nature of ordinary people and entering into the nature of enlightened people, "the path of creativity is revolutionized."

On experiencing the qualities of permanent peace and freedom, one sits on the site of enlightenment, and so "attains higher qualities." Higher qualities are naturally inherent qualities.

At the peak, it is necessary to return; those who attain buddhahood unfailingly assimilate to the flow of other realms of consciousness.

Nature needs culture; essence must have cultivation. When you produce a culture that cultivates the best in people while keeping their essential nature complete, then you see the law of the nonduality of essence and self-work.

The creative basis is that which makes beginnings and successfully carries them through. Benefit and correctness are nature and sense. Creative beginnings can benefit the world

with beautiful advantages, yet without it being said what is
gained. This is great indeed.

Before, I interpreted creativity, success, benefit, and correctness in terms of
the four qualities of humanity, courtesy, justice, and knowledge. Now I will
explain the four qualities, comprehending them through their oneness.
They all belong only to *Heaven* and are not four separate things.

The word "heaven" implies the quality of creativity, and the word "creativity" includes the four qualities. The greatness of creativity is the greatness of
Heaven.

**How great is heaven! Firm, strong, balanced, upright—it is the
pure essence of vitality. The activity of the six lines conveys
mental states indirectly.**

Heaven contains the four qualities, but that does not mean just four; so it is
great. Therefore the words "firm," "strong," and so on are repeated and profoundly extolled.

The hexagram refers to the body; the lines refer to the function. Hexagrams are based on stations; lines are based on changes. As the body is great,
the function is also great; when the body is firm, strong, balanced, upright,
the pure essence of vitality, then the function is accordingly that of the firm,
strong, balanced, upright, pure essence of vitality.

**At the appropriate times it drives the six dragons to direct
nature. Clouds roll, rain falls, the land is peaceful.**

It has already been made clear that the body of the qualities of *Heaven* must
have function—they must be useful. This section shows how sages use the
functions to attain its embodiment.

Interpreted in terms of Buddhism, this passage says that nature always implies cultivation, and cultivation is all in nature.

The eternal noumenon of the nature of enlightenment is called the creative source. There is no being that does not begin from this realm of realities,
no being that is not created and does not grow from this realm of realities.
There is also no being that does not exist and sense through this realm of
realities. There is no being whose very essence and sense is not this realm of
realities.

Therefore the eternal noumenon of the nature of enlightenment can produce all phenomena everywhere, yet in reality there is no producer or produced, no benefactor or beneficiary. In essence, this is "not changing yet
adapting to circumstances, adapting to circumstances yet not changing." It
pervades time and space, has no antithesis, and is inconceivable. It can only

be called "great" out of the need to refer to it; in reality, no idea or word can encompass it.

This nature is powerful, robust, indomitable; so it is called "firm." It is by this nature that we can aspire to enlightenment and disrupt the inertia of futile routines, so it is called "strong."

Because it is not divided into being and nonbeing, true and conventional, it is called "balanced." Because it is not partial, neither destructible nor permanent, neither void nor temporary, it is called "upright."

The nature of enlightenment is not adulterated with anything, so it is called pure. It is the quintessence of all things, so it is called "essence." The nature of enlightenment pervades everywhere, every particle of every atom of the cosmos, so it is called "vitality."

So this body of *Heaven* as the nature of enlightenment inherently includes the characteristics of the beginning and end of cultivation and realization, indicated by the six lines, which "indirectly convey mental states" of the various realms of delusion and enlightenment. This is what is meant by the inherency of cultivation in nature.

Sages drive these dragons, which are one yet six, to direct nature, which accords with six yet is one. After they have cultivated themselves in such a way as to harmonize with essential nature, then they can produce "clouds"— that is, great numbers—of concrete manifestations that are in accord with this essential nature, and use these to disburse the "rain" of true education, to cause all beings to be truly and directly aware, so that "the land is at peace." This is what is meant by the completion of cultivation being within nature.

Leaders make it their work to perfect qualities; this is work that can be seen daily. What submergence refers to is obscurity, not yet emerging, work that is not complete. This is why leaders "do not employ" it.

From here down, the six lines are spoken of only in terms of cultivating qualities, and in terms of what will work and what will thwart you.

To interpret this in Buddhist terms, perfecting qualities is practice, work done to cultivate the inherent nature of enlightenment. This means creating actions based on inherent natural qualities.

Since inherent qualities do the actions, mental aberration stops, and when it stops, one is enlightened. Therefore this practice is called "work that can be seen daily."

The reason the text still talks of submergence is that even if one discovers enlightenment, the contamination of habit is still not gone. Therefore the enlightened nature is still covered by passions based on delusions and is not yet manifest.

So practices—main and auxiliary practices—are still in the stages of contemplation and imitation, and have not yet formed the qualities of true intuition and liberation.

Therefore independent people need to cultivate qualities in order to perfect them and not just use intellectual understanding that has no substance.

Leaders study to assemble it, question to clarify it. They live by it broad-mindedly, carry it out benevolently. When the *I Ching* **says, "Seeing the dragon in the field, it is beneficial to see a great person," this refers to the qualities of leadership.**

Study is understanding through learning; living broad-mindedly is understanding through thoughtfulness; benevolent action is understanding through practice. When people attain completion through these three kinds of understanding, this opens up enlightened knowledge and vision, and these people are called buddhas. Hence the reference to "the qualities of leadership," which means the qualities of developed people.

Yang in the third place is doubly hard, and not balanced. It is not in the sky above, it is not in the field below. Therefore one works and is wary according to the time. Then there is no error in spite of danger.

To be doubly hard means to strengthen oneself unceasingly, only going forward and never withdrawing.

"Not balanced" means one does not arrive at central balance but is in a hurry to get realization.

"Not in the sky above" means one has not yet ascended to the tenth stage of enlightenment and entered the knowledge and vision of the enlightened.

"Not in the field below" means having already gone beyond the ten abodes and having opened up the knowledge and vision of the enlightened.

To be wary according to the time is properly the inconceivable method of the ten practices, entering everywhere into the realm of realities, able to master the way of enlightenment while traveling alien ways. Therefore "there is no error in spite of danger."

Yang in the fourth place is doubly hard, and unbalanced. It is not in the sky above, not in the field below, not in the person in between. Therefore there is hesitation. Hesitation means doubt; this is why there is no error.

"Doubly hard and unbalanced" is as explained above. "Not in the person in between" means having already gone beyond the ten practices, now showing enlightened knowledge and vision.

"Hesitation" means turning from phenomena to noumenon, from cause to effect, from self to others, blending in with the realm of realities, without partiality.

There is resemblance to doubt here. In this sense, "doubt" means the attempt to rationalize, so as to achieve adaptative change. Therefore, even though there seems to be cultivation and realization, in reality there is no such thing.

Great people are one with the qualities of heaven and earth, one with the illumination of sun and moon, one with the order of the four seasons, one with the good and bad luck brought on by hidden forces. In the primordial, nature does not oppose them; in the temporal, they serve the times of nature. If even nature does not oppose them, how much less do people, ghosts, or spirits oppose them?

Entry into enlightened knowledge and vision, at the tenth stage of enlightenment, is like the sky covering all, like the earth supporting all, like the sun shining at midday, like the moon shining at night, like the progression of the four seasons producing and completing myriad beings, like the determination of possibilities by good and bad luck brought on by unseen forces.

Subtle knowledge of the fundamental finds out the beginningless beginning of the realm of realities; subtle knowledge of differentiation defines the timeless times of the realm of realities. When there is inner accord, there is no opposition, so ordinary people and unseen forces are in harmony. It is not beneficial to see the unique inner design of reality unless one accords with it.

The word "peak" refers to knowing how to go forward but not knowing how to withdraw, knowing how to stay but not knowing how to disappear, knowing how to gain but not knowing how to lose. Only sages know how to go forward or withdraw, how to stay or disappear, always doing the right thing at the right time.

Those who have insight but lack stable concentration only know that the nature of enlightenment is precious, and do not know that it can get involved in ordinary states of existence. They only know that the nature of enlightenment is omnipresent, and do not know the nondisappearing disappearance that takes place when one turns back from enlightenment to harmonize with the world. They only know the gain of lofty talk of noumenal essence, and do not know the loss of neglecting cultivation and experience.

Only sages can understand the distinctions between advancing and withdrawing, staying and disappearing; and yet advance is the nature of enlightenment, withdrawal is the nature of enlightenment, staying is the nature of enlightenment, and disappearing is also the nature of enlightenment. Advance and withdrawal, staying and disappearing, never increase or decrease the nature of enlightenment, and the nature of enlightenment does not prevent advance and withdrawal, staying and disappearing.

Therefore sages produce culture while keeping essential nature complete, and complete cultivation in essential nature, always correctly. If you idly count on the nature of enlightenment, you will become conceited and will not be truly enlightened.

To interpret this in the context of the stage of ultimate realization, manifestation of attainment of buddhahood is knowing how to go forward, how to advance; manifesting other states of being is knowing how to withdraw. Manifestation of the practices of sages, religious practices, and innocent behavior, is knowing how to stay. Manifestation of aberrations out of compassion is knowing how to disappear. Yet there is no loss in the knowledge and detachment of buddhahood; this is always being correct.

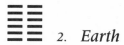 2. *Earth*

earth below, *earth* above

The creative is successful. It is beneficial to be correct like a mare. People with developmental potential have a goal; if they go ahead before this, they will get lost. If they follow, they get the benefit of the director. Companionship is found in the southwest; companionship is lost in the northeast. Stability and correctness bode well.

All six lines of this hexagram are yin, so it is called *Earth. Earth* means receptivity, docility. In the sky, it is shade; on the ground, it is softness. In people, it is humaneness. In the essential nature of consciousness, it is tranquillity. In cultivation, it is the practice of stopping the mind.

In the material world, it is support. In the physical body, it is the abdomen and the organs it contains. In the home, it is the wife. In a country, it is the ministers.

If it is receptive and docile, it will act without backlash, so this creativity too is successful; but it must take advantage of the correctness of a mare, which follows the stallion tamely. This refers to people with developmental potential embodying the qualities of *Earth* to practice the way of enlightenment.

First it is necessary to use *Heaven* knowledge to open up round understanding; then use this *Earth* practice to develop and complete this understanding.

If you practice concentration exercises without first having understanding, you will surely become an obscurantist.

Just follow knowledge and then apply it; then you will find the "director" and get the advantage of direction.

This is like the eyes and the feet working together to convey you easily into a cool pond, or like skill and strength working together to hit the target at a hundred paces.

If you go southwest, you will only get yin companions; this is like trying to complement water with water—it does not work. If you go northeast, you lose those yin companions and get in tune with knowledge; only then are you stable in correctness of balance of concentration and insight, and have a good outlook.

THE OVERALL JUDGMENT: Consummate is the creative basis of earth; all beings live on its sustenance, as it goes along in accord with the communications it receives from heaven.

Earth is thick and supports beings. Its quality is of boundlessness. Its embrace is far-reaching and its light is great; material things and living beings all succeed.

The mare is of the category of earth; she travels the earth boundlessly, gentle, obedient, helpful, faithful. This is how those with developmental potential go to the goal; if they go ahead, they lose the way; if they follow behind, they attain constancy.

To gain companionship in the southwest is to go with one's own kind. Having lost companionship in the northeast, eventually there is celebration.

The good outlook of stability and correctness corresponds to the boundlessness of the earth.

This tradition makes a detailed interpretion of the words of the judgment. First it illustrates the four qualities of *Earth* in terms of the way of the earth. Next it explains how those with development potential embody the qualities of *Earth* to harmonize with the way of the earth.

Reception of energy comes about through origination based on *Heaven*, development of form comes about through living on the sustenance of *Earth*. Because development of form only takes place due to reception of energy, this is called going along in accord with the communications received from heaven.

The quality of boundlessness means oneness with the quality of nature. Southwest indicates the trigrams *joy* ☱ , *fire* ☲ , and *wind* ☴ , all of which are in the category of yin. Northeast indicates the trigrams *thunder* ☳ , *mountain* ☶ , *water* ☵ , and *heaven* ☰ , which can be relied on for good outlook.

To interpret in Buddhist terms, *Earth* represents the essential nature of the enlightenment potential, which contains much without accumulating anything. This is called *Heaven* in terms of knowledge, but is called *Earth* in terms of noumenon. In terms of awareness, it is called *Heaven;* in terms of tranquillity, it is called *Earth.*

It can also be called *Heaven* in terms of essence and *Earth* in terms of cultivation. Also, intellectual activity in the course of cultivation can be called *Heaven,* while practical activity can be called *Earth.*

In reality, neither *Heaven* nor *Earth* takes precedence over the other; they are used to represent oneness of noumenon and knowledge, nonduality of tranquillity and awareness, interpenetration of essential nature and cultivation, the mutual adornment of virtue and wisdom.

Here the reason for speaking in a linear order where there is no linear order is that noumenon is revealed by knowledge, tranquillity is revealed by awareness, culture is developed by nature, virtue is guided by wisdom. Then noumenon and knowledge merge, tranquillity and awareness unite, culture and nature combine, virtue and wisdom blend. Therefore the text says, "Consummate is the creative basis of earth; all things live on its sustenance, as it follows the communications it receives from heaven."

Action in accord with noumenon, the inner design of reality, benefits oneself and benefits others as well. One practice is all practices, so its quality accords with boundless knowledge; "its embrace is far-reaching and its light is great."

As a mare travels the earth, though she is docile, she is strong; when meditation concentration is practiced according to knowledge and wisdom, it becomes the meditation concentration of the enlightened. Practices such as charity, discipline, tolerance, effort, and meditation are blind, and need the guidance of wisdom.

If you make welfare projects the first priority, without acquiring the wisdom and knowledge to direct them, then enlightened knowledge and vision do not open, and you will fall into a sidetrack and lose the way.

If you use knowledge to guide action, and action follows knowledge, then knowledge is constant and action too is constant. Therefore "companionship is gained in the southwest"—one only works with one's own kind; but when "companionship is lost in the northeast," one sees the whole enlightened nature in every act, and every act is the realm of realities, being in itself having no antithesis—"eventually there is celebration."

Hence the good outlook of stability and correctness; when concentration and insight are equal, one can accord with the boundlessness of the essential potential of enlightenment.

THE IMAGE: The attitude of earth is receptivity. Thus do leaders support people with rich virtue.

Inherent virtues are originally rich; therefore the attitude of earth is also rich. To richly develop virtues by means of adopting the attitude of the ground of reality, thereby to support all living beings, is the true learning through which we harmonize with our essential nature by means of cultivation.

■ *First yin:* As you walk on frost, hard ice shows up.

THE IMAGE: Walking on frost and hard ice represent the first congealing of yin. Mastering that path is coming to hard ice.

The question arises here as to why the first line of *Heaven* gives the warning not to employ it, while the first line of *Earth* gives assurance of arrival.

The answer to this is that the nature of yang is movement, and if there is arbitrary or impulsive movement, positive energy might leak away. Thus the warning not to go into action too soon.

The nature of yin is stillness, and calmness leads to success; therefore assurance is given.

Accumulating good and evil is like "walking on frost"; the resulting joys and sorrows are like "ice showing up."

In yang there are both hard good and hard evil; in yin there are both soft good and soft evil. Therefore it is not proper to interpret yin softness only as bad. Generally, to consider *Heaven* good and consider *Earth* bad was a big mistake made by the interpreters of Chin and Wei times [third to fifth century C.E.]

To interpret this in Buddhist terms, the six lines of *Heaven* are explained in terms of both essence and cultivation, nature and culture; the six lines of *Earth* are explained in terms of cultivating practices to develop good qualities and concentration.

The bottom and top lines of *Earth* represent the beginning of worldliness and the end of tasting meditation. The four lines in between represent the existence of four kinds of successful meditation.

The second line is meditation that is in the world, but is pure and reaches the manifestation of reality.

The third line is meditation that is both in the world and beyond the world.

The fourth line is meditation beyond the world.

The fifth line is meditation that is neither in the world nor beyond the world.

Now let us borrow the six lines of *Heaven* to make a complementary interpretation. In the first yang, there is insight but no concentration, so it is not to
be employed. One therefore wishes to cultivate one's concentration; the first
yin uses concentration to embrace insight, so it is like "walking on frost." If
one masters this, this is the celestial quality represented by "hard ice."

The second yang is subtle insight into the way of central balance; therefore "it is beneficial to see a great person." The second yin is subtle concentration on the way of central balance, so it is "beneficial for all."

In the third yang, intellect outstrips concentration, so there is no error
only if one is wary of danger. In the third yin, concentration has its intelligence, so one "conceals embellishments and affirms chastity."

In the fourth yang, knowledge and concentration are together, so one
"may leap" and can make progress. In the fourth yin, concentration outstrips knowledge, so one "shuts the bag, with no praise."

In the fifth yang, great knowledge and wisdom are balanced and true;
therefore one is "in the sky" and "beneficial to see." In the fifth yin, great
concentration is itself insight, so one is "dressed in gold, with a very good
outlook."

At the peak, it is because intellect has concentration that one knows to
regret. In battle, when concentration lacks wisdom, the path comes to an
impasse.

Now, if we consider *Heaven* to be the main practices and *Earth* the auxiliary
practices, then the six lines of *Earth* represent the six ways of transcendence.

Giving is like treading on ice; mastery of this can bring on "ice," which
represents celestial qualities.

Discipline is like being "upright, straight, great." One is upright because of
living according to orderly and harmonious patterns of conduct. One is
straight because of embodying good ways. One is great because of impartial
concern for all beings.

Patience is like "concealing embellishments," because it is the greatest of
strength.

Energy is like "shutting the bag," so that no truth shall escape one.

Meditation concentration is like wearing a "yellow lower garment," because the subtle concentration of central balance pervades the realm of
realities.

Wisdom is like a dragon at war, because it destroys predatory passions.

■ *2 yin:* Upright, straight, great; unfailing benefit without
practice.

THE IMAGE: The movement of the second yin is upright and
straight. Unfailing benefit without practice; the way of earth is
illumined.

Pure flexibility in correct balance is the epitome of harmonious adaptability. Because it accords with the inner design of reality, it is upright. Because it acts based on the inner design of reality, it is straight. Once it is upright and straight, it must be great. These are inherent qualities of earth, and have nothing to do with practice.

In Buddhist terms, pure meditation in the world is itself a manifestation of reality, so it is "upright, straight, great." Accurate attention to reality as it is is upright—this is the body of concentration. Goodness without lack is straight—this is the manifestation of concentration. Far-reaching virtue is great—this is the function of concentration.

Pure meditation in the world naturally contains these three qualities of reality, and can reach the manifestation of reality in the course of basic meditation; therefore "there is unfailing benefit without practice."

Spotting the inner design of reality in pure meditation is called movement or action; upon movement, the design of the three qualities becomes manifest, opening up the hidden treasury in meditation. Therefore "the way of earth is illumined."

■ *3 yin:* Hiding embellishments, affirming rectitude, if one works for the government, there will be no accomplishment, but there will be a conclusion.

THE IMAGE: Hiding embellishments and affirming rectitude mean timely activation. Working for the government means that the light of knowledge is great.

In Buddhist terms, this represents meditation that is both in the world and beyond the world, with both positivity and negativity; therefore one "hides embellishments and affirms rectitude."

If one works on the supreme royal concentration of the unique religion, then by this one can activate the highest subtle knowledge beyond the world and "have a conclusion," without any further accomplishment of graduated meditations.

■ *4 yin:* Closing the bag—no blame, no praise.

THE IMAGE: Closing the bag, so there is no blame, means being prudent so as to avoid harm.

Interpreting this in Buddhist terms, in beyond-the-world meditation it is important to refrain from grasping realization. If you grasp realization, you will fall into the states of those who opt for individual liberation; though they cannot be blamed for samsara, still they cannot be praised for helping others.

If we can be mindful of the vow to help all beings, and not grasp at small-scale realization, then individual liberation will not harm the process of universal liberation.

- *5 yin:* Yellow lower garment, great good outlook.

THE IMAGE: Yellow lower garment, great good outlook—the culture is in the center.

Yellow is the color associated with the center, the quality of the leader; clothing stands for the jobs of ministers.

In Buddhist terms, this is meditation that is neither in the world nor beyond the world, meditation identical to the manifestation of reality; this is the reason for "yellow," since yellow is a symbol of the center.

Not rising from concentration in which all sense and perception are stilled, yet manifesting ordinary modes of conduct in conformity with whatever world one is in, is like wearing a garment.

This is a genuine avenue of access to supreme enlightenment, so there is a "great good outlook."

Beautification with concentration and wisdom is called "culture." The totality of culture is in nature, so "the culture is in the center."

- *Top yin:* Dragons battle in the field. The blood is dark yellow.

THE IMAGE: Dragons battle in the field—the path reaches an impasse.

When good is consummate, then cutting off evil must come to an end; when evil is consummate, then cutting off good must come to an end. Therefore at an impasse there is inevitably a battle; and when there is a battle, there must be one casualty.

In Buddhist terms, the heaven where there are no mental images is a frozen blank that lasts for five hundred eons and then collapses; the heaven of neither perception nor nonperception lasts eighty thousand major eons, then degenerates. Ascetics practicing step-by-step meditation who fall into uninterrupted hell all use concentration exclusively, not knowing how to balance it with wisdom; therefore they reach an impasse like this.

- Using yin, it is beneficial to always be correct.

THE IMAGE: Using yin always correctly is the way to a great conclusion.

In Buddhist terms, using a static yin is like concentration that does not produce insight, whereas using a transmuting yin is like concentration that does produce insight. Concentration that does produce insight should be practiced for a long time, until consummate meditation reaches enlightenment; then it is ultimately fulfilled, so it is called "a great conclusion."

The written statement says: Earth is utterly soft, yet its movement is also firm; it is utterly quiet, yet its quality is straight. By following, it gains direction and has constancy. It embraces myriad beings and enlightens. The path of earth is obedience, being receptive to the communications of heaven and acting on them according to the time.

In Buddhist terms, this directly eulogizes the attainment of meditation. Because it abides in quiescence, it is "utterly soft" and "utterly quiet."

Because it can produce spiritual capacities that emanate manifestations to adapt to all potentials, sensitive and effective, therefore "its movement is firm" and "its quality is straight."

Because it is perfected by the guidance of transcendent wisdom, "by following, it gains direction and has constancy." That is, because wisdom is constant, therefore meditation becomes constant.

Because myriad practices are included in meditation, and each subtle practice corresponds to knowledge, guiding conscious beings, therefore "it embraces myriad beings and enlightens."

Without knowledge and wisdom, one cannot truly meditate, so "the path of earth is obedience." Without meditation, knowledge and wisdom are ineffective, so it is a matter of "being receptive to the communications of heaven and acting on them according to the time."

Those who accumulate good will have more happiness; those who accumulate evil will have more misfortune. When a minister kills the ruler, or when a son kills his father, this does not happen all of a sudden, but comes from a gradual buildup, with a failure to make clarification early on.

In Buddhist terms, good actions are good, bad actions are not good; non-contamination is good, contamination is not good; helping others is good, just helping oneself is not good; central balance is good, extremism is not good; complete balance is good, mere relative balance is not good.

Here, "good" means the ruler, "not good" means the minister; if the good controls what is not good, then what is not good is made good. If what is not good hinders what is good, then the good is obstructed by what is not good. This is like a ruler or a father being killed.

Therefore the journey of a thousand miles begins with a single step, and it is necessary to make an early clarification of how to take that single step correctly.

Uprightness is its correctness; straightness is its justice. Leaders make themselves upright within by sincerity, make themselves outwardly straight by justice. When sincerity and justice are established, their qualities are not isolated. "Upright, straight, great, unfailing benefit without practice"— thus one does not doubt what is done.

Only by correctness is one upright, only by justice is one straight; uprightness and straightness are both inherent qualities, but sincerity is the essential art for cultivation of the path. When one is sincere, one is docile and thus will be upright and straight, so these qualities will not be isolated; this can be called greatness.

In Buddhist terms, accurate awareness of objective reality is the inner body of concentration; embodiment of all that is meaningful is the outer manifestation of concentration. Once the inner body and outward manifestation of concentration are complete, then the great function will appear and the qualities of concentration will not be isolated. Thus in meditation one opens up hidden resources and clearly sees the enlightened nature, without doubt.

Although yin has beauty, one hides this. Working on governmental affairs in this way, one does not presume upon achievement. This is the path of earth, the path of the wife, the path of the minister. The path of earth has no achievement, but there is a conclusion through its agency.

In Buddhist terms, although meditation that is both in and beyond the world contains the beauty of the manifestation of reality, yet it is hidden and does not emerge. This is to be used as an aid to the royal concentration; it should not be used exclusively to reach achievement.

Generally speaking, meditation concentration is to be practiced in accord with knowledge and insight, like the earth receiving the communications of heaven, like the wife following her husband, like the minister assisting the ruler.

But if knowledge and insight lack meditation and concentration, then one cannot fulfill self-help and help for others; therefore meditation concentration can act as an agent through which a conclusion is effected.

Heaven and earth transform; plants and trees flourish. When heaven and earth are closed, the wise hide. The *I Ching* says,

"Shutting the bag, there is no blame, no praise." This means being careful.

In Buddhist terms, if concentration and insight are capable of transformation, then people of various capacities each receive nutrition and are able to grow. But if you enter into transmundane realization and obliterate yourself and your intellect, then you cannot help others. Therefore those who practice this teaching must be careful.

Leaders comprehend design in a centered and balanced way. While in the correct state, they maintain their bodies. When there is beauty therein, it rises in their limbs and comes out in their work. This is the consummation of beauty.

In Buddhist terms, one uses absorption in central balance to reach the inner design of the manifestation of reality. Although the manifestation of reality is called the "correct state," it permeates all phenomena and maintains all bodies.

Only profound experience of meditation that is neither in the world nor beyond the world can rise in the limbs and come out in work, so that the inconceivable influence of teaching is carried out through psychological assessment, appropriate instruction, and practical demonstration. This teaching benefits those in all realms of consciousness, so it is "the consummation of beauty."

Yin doubting yang inevitably leads to battle, because it is not desirable for there to be no yang. Therefore yang is referred to as a dragon. It is still not apart from its kind, so yin is referred to as blood. "Dark yellow" means mixture of heaven and earth; heaven is dark and earth is yellow.

Both yin and yang are based on the absolute, so they are based on the same substance; how can they doubt each other and battle? When the yang identifies yang as yang and does not know that it is of the same substance as yin, it doubts yin and battles. When the yin identifies yin as yin and does not know that it is of the same substance as yang, it doubts yang and battles.

Just when yin is full, it battles yang, so it is as if there were no yang; therefore it is referred to as a dragon, to make it clear that yang is never nonexistent.

When yin shifts to yang, it seems as if it has left its yin kind, so it is referred to as blood, to make it clear that yin has not left its kind. The blood is said to be dark yellow because it represents the point of movement, on the verge of change, so "dark" and "yellow" are mixed. After the change has settled, heaven is dark and earth is yellow, and these cannot be mixed up.

Someone has interpreted this passage to mean that there is no point in leaders trying to get rid of riffraff, because riffraff will just keep growing no matter how much they try to get rid of them; what they should do is provide good leadership that people will enthusiastically follow; then there will be no need for struggle. If people understood what this means, we could get rid of the curse of parties and factions right away. If the leaders doubt the people, the people will doubt the leaders, and both will be harmed.

In Buddhist terms, if the four meditations were mistaken for the four realizations in the beginning, then at the end, with the appearance of subsequent mundane manifestations, one would doubt the teaching that there is no more mundane existence after the fourth realization. Thus one would become inclined to repudiate Buddhism. This is the inevitable "battle."

Nevertheless, that does not mean there is no one in the world who has truly realized the knowledge and qualities of the four realizations; therefore the text refers to the "dragon," to make it clear that the four realizations are not in vain.

As for those who mistake meditations for realizations, they may think they have attained the four realizations, but they are just obscurantists who have tasted some meditation and really have not left the ranks of those caught up in the mundane whirl. Therefore the text refers to "blood," to define this kind.

"Dark yellow" represents injury to both concentration and insight; when you damage insight by too much concentration, since insight is defective, concentration is also defective. However, they are only defective in terms of cultivated qualities.

When it comes to the inherent nature of calm awareness, the dark is of itself dark and the yellow of itself yellow; even the incorrigible cannot cut off inherent goodness, and even if there is confusion and delusion, the truth always remains—there can be no mixup.

Now, to interpret in terms of contemplating mind, yin and yang can both refer to good and bad, but for now I will use yin for evil and use yang for good. Good and evil have no inherent nature; they are of the same one nature of the potential for coming to awareness of reality—what is there to doubt? What is there to battle?

Only for those who do not realize inherent good and inherent evil, affirmation and denial oppose each other, producing circular arguments and inevitable battle.

When we do battle, we bury the subtle nature that is natureless, the subtle, selfless self, and it seems as if there were no yang, no positive energy, so we call on the dragon to illustrate the unbroken existence of inherent good.

Once good and evil oppose each other, then both are already contaminated; therefore this fact is referred to as "blood," to show that people caught up in contests of "good" and "evil" have not left the ranks of those caught up in the mundane whirl of birth and death.

When good and evil oppose and overthrow each other, this is because of not having realized that the substance of their subtle essential nature is one, and seeing a mixture or jumble of descriptions of events.

Really heaven is dark, earth is yellow—the higher development of mind is an endless mystery; physical life on earth succeeds through balance. These cannot be changed. What is there to disapprove or doubt? What is there to do battle with?

Good and evil are not the same, yet they are the same in being of one essential nature, just as dark and yellow are not the same, yet they are the same in being descriptions of consciousness of eyesight. Heaven and earth are not the same, yet are the same one absolute. Also it is like the way the images in a mirror, beautiful and ugly, are not the same, yet it is the same one mirror.

If you know the sameness underlying dissimilarity, then you will surely not create battles by opposing differences to each other for their mutual elimination.

If you know the dissimilarity in spite of sameness, then you surely should learn to imbue yourself with good influences uncontaminated by egotism, so as to transform evil.

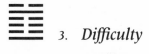 *3. Difficulty*

thunder below, *water* above

Creativity is successful. It is beneficial to be correct. Do not make use of going somewhere. It is beneficial to set up lords.

In Buddhist terms, there is the difficulty at the beginning of an age, the difficulty at the beginning of a lifetime, the difficulty at the beginning of a task, and the difficulty at the beginning of a thought. I will leave the first three aside for now, and just discuss difficulty at the beginning of a thought, when a thought first stirs.

The hexagrams *Heaven* and *Earth* represent inherent awareness, which is subtle but clear, clear but subtle. Inherent awareness must be clear, and one becomes aware of illusion by this clarity. In other words, true being-as-is does not keep to its own nature, and ignorance goes into action; when ignorance is activated, inevitably one reaches the point where objects are posited based on awareness, thus producing random subjectivity, defining variety and sameness, until difficulties arise in confusion. Therefore it is called *Difficulty.*

Were it not for random movement of mind, how could there be cultivation of virtuous qualities, to overcome error? This is why it is said that knowledge is born when ignorance acts, and nirvana appears when illusions arise. This is why when "creativity is successful, it is beneficial to be correct."

But as soon as a thought stirs, this already is the basis of entrapment in compulsive routines, so "do not make use of going somewhere." If you "go somewhere," this is following ignorance and turning away from the essence of reality.

The only thing that is beneficial at this point is to employ knowledge and wisdom to exercise profound insight into the mind; this is called "setting up lords." If you use knowledge and wisdom to observe insightfully, then you know thoughts have no definite origination, and will immediately attain peace. No secret of contemplating mind is beyond this.

THE OVERALL JUDGMENT: **In difficulty, firmness and flexibility begin to mix, and difficulty arises. Acting in the midst of danger, great success is correct. The action of thunder and rain fills; heaven creates confusion and obscurity. It is good to set up lords, but not presume on peace.**

In Buddhist terms, the first movement of ignorance is firm; defining objects based on awareness is flexible. Once there is subject and object, then there is a basis for the continuity of the process of subjectivity being mistaken for objectivity; this is how difficulty arises.

The initial random stirring of mind is the first way of entrapment in compulsive mental habits, yet it is also the barred opening to liberation; just observe the quality of the movement of mind. During this movement, the dichotomization of subject and object takes place; then the mind grasps objects, defines and labels them, and acts on and gets entangled in the subjectively constructed continuity of the perceived world. Thus the image of "thunder and rain filling, heaven creating confusion and obscurity."

It is best to immediately apply subtle observational knowledge to analyze this process; one should not sit in the nihilistic nest of unknowing. Generally speaking, when practitioners notice that random thoughts have not cropped up for a while, they mistake this for empowerment; they do not know that annihilation is the abode of production. So one should not stick to this realm of tranquillity and should break through it.

THE IMAGE: **Clouds and thunder—difficulty. Thereby leaders organize.**

To observe that the mind is not in the past, present, or future, and comes and goes without any connection to time; and to observe that mind is not inside, outside, or in between, and none knows its homeland—this is organization of meditation.

In Buddhist terms, when one is alienated from one's true nature of subtle awareness, luminous and ineffable, the characteristics of ignorant stirring of thought are "thunder." The obscuring characteristics of the objects made manifest through that stirring thought are "clouds." From these develops the continuity of idea-action-entanglement circles; this is difficulty.

Yet those who correctly practice complete all-at-once stopping and observing must go to the road in order to return home; they should realize that this very stirring of thought has the nature of awareness capable of realizing its own nature, and the objects of thought have the nature of works and qualities that can make this realization possible.

In the context of the conditions and awareness that can foster enlightenment, to explain how to stop the mind from wandering, see reality directly, and discern the qualities of all states of mind, is called "organizing." This is the foremost observation, of the realm of inconceivability.

■ *First yang:* **Staying around, it is beneficial to remain correct. It is beneficial to set up lords.**

When people have leadership qualities but do not have leadership positions, they "stay around" and will benefit from remaining correct. Since their inner qualities are fully developed and can guide the masses, it is "beneficial to set up lords" to solve difficulties.

In Buddhist terms, to "stay around" means to be immediately aware of any mental movement and not roll along, following thoughts. This is what is called "coming back before going far."

This is one who is good at cultivation and experiential realization; because accurate insight, true knowing, is in command, this is like the method of immediate enlightenment.

THE IMAGE: **Though they stay around, the action of their wills is correct. Because they value the lowly, they win many people.**

Staying around and not going forward seems like there is no will to save the world. But this world cannot be saved by force; so remaining correct is the way for action to be correct. Difficulty in society derives from communication gaps between high and low; if leaders can value the lowly, they will become "lords" even without wishing to, and will win the hearts of many people and inevitably become established.

In Buddhist terms, not following the flow of ups and downs is following the flow of the true nature of things, and doing what is correct. But even though one has all at once realized the importance of the true nature of things, yet one is able to refrain from abandoning the lowly work of actual achievements. This is what is meant by the saying that subtle contemplation of the center permeates all situations, so that basic and auxiliary ways of realizing truth are both fulfilled, and "they win many people."

■ *2 yin:* **Stopped, mounted on a horse but standing still. Not enmity, marriage. The girl is chaste and does not get engaged. After ten years she is engaged.**

In Buddhist terms, this is like the work of cultivation and realization through a step-by-step course of meditation. Here yin is in the second position, the position of balance; this represents centered, correct methods of concentration. But if one cannot immediately transcend, it is necessary to refine the mind by going through observations of different levels of reality, and practice all necessary meditations before one can see the essence of enlightenment. Therefore "after ten years she is engaged."

THE IMAGE: **The difficulty of the second yin is riding on the obdurate. Getting engaged after ten years means return to normal.**

In Buddhist terms, "riding on the obdurate" refers to the many levels of psychological problems that inhibit us from enlightenment. Without step-by-step practice of meditation in depth, it is impossible to return to the normalcy of the true nature of things.

■ *3 yin:* **Chasing deer without preparation only goes into the bush. Leaders see that it is better to give up, for to go would bring regret.**

In Buddhist terms, if you want to practice meditation concentration, you need knowledge and insight. If you have no accurate knowledge yourself and do not have enlightened teachers or associates, and practice blindly, then you will fall into a pit.

Leaders know how to see what is subtle, and would in such a case prefer to give up sitting meditation to go look for teachers who really know; if they just went on blindly, set in their ways, they would be ignorant and would bring on themselves the regret of a fall.

THE IMAGE: **Chasing deer without preparation is following the beasts. Leaders abandon this, for to go would bring regret and lead nowhere.**

In Buddhist terms, greed for experience of meditation is called "following the beasts." This is due to basic lack of sincere will for enlightenment.

■ *4 yin:* Mounted on a horse but standing still. Go to seek alliance, and the good results will benefit all.

In Buddhist terms, the yin in the fourth place is correct but not balanced; if you use this concentration method for self-cultivation, your road will be long and it will be hard to make progress. You should only go to seek alliance with enlightened teachers and associates; then the good results of the combination of practice and guidance will benefit all.

THE IMAGE: Going in search is intelligent.

In Buddhist terms, one who does not rely on meditation alone, but seeks teachers and associates who really know and are really wise, is one who truly has critical intelligence.

■ *5 yang:* Stalling the benefits. There is good outlook for the correctness of the small, bad outlook for the correctness of the great.

In Buddhist terms, balanced and accurate insight can certainly cut through confusion, but if one then grasps the absolute right away, one falls into individualistic liberation, and this means that the commitment to help everyone become liberated can no longer reach them. In the context of the Small Vehicle of Buddhism, this means rapid escape from the problems of life and death, so it has a good outlook; in the context of the Great Vehicle of Buddhism, however, it is remote from true enlightenment, so it has a bad outlook.

THE IMAGE: "Stalling the benefits" means that the giving is not yet enlightened.

It is not that there is no giving at all, just that it does not accord with greater reality.

■ *Top yin:* Mounted on a horse, standing still, weeping tears of blood.

In Buddhist terms, if you practice meditation without true insight to fulfill it, then even if you dwell on peak experiences you will not escape the calamity of going through vain repetition, and will certainly not be able to cut off confusion and get out of birth and death. Therefore you will be as though "mounted on a horse, yet standing still," not really getting anywhere, staying in trances for long periods of time, only to have them fall into nothingness. Then you "weep tears of blood."

THE IMAGE: Weeping tears of blood—what can last?

In Buddhist terms, even immensely long times spent in meditation trances ultimately come to an end. These too are impermanent.

 4. Darkness

water below, *mountain* above

Darkness. Getting through. It is not that I seek the ignorant; the ignorant seek me. The first pick informs, the second and third muddle. That which is muddled does not inform. Benefit is a matter of correctness.

Darkness is a symbol of ignorance and lack of development. This covers people's eyes and clouds their thought and behavior, but it cannot cover the essential nature of consciousness, which therefore "gets through."

But the science of enlightening the ignorant shows that it will not work if teachers approach the ignorant; they must let the ignorant come to them. When seekers are sincere, the information will get to them. When seekers are muddled, the information they find will also be muddled. Being muddled is not the correct way to enlightenment. Confucius was really a good educator; he "did not try to broaden the horizons of those who were not themselves determined to do so, and did not try to open the minds of those who had not already gone to the limit of their own understanding."

In Buddhist terms, if the mind does not stir, nothing more can be said; once it does stir, however, there is inevitably danger. When you meet danger, you must stop; when you stop, you have the opportunity to go back to the basis, to return to the source. That is why there is a way of "getting through."

If you are ignorant and want to get through it, you need the help of enlightened guides and good associates. So it is that those who would be guides and good associates have education and perfection in mind at all times, but nevertheless they must wait for the ignorant to come to them before a sense of the opportunity can be created.

Also it is necessary that the "first pick inform," to show the importance of the way to realize enlightenment. the basis of the information also must be in accord with reality and potential correctly before it can help people become wise and enlightened.

THE OVERALL JUDGMENT: Darkness—there is danger below a mountain. Stopping at danger is innocence; innocence gets through, because successful action is that which is at the heart of the time.

It is not that I seek the ignorant, the ignorant seek me—this means a correspondence of aspirations.

The first pick informs—because that which is definite is central balance.

The second and third muddle; that which is muddled does not inform, because it muddles up the ignorant. The accomplishment of sages is to take the opportunity of ignorance to educate correctly.

The reason the ignorant can get through their ignorance is that there are guides who can get them through the dark, through their skillful use of action and instruction at the heart of the time.

But even though there may be good teaching, it is necessary to wait for the ignorant to seek it; because the teaching can respond to them only if they have come because they have sensed something. The symbol for this is water being able to reflect the moon only when it is clear.

The meaning of "the first pick informs" is definite attainment of central balance, thereby being responsive to opportunity.

When it says, "that which is muddled does not inform," this does not mean fear of being muddled; it properly means fear of muddling the ignorant, thus harming them.

When people are ignorant, the work of the enlightened is to educate them properly, so that they too may become enlightened.

THE IMAGE: Under a mountain emerges a spring, in darkness. Leaders use effective action to nurture inner qualities.

In Buddhist terms, this is awakening the true aspiration for enlightenment based on the realm of inconceivability. This aspiration for enlightenment cannot be destroyed, just as a spring must flow; the commitment to universal liberation and enlightenment covers all, just as a spring provides water for plants, animals, and people.

■ *First yin:* To awaken the ignorant, it is beneficial to use punishments; if restrictions are eased, it will be regrettable to go that way.

When ignorance is extreme, it is necessary to break it down, "so it is beneficial to use punishments." And once restrictions are eased, it is proper to be conscientious in self-correction and not go forth. If you rush into something, you will regret it.

THE IMAGE: It is beneficial to use punishments, by the correct method.

The correct method of breaking down ignorance is not emotional attack.

■ *2 yang:* **It bodes well to embrace the ignorant. It bodes well to take a wife. The child becomes head of the family.**

In Buddhist terms, when concentration and insight are equally well developed, you have finished helping yourself, and therefore can embrace, protect, and educate the ignorant, with a good outlook. Through one's own development, to teach the ignorant to practice subtle concentration is called "taking a wife," which "bodes well."

Concentration can give birth to insight, and insight can succeed to the lineage of buddhas; this is the child becoming head of the family. The wife is concentration; the child is insight.

THE IMAGE: The child becoming head of the family is firmness and flexibility meeting and joining.

The reason that the text speaks of taking a wife and says that the child becomes head of the family is that concentration must produce insight, and insight must be equal to concentration, so that they are not imbalanced.

■ *3 yin:* **Do not take a girl to see a moneyed man, or she will lose herself, to no one's benefit.**

When people are mixed up they should seek firm guidance to break through their ignorance, for only thus can their affliction be cured. If in this state they wish only to be accepted and treated nicely, then they will be like a girl who meets a moneyed man and loses her chastity.

In Buddhist terms, if they are not correctly centered, concentration and insight are both of a low quality. If they are put in a dominant position, they will lose all possibility of rectification, and there will be no benefit.

Also, when people who are inclined to sport their cleverness are for the moment in high positions, they have already become so mechanical that if they were to practice meditation now, acutely compulsive, deluded views would surely arise in their meditation; and once acute compulsions arise, then the root of good is cut off. So the girl is meditation, and the moneyed man is the arrogant ego; meditation loses its true character when it is practiced while under the influence of the arrogant ego, and it loses all benefit.

THE IMAGE: **Do not introduce the girl, because his conduct is not harmonious.**

When action is not harmonious, it is necessary to use abrasive and uncomfortable methods to refine it before it is useful to practice meditation.

■ *4 yin:* **Stuck in darkness, regretful.**

The yin lines are all emblematic of darkness, or ignorance. The first stands for ignorance that is ready to be cleared up; the third stands for ignorance that should be attacked; the fifth stands for ignorance that should be embraced. This fourth stands for those who have no enlightened guides or good companions at all, and so are stuck in ignorance. What could be more regrettable?

THE IMAGE: **The regret of being stuck in darkness is having strayed from reality on one's own.**

Real teachers do not avoid us; we ourselves avoid real teachers. As long as we avoid real teachers, what can they do for us?

■ *5 yin:* **Innocent ignorance has a good outlook.**

When an adult does not lose the heart of a baby, this is innocent ignorance and has a good outlook, because of being near to strict guides and good associates.

THE IMAGE: **The good outlook of innocent ignorance is in harmonizing smoothly.**

The inherent rule of the way to really learn is that you have to harmonize with the way in order to get into it; even if you try, as long as your actions do not harmonize with the way, you will have no way to get into real learning.

■ *Top yang:* **Attack ignorance. It is not beneficial to be a robber; it is beneficial to ward off robbers.**

When one is firm but not excessive, one can use the power of concentration and insight to break through the barriers of ignorance.

But the way to teach the ignorant does not have dogmas to bind people. As it is said, there are only ways to remove blindness, no special ways to give sight.

So if you want to hand on your own personal doctrine, then you are being a robber.

If you give medicines to suit ailments, freeing people from their bonds, then you are warding off robbers.

THE IMAGE: It is beneficial to ward off robbers, for then above and below are in harmony.

When there is no dogma binding people, then all types of people can be contacted, in harmony with truth and in harmony with the potential inherent in the opportunity of the moment; therefore "above and below are in harmony."

 5. *Waiting*

heaven below, *water* above

Waiting with truthfulness lights up success in correct orientation toward good. It is beneficial to cross a great river.

The way to educate the ignorant cannot be rushed; it is necessary to await the appropriate times and conditions. If the time comes,the truth becomes self-evident.

But it is important that the cause be true, so the effect is right; therefore it is when the waiting has truthfulness that it lights the way to success that is correctly oriented toward good.

In the beginning the text speaks of waiting, but in the end one can cross the great river of birth and death, and climb up onto the shore beyond, which is great ultimate nirvana.

THE OVERALL JUDGMENT: Waiting is necessary; danger lies ahead. When firmness is strong and not overthrown, its justice is not frustrated.

Waiting with truthfulness lights up success in correct orientation toward good, in that it is posited on celestial order and thus correctly centered.

It is beneficial to cross a great river in the sense that progressive action is successful.

Knowing the need to wait when danger lies ahead is characteristic of firmness that is strong, not bringing about its own overthrow by wrong action.

In Buddhist terms, long, unpleasant stretches of danger and difficulty are called "danger ahead." The power of knowledge and wisdom is not over-thrown by problems, so in the end it is possible to be liberated and not be frustrated.

The yang in the center of the trigram *water* is based on the body of *Heaven;* this symbolizes how the essential nature of dangerous paths or problems is based on the potential for realization of being-as-is.

If you use this unborn, imperishable essential nature as the basis, then from beginning to end you will be in harmony with the disposition of celestial events.

From the essential nature, the right basis, you gradually flow into the ocean of all knowledge. Therefore "it is beneficial to cross a great river." Going from the state of the ordinary man to that of the sage, there is accomplishment.

THE IMAGE: Clouds rise in the sky—waiting. Leaders make merry with food and drink.

In Buddhist terms, practical actions to aid the way to enlightenment are "drink." The activity of wisdom, the main way to enlightenment, is "food." Using activities and wisdom in accord with essence to adorn the essence is like the image of clouds rising in the sky.

To complete nature, we produce culture; the completion of culture is in nature. It does not depend on working hard to get through the grist, to "practice" and "realize." Therefore it is called "making merry."

This is skillful resting of the mind in calm and clarity whatever the circumstances. The nonduality of calm and clarity is like the harmony of food and drink.

■ *First yang:* Waiting on the outskirts, it is beneficial to employ constancy. No blame.

In Buddhist terms, the stage of merely ideal buddhahood cannot really be called "waiting." In the stage of intellectual understanding of buddhahood, it is for the time being good to use the power of the influence of learning as sustenance for the intellect. At this stage one has not yet battled with the forces of delusion in afflictions.

THE IMAGE: "Waiting on the outskirts" means one has not entered into difficult actions. "It is beneficial to employ constancy; no blame" means one has not yet lost normalcy.

■ *2 yang:* Waiting on the sand, there is some criticism, but the end is auspicious.

In Buddhist terms, in the stage of contemplation practices, once you have put down confusion, then the forces of delusion are shaken up; so "there is some criticism."

THE IMAGE: **Waiting on the sand is because there is useless excess within. Though there is some criticism, it is to make the end auspicious.**

- *3 yang:* **Waiting in the mud brings enemies.**

In Buddhist terms, in the stage of conformity, one is about to cross the great river of birth and death; there is something about this that brings on the forces of delusion, and there is something about this that subsequently conquers them.

THE IMAGE: **Waiting in the mud, calamity lies without. Once I have brought on enemies, I am careful not to be defeated.**

Since the "calamity lies without," the autonomous self does not get lost, and nothing that comes from outside can take advantage of you. You just use the power of aspiration to bring the forces of delusion, so as to show the power of conquering delusion and attaining enlightenment. If the work of contemplating the absolute, the relative, and their unity is carried out with respect and care, there will certainly be no failure.

- *4 yin:* **Waiting in blood, coming out from one's cave.**

In Buddhist terms, when the forces of delusion have been defeated, you come out beyond the lairs of all physical and metaphysical realms and attain true awareness.

THE IMAGE: **Waiting in blood means listening receptively.**

Without even using force to conquer delusion, only the power of concentrated compassion, one can see to it that the forces of delusion retreat of themselves, and enlightenment is achieved of itself.

- *5 yang:* **Waiting in the midst of wine and food, it is good to be correct.**

The suchness of the realm of delusion is the same as the suchness of the realm of enlightenment. Only liberating people through the development of powers of concentration and insight can be "waiting in the midst of wine and food."

THE IMAGE: **With wine and food, it is good to be correct, in the sense of being centered correctly.**

■ *Top yin:* **Entering a cave, three unhurried guests come. Respect them, and the end is auspicious.**

In Buddhist terms, this means not only going into the realm of enlightenment, but also being able to go into the realm of delusion, coming back into the realms of emotions, physical events, and metaphysical states, to liberate as many people as possible, observing the elements of the subjective and objective causes and effects of these realms. This is the unified mind with three perspectives, which enables people to be free benefactors. Those who respect these enlightened benefactors end up well.

THE IMAGE: **Three unhurried guests come. Respect them, and the end is auspicious. Even though you do not reach rank, still you have not lost much.**

Once you are integrated with the emotional, physical, and metaphysical worlds, though you are not in the position of buddhas, yet you can liberate people according to their type. Even if people do not know or respect you, you can still make conditions for their liberation from a distance, and you have not lost much.

 ## 6. *Contention*

water below, *heaven* above

Contention; there is blockage of truth. Wariness within leads to good results, but ending up that way is unfortunate. It is beneficial to see a great person. It is not beneficial to cross a great river.

In Buddhist terms, a good way to educate the ignorant is to wait for them with comprehensive all-at-once calmness and perception; this is sufficient. But if the habit of mental affliction is strong, one cannot do without effort to contend with oneself.

In this sense, contention means self-criticism, reforming in ever better ways. We have true hearts, but they are blocked by the harmful action of moods, desires, and opinions. So we should criticize ourselves and be aware of that which is within—this will lead to good results.

But if we keep regretting the blockage of truth and have no means of doing something about it, then we just wind up stifled by regret and end up unfortunate.

It is appropriate to see a great person, to get rid of doubts and regrets with certain exposition. It is not beneficial to try to cross the great river of arising and passing away of afflictions, and wind up sinking.

THE OVERALL JUDGMENT: Contention. Above, adamant; below, dangerous. Strong in the face of danger, contend.

When there is contention, there is blockage of truth. To be wary of what is within leads to good results—strength comes and finds balance.

Ending up unfortunate means that the suit could not be completed.

It is beneficial to see a great person—this is valuing central balance that is true.

It is not beneficial to cross a great river, because it would mean entering an abyss.

If you are strong but there is no danger, it is not necessary to contend with yourself. If there is danger and you have no strength, then you cannot contend with yourself.

Now we are in the dangerous, miserable cave of afflictions, yet the intelligence is brave and strong, enabling us to intend to criticize ourselves and change for the better.

When the text says that there is blockage of truth but that wariness of what is within leads to good results, this is because the quality of firm strength comes back to flawlessness.

It is enough to get the fault to disappear; do not stifle yourself by too much regret. "Ending up unfortunate" means that the arrow of regret has entered the heart. This creates a great loss, so the reform cannot be completed.

The reason it is beneficial to see a great person is that the qualities of correct balance have ways of resolving doubts and getting away from faults.

The reason it is not beneficial to cross a great river is that as long as the dust on the heart has not yet been cleaned away, and the film of deposit on the mind has not been removed, if one enters the oceans of birth and death, one will surely come to a point where one will fall and not get out.

In terms of contemplating mind, cultivating the exercise of insight is called seeing a great person; cultivating meditation concentration is called crossing a great river.

Waiting refers to people without excesses, who are therefore in a proper condition to practice concentration. *Contention* refers to people with excesses, who will become deluded if they practice concentration.

THE IMAGE: **Sky and water go in opposite directions—contention. When leaders do things, they plan to begin with.**

Sky and water—that is, intellect and desire—are both of the absolute and have no essential opposition. When intellect is unified, it produces desire, so there is no opposition in this sense either.

But now that we are pursuing false appearances, one is above and one is below; they go in opposite directions. This is what is referred to as intellectually desiring purity but being thoroughly polluted.

It only takes a moment of thought in which one is unable to be careful of the beginning in order to bring about mental problems produced from nature. Those problems become habitual and grow so strong that they deviate from nature.

Therefore leaders must be careful of themselves even when they are alone, aware of the beginning of each act, each thought, not letting anything develop insidiously to the point where it becomes hard to handle. This is what is called being good at self-criticism.

In Buddhist terms, this represents a method of breaking through all phenomena, by questioning whether they arise from themselves, from something else, from both themselves and something else, or from no cause. The result of this contemplative method is to realize that fundamentally there is no origination.

■ *First yin:* **Not persisting in an affair, there is some criticism, but the end is auspicious.**

In general, good should be strong and progressive; evil is best when it is weak and recessive. The first yin is weak and recessive, so it is used to represent evil that has not yet fully developed, when reform is also easy. All that is needed is a little criticism. This is like the repentance practices in Buddhism.

THE IMAGE: **Not persisting in an affair means that contention should not go on long. Though there is some criticism, the explanation is clear.**

■ *2 yang:* Not victorious in contention, one goes home and hides. The local people number 300 families. There is no mistake or calamity.

If one is strong but not right, one cannot master oneself and so comes to contention. Having made serious mistakes, one cannot avoid loss; one can only escape, lie low, and lead a simple life, in hopes of avoiding calamity.

In Buddhism, this is like when initiates regress to become student novices.

■ *3 yin:* Living on past virtues, if you are upright in danger, the end will be auspicious. If you pursue political affairs, nothing will be accomplished.

This represents weakness in the sense of not daring to do anything wrong and just prudently keeping to standard rules; by being very careful this can turn out well. Petty-minded people, however, probably are not up to accomplishing anything great.

THE IMAGE: Living on past virtues is the luck of following the high.

If you cannot do it on your own, you will be lucky if you stick with other people. This is what is referred to as the vine climbing the tall pine soaring to the heights.

In Buddhist terms, even if it is not a teaching of the universalist school, if you take away the temporary presentation to show the underlying reality, then that practice too is a path of enlightenment. Therefore it is necessary to follow the highest method of complete all-at-once understanding in order to have the fortune to realize this.

■ *4 yang:* Contending unvictorious, return to destiny, change to rest in rectitude; then the outlook is good.

This also represents strength that is not oriented correctly or used properly, which makes one unable to master oneself and so come to contention. But this line is in the body of *Heaven,* the realm of intelligence, so the power of reform is strong, so one can return to perfection and awaken to the profoundly subtle body of nature and life.

In Buddhism, this is like awakening to beginninglessness by means of repentance through mental picturings.

THE IMAGE: Returning to destiny, changing to rest in rectitude, means not getting lost.

■ *5 yang:* Contention is very auspicious.

When firm strength is balanced and correct, one is always aware of the existence of anything that is not good, and being aware of it, one does not do it. One is extremely wary of making even the slightest wrong move. This is a way to great goodness, very auspicious.

In Buddhist terms, this means when all actions, those that come naturally and those that are invented, are thoroughly pure.

THE IMAGE: Contention is very auspicious when it is balanced and correct.

■ *Top yang:* Even if one is given a belt of honor, before the day is out it will be taken away three times.

Strength that is too extreme is neither balanced nor correct. If one keeps making mistakes and keeps repenting and reforming, the thin robe of regret in the repentance is like a belt of honor; but repeating mistakes, without a day of clean living, is like the belt of honor being taken away three times.

THE IMAGE: One receives the robe through contention and is not worthy of honor.

Having a fault and then reforming is called repentance; already this is not as honorable as having no faults. Why must we be dishonored repeatedly before we are ashamed? This is a grave warning to people not to carelessly go wrong.

7. *The Army*

water below, *earth* above

**For the army to be right, mature people are good.
Then there is no error.**

If one can contend with oneself, then one will not get into contention with others. When there is contention among two or more parties that is not settled, this is called disorder.

Disorder inevitably leads to the use of arms; it is the force of events that brings this unavoidably about, and arms are indeed a way to get rid of disorder.

However, weapons are unlucky and battle is dangerous; how can anyone but mature people of character be capable of carrying this out?

In Buddhist terms, if people are ignorant but have made no mistakes, then one educates them with patience, waiting; if they are ignorant and have made mistakes, one contends with them to improve them.

But people's afflictions are infinite, so the methods of curing them are also infinite. These infinite methods of curing afflictions are called "the army."

Of course, it is necessary to cure aberrations correctly, so it is necessary to have profound knowledge of the relationship between medicine and disease, and to give the medicine to suit the illness.

So one must be like an old general, a skilled strategist who knows what will work and what will not; only then can there be good results, without error.

Otherwise, if the teaching or method is not appropriate to the potential of the person and the situation in which it is applied, then the medicine will not cure the illness, and will instead do harm.

THE OVERALL JUDGMENT: **The army is a group; being right is being correct. Those who can use groups correctly can be kings. When strength is balanced and responsive, it may act dangerously yet still be in accord with the right way, so this may poison the country, yet the people will still go along with this. Good fortune, and what blame?**

Arms are used when there is no other choice; this is like using medicine to cure illness. Therefore it is called "poisoning the country."

In Buddhist terms, the army is the manifold methods of liberation, being right is the true certainty of having transcended the world.

If one can use the many liberative methods to correct one's innumerable delusions, one helps oneself and helps others, and can thereby be a spiritual monarch governing the spiritual realm.

Strength in balance refers to the adornments of concentration and insight sensing and responding; though they operate in the dangerous paths of birth and death, yet at no time are they not in harmony with nirvana.

Using this complete, all-at-once metaphysical medicine is like poison milk poisoning everyone in the country, and the people in all states of mind go along with it. Good fortune, and what blame?

THE IMAGE: **There is water in the earth—the army. Leaders develop a group by admitting people.**

In Buddhist terms, within all phenomena without exception there is the essence of ease and bliss, and all phenomena include their antitheses. This is like the image of the presence of water in the earth.

Therefore progressive people realize that all the countless problems experienced in the course of life in the world are also so many ways to enlightenment, so they do not cling to anything, nor do they reject anything.

This is expert knowledge of what works and what does not. An ordinary example of this is that if you treat the people well, they will take up arms, but if you lose their goodwill, they will become bandits and enemies.

■ *First yin:* **The army goes forth in an orderly manner;**
negating the good leads to misfortune.

In Buddhist terms, the best method of curing the personality imbalances of beginners is communal and individual order. If one cannot lead an orderly life, one's actions, speech, and thoughts will be no good and will lead to misfortune.

THE IMAGE: **The army goes forth in an orderly manner,**
for if it loses order, there will be misfortune.

■ *2 yang:* **Being in the middle of the army is lucky, blameless.**
The king gives orders thrice.

In Buddhist terms, concentrated insight universally applying all ways of access to truth enables one to heal oneself and others; therefore it is lucky and blameless. When one has attained this, one will receive directions from the dispenser of the spiritual order.

THE IMAGE: **Being in the middle of the army is lucky, for one**
receives celestial favor. The king gives orders thrice, thinking
of all the provinces.

In Buddhist terms, to take up celestial action, and make it into wise and pure, compassionate and innocent work, is what is called keeping all this work in one mind. This is how one receives the favor of the dispenser of the spiritual order and receives directions in order to spread true civilization through all nations.

■ *3 yin:* **The army may have casualties; misfortune.**

In Buddhist terms, if you apply corrective methods arbitrarily, without knowing when they will work, you will on the contrary damage your own and others' mental life.

THE IMAGE: **When the army has casualties, that is great lack of**
success.

■ *4 yin:* **The army retreats and camps. No blame.**

In Buddhist terms, this is like a master of precepts for conduct not claiming to be universal in approach.

THE IMAGE: **Retreating and camping, without blame, means that one has not lost the constant.**

■ *5 yin:* **There are animals in the fields. It is beneficial to take up words. No blame. A mature person leads the army. If the leader is immature, there will be casualties, and even if the leader is right, the prospects are bad.**

In Buddhist terms, animals in the fields damaging the crops are like mental afflictions damaging the sprouts of enlightenment.

It is beneficial to take up words in the sense that it is good to read the teachings to clearly understand this.

However, the principles for reading scriptures are to rely on the meaning, not on the words; to rely on the complete teaching, not on incomplete teachings; to rely on true knowledge, not on conditioned discrimination.

If you can make a deep search of the meanings and principles in the scriptures, and go into contemplation along with the scripture, then you are like a mature person leading the army.

If you just stick to words and letters and do not go by the real meaning, that will be like the immature sustaining casualties; even if you are right, there is no real hope.

This is like Buddhist scholars today.

THE IMAGE: **A mature person leads the army, with balanced action. The immature sustain casualties because their mission was not appropriate.**

■ *Top yin:* **A great leader has orders to establish states and families that continue. Small people are not to be employed.**

In Buddhist terms, when it is appropriate to use corrective measures, one may go along with something or oppose something to correct it. An obstacle may arise in something that should work, or an obstacle itself may become a way through; so the matter cannot be generalized.

Now, when the correction has been successfully made and we can enter into attunement with ultimate truth, we are about to "establish states and families that continue," set up common and individual approaches to education that would truly civilize people, only using good things, not using anything bad.

If we do not weed out aberration and keep what is right, put aside sentimental views and show the seal of emptiness, selflessness, and nirvana, then
Buddhism and other teachings will be nearly without distinction.

THE IMAGE: A great leader has orders through appropriate
achievement.
Small people are not to be employed, because they will disrupt
the nation.

 8. *Accord*

earth below, *water* above

Accord bodes well. Make sure the basis is always right,
so that there will be no fault. Then the uneasy will come.
Latecomers are unfortunate.

In Buddhist terms, when you have skillfully applied corrective measures and
have become enlightened, those in other states of mind regard you as a reliable guide. This is called accord.

In terms of contemplating mind, once you know which corrective methods will work and which will not, it is necessary to adjust and harmonize
the elements of the path to enlightenment. The coordination of these elements is called accord.

Then it is still necessary to contemplate the practice itself, to see to it that
it is in accord with the unborn, imperishable, fundamental essence. This is
called making sure the basis is always right, so that there will be no fault.

This means practicing comprehensive meditation, wherein the perfection
of cultivation lies in nature. All the right efforts, spiritual faculties and powers, and other elements of the path follow along in order. This is called
"Then the uneasy will come."

All afflictions caused by emotional views, which are not in accord with
the correct method for liberation, will be forever destroyed and so are
"unfortunate."

THE OVERALL JUDGMENT: Accord is auspicious. Accord is
assistance; it is the lowly following docilely.

Make sure the basis is always right, so that there will be no
fault; then firmness is balanced.

Then the uneasy will come—above and below respond.

Latecomers are unfortunate—their path comes to an end.

In Buddhist terms, in terms of the person, those in unenlightened states of mind are the lowly. When they follow the realm of the enlightened docilely, they are assisting.

In terms of the teaching, practical activities are the lowly. When they follow the exercise of insight, then they are assisting. It is because of firmness in balance that one can produce culture with the whole nature and can complete culture in nature.

As for the responding of above and below, in terms of person this means people in all mental realms alike receiving the influence of the way of enlightenment. In terms of the teaching, all the elements of the way of enlightenment combine in round understanding.

The path comes to an end for people in the sense that they become deluded or wander off and suffer a fall, not following the teaching of enlightenment. In terms of teaching, this means being eliminated because of emotional ideas not in accord with the right way.

THE IMAGE: **There is water on earth—accord. The kings of yore thus set up myriad nations and associated with the lords.**

In Buddhist terms, earth is like objective realities, water is like perceptive insight; earth is like the realm of silent light, water is like the different realms of common presence, expedient purification, and true reward. Both have the image of accord.

In terms of teaching others, the realms of common presence, expedient purification, and true reward are set up, to have the enlightening beings transmit the teaching.

In terms of contemplating mind, objects such as the mental and physical elements are set up to provoke contemplative insight. This contemplative insight is called "the lords."

This stands for the harmonization of the various elements of the way to enlightenment, so that they are in accord, without any rift.

■ *First yin:* **When there is truthfulness, accord with it is blameless. When there is truthfulness filling a plain vessel, when the end comes there is other good fortune.**

In Buddhist terms, the first yin is like the human path, the second yin is like the heavens of desire, the third yin is like the heaven of delusion, the fourth yin is like the heavens of meditation, the fifth yang is like a Buddha being a spiritual monarch, and the top yin is like the heaven where there is neither perception nor nonperception. On the human path, represented by this first yin, it is easy to proceed toward enlightenment, so "there is other good fortune."

In terms of contemplating mind, the first yin is like the teaching of individual liberation, the second yin is like the teaching of universal emptiness, the third yin is like a sentimental teaching, the fourth yin is like the teaching of infinite ways of liberation for infinite types of people and problems, the fifth yang is like real true complete teaching, and the top yin is like false teaching of emptiness that disregards causality.

This line represents the teaching of individual liberation, which focuses on accurate perception of causal relations. When you open this up, it is none other than ineffable truth, so "there is other good fortune."

THE IMAGE: The first yin of accord has other good fortune.

■ *2 yin:* Accord coming from within is auspicious if correct.

In Buddhist terms, this can be interpreted to mean that people in the heavens of desire have virtues, and they also have intelligence, but they need to cultivate profound concentration.

Also, this is the skillful manner of liberation according to the teaching of universal emptiness as applied to that which is within one's own realm. It is the same as the totality of phenomena being identical to noumenon, as elucidated in the complete teaching; all that is needed is to reach the outside from the inside.

THE IMAGE: Accord coming from within means not losing oneself.

■ *3 yin:* The wrong person to accord with.

If one is not balanced correctly, and one is in a position of minor authority but has no strong critical guidance, one is "the wrong person to accord with."

In Buddhist terms, this means the devil hasn't a thought of good, and also that emotional opinions certainly do not accord with the way to enlightenment.

THE IMAGE: The wrong person to accord with; will there not be injury?

■ *4 yin:* According with the wise outside, correctness brings good results.

In Buddhist terms, this means that the realm of pure form has many meditation states in it. One should just awaken the aspiration for enlightenment and cultivate all facets of knowledge of differentiation outside.

Also, the teaching of infinite means of liberation for infinite types of people and problems involves dogged liberation of those outside one's own realm. It is appropriate to deal with this by accurate observation of complete integration.

THE IMAGE: **Accord with the wise outside is the way to follow the advanced.**

When there are people of wisdom in positions of leadership, for those below them to accord with them outside is simply the way things should be in theory and in fact.

■ *5 yang:* **Manifest accord. The sovereign uses three chasers. He loses the game before him. The local people are not warned. Auspicious.**

To interpret this in Buddhist terms, when a spiritual sovereign appears in the world, like the sun in the sky, this is called "manifest accord."

The "civilization" is effected by three means—mind-reading, appropriate instruction, and demonstration. Also, elementary, intermediate, and advanced teachings lead people to liberation, and enable the seeds of development to ripen, shed the husk of the worlds, and gain enhancement. These may be called "the sovereign using three chasers."

In regard to people with no affinity, the enlightened skillfully employ concentrated equanimity. So even the disciples of Buddha did not forcibly convert people with no affinity. That is called "He loses the game before him. The local people are not warned."

In terms of contemplating mind, when real insight opens out, it is like the bright sun in a clear sky; this is called "manifest accord."

When perception of the ultimate emptiness, conditional existence, and balance of all things is present in one mind, then one can absorb and understand the preparatory three teachings, each of which dealt with one aspect of this totality. This is called "the sovereign using three chasers."

Concentration on wakeful attention, in which one observes thoughts as they arise and does not fear the arising of thoughts but fears delay in noticing them, enables one to return to correct mindfulness as soon as one notices a thought, so that one does not keep the error of prior thoughts on one's mind. This is called "He loses the game before him. The local people are not warned."

THE IMAGE: **The good fortune of manifest accord is the correct balance of state. Giving up the opposition and taking the harmonious is losing the game before one. The local people are not warned, because the ruler has effected balance.**

■ *Top yin:* Accord without leadership bodes ill.

In Buddhist terms, this refers to ultimately vain circling in routines and being unable to perceive the enlightened or hear their teaching. Even if you go on for eighty thousand eons, you will not escape falling into nothingness.

In terms of contemplating mind, if you suddenly realize emptiness and disregard causality, believing yourself to have transcended everything, you are not really in accord with the true vehicle to the source. Your habitually active consciousness is vague, with no basis to rely on, and in a life-and-death crisis you are bound to be like a lobster plunged into boiling water.

THE IMAGE: Accord without leadership has no conclusion.

The six hexagrams from *Difficulty* to *Accord* have each contained the trigram *water* ☵ . *Water* ☵ has the center line of *heaven* ☰ , which stands for subtle insight into the center of everything. The reason that its quality, that of water, is overpowering and dangerous is that the ocean of passions and the ocean of all knowledge are not really two in essence.

Furthermore, from ancient times until now, none have not been born in suffering and died into peace; so the truth of suffering is placed first among the four truths elucidated by the Buddha. The Buddha called eight kinds of suffering teachers. Suffering causes anxiety and unease, and when one is anxious and uneasy, the ocean of passion stirs, so particularized knowledge appears.

The meaning of the order of the hexagrams as arranged by the sages is profound indeed.

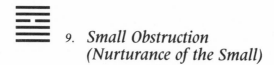

9. *Small Obstruction (Nurturance of the Small)*

heaven below, *wind* above

**At small obstruction, nurturing the small succeeds.
Dense clouds, not raining, come from one's own western region.**

The word for obstruction can also be read to mean nurturance; when you encounter situations that obstruct you and bog you down, if you do not get resentful or bitter, but just nurture yourself to digest them, you will be successful.

However, one must not seek to obtain results too rapidly. In worldly terms, this is like an orderly and peaceful country with a noninvasive government, to which some people nevertheless will not come.

In Buddhist terms, this is like when the mental center of delusion appears, as yet not under control.

In terms of contemplating mind, when the factual obstructions to enlightenment that have been there since beginningless time are overpowering even after the harmonizing of the elements of the path to enlightenment, they block perceptive insight, so that it cannot realize the truth.

However, when sages direct the age, they do not reject the ignorant masses. The educational and liberative activities of buddhas do not reject the deluded. As the contemplating mind progresses, why fear earlier obstructions?

Indeed, events and situations that formerly obstructed you can become means of self-development; this is how you succeed.

But now, though you need not fear the situation, still you should not grab for easy success. You should be like "dense clouds, not raining, coming from your own western region." That is, you should only go into action after harmonization of yin and yang. Usually clouds that rise from the east rain right away, whereas those that rise in the west hardly ever rain. This line indicates the value of not grabbing for easy success and the value of long-term results.

THE OVERALL JUDGMENT: **Nurturing the small at small obstruction, flexibility finds its proper position, so above and below respond to it. This is called nurturing the small. Strong yet obedient, firmness balanced, determined in action, one then succeeds.**

Dense clouds not raining are still moving. Coming from one's own western region means that the actualization has not yet taken place.

Once one is at an impasse and needs development, this is "small" in the sense that it is a matter of being correctly flexible. There is also firm strength above and below responding to this, so no external difficulties are sufficient to disturb one's stable, firm certainty. Then one uses this to develop oneself a little.

The quality of firmness, represented by the lower trigram, *heaven,* means there is no aberration caused by material desires; the quality of obedience, represented by the upper trigram, *wind,* means one makes no mistakes through impulsiveness.

When firmness is balanced, then insight accompanies concentration, so one's will can be carried out successfully.

Though the clouds are dense, they are still moving—this means that cultivation of inner qualities could be more progressive. Coming from one's own western region means that the actualization has not yet taken place—that is, one should not desire to obtain results quickly.

THE IMAGE: Wind moving up in the sky, nurturing the small.
Thus do leaders beautify cultured qualities.

Nothing has a more subtle influence on things than wind. Beautifying cultured qualities is like when they say that if people at a distance do not take to
you, you cultivate cultured qualities to attract them, just as an ancient chief-
tain won over a hostile tribe by doing dances representative of war and
peace.

In terms of contemplating mind, using generosity, self-discipline, patience, diligence, meditation, and insight to correct perceptive flaws, aid in
psychological development, and open the mind, is called beautifying cultured qualities.

First yang: Returning by the path, how could that be
blameworthy? It is auspicious.

THE IMAGE: Returning by the path, it is right that there should
be good fortune.

■ *2 yang:* Leading back bodes well.

THE IMAGE: Leading back into the center, and not losing
oneself.

■ *3 yang:* The wheels are detached from the cart. Husband and
wife look away from each other.

THE IMAGE: When husband and wife look away from each
other, they cannot cohabit.

■ *4 yin:* If there is truthfulness, blood goes and fear leaves,
and there is no blame.

THE IMAGE: Fear leaves when there is truthfulness, because
there is a consonance of will with on high.

■ *5 yang:* There is truthfulness in companionship. Blessings are
shared with the neighbors.

THE IMAGE: There is truthfulness in companionship, in the
sense that one does not enjoy blessings alone.

■ *Top yang:* It having rained and settled, exalted virtue is full.
Even if the wife is chaste, she is in danger.
The moon is almost full.
It is unlucky for a leader to go on an expedition.

THE IMAGE: It having rained and settled represents full
development of inner qualities. It is unlucky for a leader to go
on an expedition, as there is some doubt.

To interpret this hexagram in terms of mental states in Buddhist contemplation, when we practice a true way, there may be powerful factual obstructions that require specific remedies to help clear them away. But though we
use remedies to help clear away obstructions, still the guidance comes from
perceptive insight into the right way.

In the first yang, accurate knowledge is strong, so obstacles caused by
events cannot do any harm, and so one "returns by the path."

In the second yang, concentration and insight are balanced, so one can
make obstacles into one's own assistants and not lose oneself.

In the third yang, one relies on unfertile intellect and so is stymied by
obstacles that arise in the course of events; concentration and insight are
both damaged.

In the fourth yin, one skillfully uses correct concentration to awaken
competent insight, so "blood goes and fear leaves."

In the fifth yang, subtle insight into the true center of everything understands that obstacles lead to the qualities to overcome them, so they can
"share the blessings with the neighbors."

In the top yang, concentration and insight are equal, so concrete obstacles
melt away and you are freed of them. This is like when it has rained and
settled—the cultivation of inner qualities has been successful.

When concrete obstacles are set aside through corrective auxiliary measures, there will be an experience of utmost ease. This is called "the wife."

One should not savor this ease, because to savor it would give rise to pride,
and one would think oneself the same as a consummate sage. This is called
"the moon almost full." If you believe in this and proceed in this way, then
this will be a great falsehood, which bodes ill. How can we be careless?

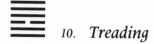

10. Treading

lake below, *heaven* above

Someone treads on a tiger's tail without being bitten, thus getting through.

In Buddhist terms, this is when the center of delusion comes under control, and the way of transforming it is working and can be trodden in the sense of being carried out.

Because one uses kindness to absorb the violence of the center of delusion, therefore it does not bite the person.

In terms of contemplating mind, after effecting specific remedies, it is necessary to clearly recognize successive stages, in order to accomplish true attainment of real application. To see mind as in itself enlightened is like treading on a tiger's tail; not getting conceited is like getting through without being bitten.

THE OVERALL JUDGMENT: **Treading is the flexible treading on the firm. There is joy that is in accord with heaven; this is how to tread on a tiger's tail and get through without being bitten. If one can exercise the position of the overall ruler and not be remorseful, this is illumination.**

In Buddhist terms, the flexible treading on the firm may represent using concentration to awaken insight, using culture to harmonize with nature, using awakening to seek the highest integration with original awareness, learning to be enlightened while an ordinary person.

Attaining delight in truth is called joy. To realize the essence of the cosmic design is called being in accord with heaven.

If one can progress to the state of truth without becoming conceited, then one can use culture to harmonize with nature and can manage the noble position of spiritual director.

THE IMAGE: **Above, sky; below, lake—treading. Leaders stabilize the wills of the people by distinguishing positions.**

In Buddhist terms, when we have deep knowledge of the eternal diversity of conscious states in spite of the identity of consciousness with itself, then we will not mix up steps in the procedure of full realization of complete consciousness. This is stabilizing the wills of the people by distinguishing positions.

■ *First yang:* Plain treading; to go is blameless.

THE IMAGE: To go treading plainly means to carry out your vows alone.

In Buddhist terms, this means having the power of accurate insight, thus profoundly knowing rankless ranks. Going on this way does not produce conceit.

■ *2 yang:* Treading the road; it is level. The person in obscurity is fortunate if upright.

THE IMAGE: The person in obscurity is fortunate if upright in the sense of not becoming personally deranged within.

In Buddhist terms, this is when concentrated insight into the center of everything progresses toward consummate enlightenment and does not become complacent but inwardly cultivates the mind so that it can personally witness truth, without seeking the recognition of another. This is the reason for being fortunate.

■ *3 yin:* The squint-eyed can see, the lame can walk. Treading on a tiger's tail, they get bitten, unfortunately. A military man becomes a civil leader.

THE IMAGE: The squint-eyed can see, but not clearly; the lame can walk, but not well enough to be companions on a journey. The misfortune of being bitten is that of being in an inappropriate place. When a military man becomes a civil leader, his determination is adamant.

In Buddhist terms, to know about inherent qualities but not know about cultivated qualities is like squinting an eye; to value the exercise of insight but not the exercise of action is like being lame in one leg. You may think you can see, but you do not really see true reality; you may think you are a practitioner, but you cannot really reach the ultimate goal. You talk in lofty terms about buddha-nature, but you are in fact adversely affected by these words. Originally a crude soldier, you falsely declare yourself a leader of the people. Few who do so escape falling into hell.

■ *4 yang:* Treading on a tiger's tail with utmost caution turns out lucky.

THE IMAGE: Utmost caution turning out lucky is determined action.

In Buddhist terms, when concentration and insight balance each other, even if one has not yet realized the center of everything, nevertheless one will progress relentlessly.

■ *5 yang:* Decisive treading is correct yet dangerous.

THE IMAGE: Decisive treading is correct yet dangerous; the position is appropriate.

In Buddhist terms, when firm strength is balanced correctly and one is certain to realize the enlightened nature, from this point on one uses up one's life to enhance the possibility of enlightenment for all, appearing and disappearing to influence people, not taking nirvana for personal comfort.

■ *Top yang:* Observing the treading, considering what is felicitous, the return is very auspicious.

THE IMAGE: When great good fortune is above, there is much celebration.

In Buddhist terms, effect permeates cause; when all virtues are completely fulfilled, we return to our original nature. Because we attain our original aspiration for awakening, this is very auspicious.

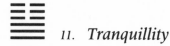

11. *Tranquillity*

heaven below, *earth* above

Tranquillity. The small goes and the great comes, getting through auspiciously.

In worldly terms, this is when there is true communication of mind between rulers and ruled, so that the country is tranquil.

In Buddhist terms, this is when the way of enlightenment is in effect and the methods it uses are working calmly.

In terms of contemplating mind, this means profound understanding of the various grades of self-realization, and cultivating experience surely without becoming conceited.

This also can be taken to refer to calm endurance of both strong and weak demons, so that the demons recede and the way of enlightenment goes through.

The inability of strong and gentle demons to cause trouble is what is meant by "the small goes." The complete development of the power of patience is what is meant by "the great comes."

THE OVERALL JUDGMENT: **In tranquillity the small goes and the great comes, getting through auspiciously. This is the development of myriad beings due to the combination of heaven and earth. Above and below communicate, so their wills are the same. Yang inside and yin outside, strong inside and docile outside, a leader inside and an ordinary person outside; the path of a leader goes on and on, while the path of an ordinary person vanishes.**

In Buddhist terms, if you get the small to go and the great to come, then the heaven inherent in you combines with the earth that you have cultivated, so that all things develop together. Transcendental mystic enlightenment and active work in the world combine, so that understanding and action are not separate.

Inwardly you now have the firmness represented by yang, and outwardly you display the flexible patience represented by yin. Inwardly you have the power of strong action unceasing, while outwardly you have the means to adapt to the world. Inwardly you are a leader on the way to enlightenment, while outwardly you are an ordinary person in the same continuum of mental experiences.

Because it can transform all realms of mental experience, so that they become objects of enlightenment, the path of such a leader goes on and on, while the path of an ordinary person dies out.

THE IMAGE: **When heaven and earth commune, there is tranquillity. Thus does the ruler administer the way of heaven and earth and assist the balance of heaven and earth, so as to influence the people.**

In Buddhist terms, the way of heaven and earth is inherent concentrated insight; the balance of heaven and earth is the balanced use of concentration and insight. Administration and assistance mean using culture to supplement nature. Influencing the people means that one is not destroyed by demons, strong or weak, and so can use these two kinds of demons as servants.

■ *First yang:* **Pulling out a reed by the roots, other reeds come with it. It is auspicious to go forth.**

THE IMAGE: **Pulling out reeds, going forth to success, means focusing the will beyond.**

Positive strength is at the beginning of tranquillity; but does that mean one should spend one's whole life in a low state? It is by taking similar people along to progress, the will not being limited to personal or family concerns, that it is possible to guarantee the tranquillity of the world in the end.

■ *2 yang:* **Accepting the uncultivated, employing those who can cross rivers, not overlooking the remote, free from partisanship, one can seriously perform balanced action.**

THE IMAGE: **Accepting the uncultivated and seriously performing balanced action are due to greatness of illumination.**

Here strength is balanced and in harmony with the fifth yin of this hexagram. This represents when someone who is wise is also in charge of carrying out tasks relating to the organization and operation of government and society, and does so in the best possible manner, with the most appropriate timing.

So here it is good to be tolerant, and accept the uncultivated and unskilled, and see after their welfare. As for those of talent, who can, so to speak, "cross rivers," employ them. Do not overlook those who are far away. Do not just be a partisan of other strong people, but cooperate seriously with those on a higher level who are flexible yet balanced and sane, so that enlightenment will become widespread.

■ *3 yang:* **There is no level without incline, no going without returning. Be upright in difficulty, and you will be blameless. Do not grieve over your sincerity; there will be prosperity in sustenance.**

THE IMAGE: **There is no going without returning—this refers to the border of heaven and earth.**

No individual or society has ever had enduring tranquillity and not gone bad. The point is simply to be aware of what that which is maintaining it is like. The third yang represents strength being correct, enabling one to be upright in difficulty and have prosperity, pulling back this border of heaven and earth.

■ *4 yin:* Unsettled, not prosperous, one works with the neighbor. Sincerity is exercised, without caution.

THE IMAGE: Being unsettled and not prospering are both due to loss of the real. Exercise of sincerity without caution is the heart's true desire.

This line represents the quality of being flexible but correct at a time when tranquillity has already passed midway. Although one has no real true ability or power to effect order, still if one relies on those with the same aspiration, it is thereby possible to prevent disastrous confusion. So among people of the same aspiration there is mutual trust, without any formal pact; therefore it is still possible to preserve this tranquility.

■ *5 yin:* The emperor marries off his younger sister, whereby there is good fortune, very auspicious.

THE IMAGE: That by which there is very auspicious good fortune is the balanced carrying out of deliberate, purposeful undertakings.

Flexible but balanced people in high positions who are open to the advice of the wise and do not consider leadership a personal monopoly are symbolized by the emperor marrying off his younger sister to a minister. If the ruler is able to recognize good advice and is open to it, then it is easy for the wise to work for such a ruler so as to maintain tranquillity permanently.

■ *Top yin:* The castle walls crumble into the moats. Do not use the army. Announcing order in one's own locality is shameful, in spite of correctness.

THE IMAGE: The castle walls crumbling into the moats means that order is in disarray.

When tranquillity culminates, there must be obstruction; the forces of time assure us of this. Passive flexibility has no ability to get rid of confusion, hence the caution not to use the army.

Those who have lost their authority above will make much of their orders to those below them, so there are those who give orders in their own localities. This is not the place to give orders, yet they are arbitrarily giving out orders—this is shameful.

However, the state represented by this top line is simply one of inability; since yin rests on yang, it is still correct, so it is not entirely without merit. It is just that in such a situation—the culmination of tranquillity—order is disturbed and comes from personal bailiwicks.

Now to interpret the six lines in Buddhist terms. If you want to calmly endure strong and weak demons, you must depend on the power of concentration and insight. The first yang is strong and upright, so once inner demons are conquered, outer demons will also submit, as when one pulls out a reed and takes others along with it.

In the second yang, strength is balanced, so once outer demons are transformed, inner demons do not arise. This is like "seriously performing balanced action," so that "enlightenment is widespread."

The third yang is too strong, so it is necessary to be upright in difficulty before one can be blameless. Because the basis is accurate insight, one will surely be able to attain concentration, so it is "the border of heaven and earth."

The fourth yin represents correct concentration truthful to accurate insight, so even though it may not be rich, it can "work with the neighbor." When one knows that demons have no reality, the demons become one's assistants and are like neighbors.

In the fifth yin, concentration has the right insight, so one can identify the realm of demons with the realm of enlightenment and become imbued with the twin adornments of blessings and wisdom, like the emperor marrying off his daughter so that there is good fortune that is very auspicious.

The top yin shows how demons can come out and cause disturbance because one persists in a low level concentration.

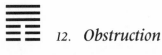 12. *Obstruction*

earth below, *heaven* above

Obstruction's denial of humanity does not make the leader's correctness beneficial. The great goes and the small comes.

In Buddhist terms, this is when the teaching becomes popular and there are many professional monks and nuns, and contaminated teachings and practices arise.

In terms of contemplating mind, after calmly enduring demons, one attains a semblance of realization; there is a tendency to give rise to religious attachment to an imitative path and not progress further.

If you give rise to religious attachment, then it is not the way of transcendental true tolerance and true knowledge; therefore it denies humanity and thwarts the correctness of the leader, because you are turning away from the universalistic way and falling back into the perspective of temporary personal concerns.

THE OVERALL JUDGMENT: Obstruction's denial of humanity does not make the leader's correctness beneficial. The great goes and the small comes. This means that heaven and earth do not commune, so myriad beings do not develop.

When above and below do not communicate, no country can exist. When inwardly weak while outwardly strong, inwardly a small person while outwardly a leader, then the way of the small will be fostered, and the way of true leadership will wane.

In Buddhist terms, if you give rise to religious attachment to an imitative path, then your cultivated qualities will not accord with the heaven of inherent qualities, and none of your practices will be developmental.

If transcendence is not combined with integration, you cannot emanate the "countries" of common presence, expedient liberation, and true reward from the realm of silent light.

If you inwardly attain passive, flexible, docile tolerance and place positive, strong enlightened nature beyond you, inwardly you are the same as small people who are mainly concerned with personal liberation, and you place the enlightened leaders beyond you. Unable to attain enlightenment yourself, you cannot influence others to attain enlightenment; therefore the way of the small will be fostered and the way of true leadership will wane.

People always fear demons, strong and weak, so the tradition on *Tranquillity* uses words of utmost felicity to comfort them and enable them to avoid shrinking back, intimidated. People always love religious attachment in following a way, so the tradition on *Obstruction* uses words of utmost lament to warn them not to become attached.

THE IMAGE: Heaven and earth do not commune—obstruction. Leaders therefore use power parsimoniously to avoid trouble, and should not prosper on wages.

In Buddhist terms, this means that one observes this religious attachment in following a path, and it is trouble like a dangerous pitfall, and so one does not grasp the taste of the experience. This is what is meant by "should not prosper on wages."

■ *First yin:* Pulling out a reed by the roots, taking other reeds
with it, correctness is auspicious and successful.

THE IMAGE: Pulling out a reed, correctness is auspicious—
the will is in the leader.

All six lines involve the responsibility for rescue from obstruction, and all
speak of methods of rescue from obstruction, so one should not take the
bottom three lines as denying humanity.

The first line represents passivity or weakness, or flexible docility, being
put in a position where firm, active strength is called for; there are those of
like mind who can help, so "pulling out a reed by the roots takes other reeds
with it," and this bodes well and is successful.

The time, however, is at the beginning of obstruction, so it is best to think
of troubles that may occur and prevent them; that is why the text cautions
with the word "correct."

■ *2 yin:* Embracing service, small people are lucky; great people
get through obstruction.

THE IMAGE: Great people get through obstruction in the sense
that they are not deranged by the crowd.

This line represents flexible docility balanced correctly, responding to the
leader with positive firmness balanced correctly, represented by the fifth
yang above, who develops people's hearts with humaneness and kindness,
bringing back the celestial fortune. So small people who embrace service to
enlightened order are lucky.

But from the point of view of the great person in the position of this second yin, this is where one sees the world not yet at peace and is still choked
and uneasy at heart; yet it is precisely because of this unease that one can
bring about a successful way through impasses and be invulnerable to mass
derangement.

■ *3 yin:* Embracing disgrace.

THE IMAGE: Embracing disgrace means that the position is not
appropriate.

This represents being inwardly strong while outwardly weak. If there is anything you can do to help the rescue of people from obstruction, you will do
it, without concern for petty reputation or petty manners.

■ *4 yang:* If there is order, there is no blame. The companions
cleave to blessings.

THE IMAGE: If there is order there is no blame because
the will is carried out.

When one is strong but not upright, if one is in a high position one would
be likely to go wrong. But when obstruction culminates and tranquillity
comes, one also gets companions together, cleaving to blessings, so the determination to rescue people from obstruction is carried out.

■ *5 yang:* Putting a stop to obstruction, great people are
fortunate. But they still keep destruction in mind.

THE IMAGE: The fortune of great people is when their position
is truly appropriate.

This represents positive strength balanced correctly and put in the position
of leadership, corresponding with ministers below in whom flexible obedience is balanced correctly. Therefore it is possible to put a stop to obstruction and be fortunate.

However, trouble is always overcome when it has not yet happened, and
disturbance always arises in what is overlooked. Therefore it is necessary to
be calm yet not forget danger, to live without forgetting death, to be orderly
but not forget disorder. This should be kept firmly in mind. Who but great
people can do this?

■ *Top yang:* Overturning obstruction. First there is obstruction,
afterward joy.

THE IMAGE: When obstruction ends, it collapses.
What can last?

When strength is not balanced correctly, first there is obstruction. But when
obstruction ends, then it collapses; it definitely cannot last. Therefore there
can be joy afterward.

In Buddhist terms, religious attachment following a path cannot be up-
rooted without positive strong knowledge.

In the first yin, religious attachment is not too deep-rooted, but it is in a
position for positivity; if you can root it out from this one, then all will come
out together. Therefore one strives to be correct, for by working correctly
one will get through auspiciously. Inspiration is a matter for the leader,
which here is the true experience of reality.

In the second yin, religious devotion has gradually become deep, so it is good for small people. Great people should at this point visualize choking obstruction, so that they can find a way to progress and get through successfully.

In the third yin, religious attachment is most profound. One also has a small intelligence, and mistakenly takes an imitative path for a real one. So this is called "embracing disgrace."

The fourth yang is strong but not right. Though one gives rise to religious attachment for a while, ultimately one can uproot it and carry out one's true aim.

In the fifth yang, firm strength is balanced correctly, so it enters directly into the proper position and is fortunate. But there are still many kinds of ignorance that have not been cut off, so one will not stay in any state—this is here called "keeping destruction in mind." From this, every state of mind enters the ocean of all knowledge, and the witnessing awareness does not recede.

In the top yang, yang is in a yin place; although in the beginning one may not have escaped religious attachment, in the end the power of knowledge and wisdom were so strong that they could overturn it.

 13. **Sameness with People**

fire below, *heaven* above

Sameness with people in the wilderness is successful.
It is beneficial to cross a great river. It is beneficial
for a leader to be correct.

In sociopolitical terms, this means that to overcome obstruction it is necessary to cooperate with people, sharing the same aim.

In terms of contemplating mind, this is when one has become detached from religious attachment following a path, and now for the first time enters into sameness with all life, joining with the power of compassion of the buddhas above, sharing the same sorrowful longing as people below; therefore it is called "sameness with people."

"The wilderness" means beyond the realms of desire, form, and formlessness. It also means the unobstructed realm of silent light. Once one has gone beyond birth and death, one should return to cross the great river of birth and death, to bring other people across.

Only using enlightened knowledge and enlightened vision to teach people is referred to here by the statement "It is beneficial for a leader to be correct."

THE OVERALL JUDGMENT: In sameness with people, flexibility finds its place and gains balance, so to correspond with the creative. When it says that sameness with people in the wilderness is successful, and that it is beneficial to cross a great river, this is creative action. Health through civilization and enlightenment, responding with balance correctly is the correctness of a leader. A leader is one who can communicate with the wills of the world.

In terms of contemplating mind, being an ordinary person who has not yet witnessed true reality is called flexibility. Now gaining access to the absolute and actually witnessing the center of everything, we are united with the body of creative power that is the real body of buddhas, so this is called "sameness with people."

Once we have witnessed the true being of buddhas, we must exercise enlightened qualities to liberate people; this is called creative action.

Health through civilization and enlightenment, responding with balance correctly is like the sun and moon shining in the sky, their reflections spontaneously appearing wherever there is clear water. This is the correctness of leaders.

Leaders are those who have already cut off ignorance and found the center of reality, and who adapt the inherent ability to command any of the roles or states open to humankind. Therefore they can communicate with the wills of the world, joining all people and all beings in the same sorrows and longing for release that are shared by all forms of life.

THE IMAGE: Sky with fire—sameness with people.
Leaders distinguish beings in terms of classes and families.

Without differences, how could sameness be shown? Make sure the different do not lose their differences, so that sameness can rest in great sameness.

In Buddhist terms, just as sky and fire are similar yet dissimilar, dissimilar yet similar, the various states of being each have their families, each of which acts as one being with one mind.

One mind has all possible states of being inherent in it, and every state of being has every other state of being inherent in it, so there are countless differences in the points of interpenetration of these states of being, which are representative of our states of mind.

So all these states of being are ultimately based on just one mind. This is the final attainment of sameness without sameness, nonsameness with sameness.

■ *First yang:* Sameness with people at the gate is blameless.

THE IMAGE: And if you are the same as people outside the gate, who can blame you?

The way of sameness with people calls for impartiality and impersonality. Here there is correct strength in the beginning without a linking correspondent at a higher level, so if one goes "outside the gate," one can thus get to the wilderness, so there is no blame.

■ *2 yin:* Sameness with people in the clan is regrettable.

THE IMAGE: Sameness with people in the clan is the road to regret.

The second yin is in its place, in balance, so it can correspond with the creative. This is why this hexagram is called *Sameness with People.* But since recessive flexibility cannot get far, if you are this way at any given time, you may fall into the company of whoever happens to be around and become one of them willy-nilly. Eventually you will regret this.

■ *3 yang:* He hides fighters in the bush; he climbs the high hill. Three years without flourishing.

THE IMAGE: One hides fighters in the bush because the enemy is strong. Three years without flourishing is calm activity.

The second place in a hexagram corresponds with the fifth place. Here, the second yin is not something that the third yang can force sameness with. The third yang wrongly seeks the sameness, so he hides fighters to lie in wait and climbs the high hill to spy.

The fifth yang represents strength that is balanced and correct, both in name and reality. This cannot be opposed by the irrational strength of the third yang.

■ *4 yang:* He mounts the wall but does not succeed in the attack. This is lucky.

THE IMAGE: It was right that he did not succeed when he mounted the wall. The luck is that he will return to order when he reaches the impasse.

The image of *fire* is that of a wall. The fourth yang also wrongly desires sameness with the second yin, so he tries to climb the wall of the third yang to attack her. But justice informs him that he must be thwarted, so he can return to order and not attack anymore.

- *5 yang:* In sameness with people, first there is weeping, later laughter. The great general conquers, and meets others.

THE IMAGE: The reason sameness with people is in front is that it is the middle way. In a meeting with the great general, his words overcome.

In the second yin, recessive flexibility is balanced correctly; this is the guideway for *fire,* the intellect. This corresponds with the fifth yang, in what is called sameness in spite of nonsameness, which is true sameness. True sameness was blocked by the third and fourth yangs, so it was impossible to avoid weeping and employing the great general to overcome them.

The fifth yang is balanced, so he meshes perfectly with the second yin and does not doubt what he had to do. He is honest, so he weeps and uses arms, without any qualms.

- *Top yang:* Sameness with people in the countryside involves no regret.

THE IMAGE: Sameness with people in the countryside is when the aspiration has not yet been attained.

One commentator says that there is no regret because one does not try to force sameness unreasonably, but the aspiration is not yet attained because no one stands with one.

Interpreted in terms of contemplating mind, each of the six lines again illustrates the efforts inspired by desire to realize sameness with people.

If you want to experientially enter the reality nature that is the same for all people, you need to use the power of concentrated insight. You cannot do it by conscious seeking, but you cannot get it by mindlessness either. As they say, when the right time comes, the design will be self-evident. This is the secret of cultivating the mind—do not forget, but do not try to help.

The first yang represents accurate insight and true wisdom appearing, without effort; then one can go out of the gate of birth and death.

The second yin represents having correct concentration but lacking sufficient power of insight, still not escaping being fascinated by meditation, and not getting out of the old "clan" of the realms of desire, form, and formless experience.

The third yang represents only using insight, claiming to be right, but not having any concentration to sustain it. Therefore it is like climbing to the top of a high hill and becoming one of the bodhisattvas that fall at the peak, "not flourishing for three years."

The fourth yang represents concentration and insight evenly balanced; whereas there was a sense of anticipation at first, now one knows that expectations cannot match reality, so one has good fortune by finally entering integration with reality nondeliberately.

The fifth yang represents firm strength balanced correctly yet insufficient in concentration power; though one sees the enlightened nature, it is not perfectly clear. Therefore it is necessary first to cultivate many practices, accumulate resources for enlightenment, and rely on the power of innumerable good qualities and works; only after that will one discover the true way to reality. It is because this is direct focus on the essence of complete awareness at the center of everything, whereby it is possible to go far beyond the truths of emptiness and conditionality, that there is "first weeping, afterward laughter."

In the top yang, though concentration and insight are again equal, nevertheless one is at the culmination of creativity and can only get the empty experience of nirvana, incapable of entering the ordinary world and extending help to others; therefore "the aspiration is not yet attained."

14. Great Possession

heaven below, *fire* above

Great possession is great success.

In political terms, this means inheriting the earth after people of like mind overthrow injustice.

In Buddhist terms, this is when transformative practice is widely carried out after establishment and explanation of the necessary disciplines.

In terms of contemplating mind, this is self-adornment with achievements, qualities, knowledge, and wisdom, after experiencing the universal essence of reality.

All of these are ways of great success.

THE OVERALL JUDGMENT: **In great possession, flexibility is in an important position. Greatness is balanced, and above and below respond to it. This is called great possession. Its qualities are firm strength and civilized intelligence. It responds to nature and acts according to the time; therefore it is greatly successful.**

In Buddhist terms, "great possession" means when you enter directly from the state of an ordinary person into the exalted state of actualized buddhahood and witness the center of all things, to which all states of being are subordinate.

"Firm strength" and "civilized intelligence" refer to the accomplishments of wise and pure practices.

"Responding to nature and acting according to the time" means realizing a multitude of enlightening practices within one mind, using celestial action as the substance from which to produce the functions of innocent and compassionate actions.

THE IMAGE: **Fire in the sky—great possession. Leaders obey nature and accept its order by stopping the bad and promoting the good.**

In Buddhist terms, when you cultivate the bad, you should cut it off completely; when you cultivate the good, you should fulfill it. Only then are you going along with the good order of the ultimate essence of things. All states of being have this essence inherent in them and are indeed made of this essence, but all states other than that of complete enlightenment are out of harmony with this essence in some way. Buddhahood is when you accord with this essence.

■ *First yang:* **As long as there is none of the harm that comes from association, this is not blameworthy. If one struggles, there will be no blame.**

THE IMAGE: **The positivity in the beginning of great possession is the absence of the harm that comes from association.**

A problem of people whose possessions are great is to cause harm by associating with too many people. If they struggle, then the end will also be like the beginning.

■ *2 yang:* **Using a large car for transport, there is a place to go. No fault.**

THE IMAGE: **Using a large car for transport, if the load is balanced you will not fail.**

The "large car" refers to the fifth yin, which represents receptive openness. Even if there is a wise ruler who is able to listen to advice, if there are no wise ministers to work with the ruler, how can there be no failure? Here, "the load is balanced" means that the guidance received is wise.

■ *3 yang:* **Impartial action gets through to the ruler. Small people are incapable of this.**

THE IMAGE: **The action of the baron gets through to the ruler. Small people would be harmed.**

It is possible to get through to a ruler by being firm, strong, upright, correct, and in an important position. How can small people do this?

- *4 yang:* **Negating self-inflation, there is no blame.**

THE IMAGE: **Negating self-inflation, there is no blame, because the understanding is clear.**

The fourth yang is firm and strong, but not excessively so. It is also in the body of *fire,* which represents understanding being clear and negating self-inflation, so that one can work for enlightened leadership.

- *5 yin:* **This trust is mutual. It is fortunate to be awesome.**

THE IMAGE: **This trust is mutual; aspirations are aroused through faith. The good fortune of being awesome is ease and freedom from preparation.**

Flexibility in balance in the honored (fifth) position single-mindedly trusts the balanced strength represented by the second yang; the world trust this, so the people are awed without anger, and it is not necessary to make any special effort to awe them.

One commentator explains that freedom from preparation indicates more than sufficiency, because preparation arises from insufficiency, and thus is a manifestation of insufficiency, which causes awesomeness to be diminished.

- *Top yang:* **Good fortune that is a blessing from heaven is beneficial to all.**

THE IMAGE: **The noble good fortune of great possession is a blessing from heaven.**

This tells how good fortune from heaven is beneficial to all, most abundantly, but it does not tell how to bring good fortune. Could there be no way to explain it? It must be because the way to bring good fortune is remote.

Confucius said that what heaven helps is obedience, and what people help is trust. Acting on trust and conscientiously obeying the order of nature is also the reason for respecting the wise. Therefore the good fortune that is a blessing from heaven is beneficial to all.

Trust, obedience, and respect for the wise—these are the qualities represented by the fifth yin here. What is easy and needs no preparation is the obedience of balanced flexibility; the mutuality of trust is the trust of balanced flexibility; being the resort of all positive forces is balanced, flexible respect for the wise. The top yang represents acting on this.

Those who can act on this themselves can obey and trust, and can therefore respect the wise; so where does the help of heaven and humanity end up? This is why it is said that the sage has no success, the spiritual human has no name.

The lines may be interpreted in Buddhist terms in two senses: one according to educational outreach after realization and the other according to progressive practice of educational method.

First, in terms of educational outreach after realization, the first yang represents appearing in states conditioned by emotional confusion, without being affected by the anxieties of these states, just commiserating with people out of compassion.

The second yang represents appearing among civilized people, among whom it is possible to effect widespread liberation of all kinds of people by means of methods of collective enlightenment. Therefore "there is a place to go," and this "will not fail."

The third yang represents working on the celestial plane without being affected by celestial bliss or by meditation trances. Therefore "small people are incapable of this." If small people entered celestial states, they would be harmed by bliss or trance.

The fourth yang represents manifesting forms of methods for individual liberation, therefore "negating self-inflation," yet not taking experience of total extinction for personal liberation, so having "understanding that is clear."

The fifth yin represents appearing as an enlightening being. Enlightening beings initiate those who are ready to be initiated; therefore "this trust is mutual." They break down those who need breaking down, so "it bodes well to be awesome." In the sense that they guide people with basic goodness, "aspirations are aroused through faith." The way they break down people in bad states is "easy, free from preparations."

The top yang represents manifestation as a realized buddha, wherefor "the good fortune of blessings from heaven is beneficial for all." This is what is known as appearing as a guide based on the ultimate truth.

In terms of progressive practice of educational method, the first yang represents taking up the study of discipline, whereby one does not associate with aberrated mental states.

The second yang represents taking up the study of concentration, whereby one includes all truths in meditation without fail.

The third yang represents taking up the study of knowledge, whereby one can get through to the ruler. This knowledge cuts through emotional understandings of the ordinary and the holy, sweeps away emptiness, and washes away existence; people who misapprehend emptiness make a pretext of having this knowledge. So even the slightest error means enormous deviation; small people cannot use this knowledge and would only be harmed if they tried.

The fourth yang represents taking up the teaching of universal relativity, according to which everything is conditional and has no inherent being of its own. This is the introduction to the methods of collective enlightenment, so it "negates self-inflation." Though in the practice of this teaching people contemplate beginninglessness, just as those striving for individual liberation do, nevertheless they do not experience it in the same way as individual escapees, so their understanding is clear.

The fifth yin represents taking up the teaching through which the countless varieties of suffering and release are studied. Here there is a respectful belief in balance, so "this trust is mutual." Because through this teaching people particularly cultivate activities and understanding that foster enlightenment, it is awesome and bodes well.

The top yang stands for taking up the method of complete teaching, where the whole of nature produces developmental culture and the completion of culture is in nature. Therefore the good fortune of blessings from heaven is beneficial to all.

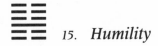 *15. Humility*

mountain below, *earth* above

Humility gets through. A leader has a conclusion.

In political terms, this means not being self-satisfied at good fortune when the earth is at peace and has become a paradise.

In Buddhist terms, this means still being impartial and respectful to all people after the true way has gone into action.

In terms of contemplating mind, this means returning to nonacquisitiveness on fulfilling enlightenment.

All of these are ways through to success; this is how leaders conclude what they have begun, the conclusion being in accord with the beginning. This can be called the result permeating the source of the cause.

THE OVERALL JUDGMENT: **Humility gets through. The way of heaven, descending to save, radiates light. The way of earth,** lowly, goes upward. The way of heaven diminishes the full and enhances the humble. The way of earth changes the full and spreads humility. Spirits injure the full and bless the humble. The way of humans is to dislike the full and like the humble. Humility is noble yet enlightened, low yet unsurpassable. This is the conclusion of leaders.

In Buddhist terms, this refers to the infinity of the vows of enlightening beings. Only when all beings are liberated will the enlightening beings realize complete enlightenment themselves; as long as hell is not emptied, they will not accept the peace of extinction for themselves.

Therefore there is basically no fulfillment of either worldly or transmundane laws. If you think you are fulfilled, then heaven will diminish you, earth will change you, spirits will harm you, people will dislike you.

To appear in all states of being with the quality of humility is to manifest the nobility of buddhahood; this is of course enlightened. Even if one manifests the lowliness of a being in hell, still one is unsurpassable.

THE IMAGE: Mountain in the earth—humility.
Leaders assess people and give impartially, by taking
from the abundant and adding to the scarce.

In Buddhist terms, this means taking from the mountain of infinite virtues of buddhahood to add to the earth of sentient beings, realizing that all beings have the mountain of virtues of buddhahood within them, assessing people's potentials and what suits them, impartially giving out the bliss of buddhahood, not letting anyone attain extinction alone.

■ *First yin:* Extreme humility. It is fortunate if leaders use this
to cross great rivers.

THE IMAGE: In extreme humility, leaders manage themselves
with lowliness.

This is excess of humility. There is no use for this but to cross great rivers. There is great difficulty, and one cannot effect this function unless one restrains oneself profoundly. Managing oneself means developing oneself until one can act.

■ *2 yin:* Expressing humility is good if correct.

THE IMAGE: Expressing humility is good if correct in the sense
of attainment in the heart.

This is the expression of humility to harmonize with the humility of those who work selflessly for others; it is correct insofar as it comes from one's true nature.

■ *3 yang:* Leaders who work and achieve yet are humble have an auspicious conclusion.

THE IMAGE: The people submit to leaders who work and achieve yet are humble.

Those who work and achieve yet are not overbearing, who are successful but do not congratulate themselves, are those who have attained complete humility.

■ *4 yin:* Beneficial to all, the exercise of humility.

THE IMAGE: Beneficial to all, the exercise of humility— this is the way it is supposed to be.

Being above those who are successful yet humble, as represented in the third yang, yet being correctly flexible and agreeable, is beneficial to all and is the exercise of humility. Exercising humility toward the humble is truly the way it is supposed to be.

■ *5 yin:* Not rich, employing the neighbors, it is beneficial in invasion and attack; all will profit.

THE IMAGE: It is beneficial to invade and attack in the sense of overcoming the unruly.

The fifth yin represents neither pride nor humility; it is in the center. Therefore the five aspects of humility represented by the other lines are all its servants. But if you look for what makes it able to employ these five aspects of humility, there is nothing; so it is "not rich, employing the neighbors." Ultimately, invasion and attack do not destroy humility, so "it is beneficial in invasion and attack." All work for it, so "all will profit." Overcoming the unruly is humility in the sense of taking away excess.

■ *Top yin:* Expressing humility, one profits from military operations attacking the country.

THE IMAGE: Expressing humility, the aspiration has not been attained; one can use military operations to attack the country.

This is claiming sympathy with the humility of the workers and achievers represented by the third yang, but actually only putting on an appearance of humility and not really being humble. For this reason few will accept you, so even if you have a country, there will be rebellion. But even though the reality of humility is not there, the name of humility is there, so those who rebel will not gain the advantage; the attacker will profit.

The six lines may also be interpreted in Buddhist terms, in two senses: in terms of characteristics of buddhahood, and in terms of people involved in Buddhism in some way.

First, in terms of characteristics of buddhahood, the first yin represents manifestation of spiritual descent into the womb and subsequent birth on earth. Because a buddha has already realized birthlessness long ago, yet still manifests birth, this is called "managing oneself with lowliness."

The second yin represents manifestation of renunciation of social status. Buddhas are already liberated from birth and death, yet they say they are leaving behind their social status because of birth and death. This is "expressing humility."

The third yang represents manifestation of overcoming demons and attaining enlightenment. Buddhas have already transcended the realm of demons and realized great enlightenment, yet they manifest these accomplishments for the benefit of other beings, to cause those who observe this to accept it in their hearts.

The fourth yin represents manifestation of reflection after enlightenment. Buddhas already perceived potentials and set up teachings accordingly; this is "the way it should be."

The fifth yin represents manifestation of activation of teachings. Originally there is no real teaching; all teachings are beneficial techniques, provisionally demonstrated: so the buddhas are "not rich." All buddhas can invoke the testimony of all other buddhas, since reality is one, so this is "employing the neighbors." Buddhas break through people's confusions to enable them to return to inherent enlightened qualities and obey them, so "it is beneficial to invade and attack."

The top yin represents manifestation of extinction. Because people's potential is exhausted, the response to it dies out; this is "the aspiration not attained." But buddhas actually do perform buddha-work by extinction, in that they cause people who have not yet planted roots of goodness to plant them, they cause people who have planted roots of goodness to mature them, and they cause mature people to be emancipated; this is "attacking the country."

Now, in terms of people involved in Buddhism, the first yin represents novices, who "manage themselves with lowliness." The second yin represents initiates who preserve the teaching; this is "expressing humility, good if correct." The third yang represents initiates who spread the teaching, in charge of the mystic order; they are therefore "leaders who work and achieve yet are humble."

The fourth yin represents outside protectors, who always humbly defer to all initiates in all phases of practice; this is "exercising humility," which is "the way it should be." The fifth yin represents higher desires that protect the teaching, whereby it is possible to crush aberration and reveal sanity, thus "conquering the unruly." The top yin represents higher states in the realm of form and the formless realm; though they also protect sanity and crush aberration, yet as there is no sign of anger in meditation trances in these realms, it is impossible to carry out liberative practices that involve breaking down illusions. So "the aspiration is not attained."

 ## 16. *Joy*

earth below, *thunder* above

Joy. It is beneficial to set up rulers and mobilize the army.

In political terms, this is when an enlightened ruler deals with the people humbly, so that those above and those below are pleased with each other.

In terms of Buddhist influence, this is when methods of enlightenment are popularly carried out and people rejoice with each other.

In terms of contemplating mind, this is the realization of the truth that nothing is as pictured by the imagination, and the experience of indescribable bliss.

In politics, once there is joy, it will not do to forget cultural affairs and military preparedness, so it is appropriate to "set up rulers" so as to disseminate good influences, and to "mobilize the army" to be prepared for the unexpected.

Once methods of enlightenment are in practice, it will not do to forget instruction, guidance, admonition, and exhortation, so it is appropriate to set up rulers to direct the influence of enlightenment, and to mobilize the army to prevent the beginnings of decadence.

When people have personally experienced the joy of truth, it will not do to neglect transformation guidance of others, so it is appropriate to set up rulers to deal with other people, and mobilize the army to overcome people's delusions.

Also, the practice of insight is like setting up a ruler, while practical activities are like mobilizing the army.

Creating good is also like setting up a ruler, while destroying evil is like mobilizing the army. All those who have first attained the joy and bliss of ways to enlightenment should do this.

THE OVERALL JUDGMENT: **In joy, strength responds and its will is carried out. Acting obediently is joy; joy acts obediently, so even heaven and earth conform to it, to say nothing of setting up rulers and mobilizing the army. Heaven and earth act obediently, so the sun and moon are not excessive, the four seasons are not out of order. Sages act obediently, so punishments are clear and the people accept. The duty of the time of joy is great.**

Each of the sixty-four hexagrams of the *I Ching* represents a time, and every time has its duty, and the duty must be important; this does not apply only in the time of joy, but in a time of joy it is easy to get lazy and careless, so special mention of duty is made here.

In Buddhist terms, when one only acts obediently, action is therefore always obedient. This means that in the cultivation that is produced in accord with essential nature, the completion of cultivation after all lies in essential nature. Is the duty of time not great?

THE IMAGE: **When thunder emerges, the earth stirs—joy. Thus did the kings of yore make music to honor virtue, offering it in abundance to God, thereby to share it with their ancestors.**

In Buddhist terms, making music is like the natural playing of holy songs as in the scriptures. Honoring virtue is beautifying nature by cultivation. Offering it in abundance to God refers to the inherent essential nature that is the original source, here called "God." Ancestors are the enlightened ones of the past.

■ *First yin:* **Trumpeting joy bodes ill.**

THE IMAGE: **Trumpeting joy bodes ill when the aspiration reaches an impasse.**

When prosperity reaches a climax, there must be decline; when happiness culminates, there must be suffering. In joy it is necessary to be careful, so the six lines have a lot of warnings. This is also the message of the judgment, about setting up rulers and mobilizing the army.

The first yin harmonizes with the fourth yang above and rejoices in this; having no real qualities in oneself, only aspiring to cleave to others, how can one not come to an impasse?

■ *2 yin:* Firm as a rock, not procrastinating, correctness bodes well.

THE IMAGE: Not procrastinating, correctness bodes well, because it is balanced in the right way.

This yin, in between two other yins, stands for the ultimate of darkness and stillness; using darkness to observe light, using stillness to observe activity, one can see what will happen.

Being "firm as a rock" is the accomplishment of stillness, "not procrastinating" is the accomplishment of activity. Knowing the results of activity and inactivity is what is called knowing the potential of the moment.

■ *3 yin:* Looking up in joy, repent. If too late, there is regret.

THE IMAGE: Looking up in joy, there is regret, because the position is not appropriate.

The third yin also represents one who lacks real qualities finding joy in looking up to another; this presents an opportunity to repent and reform oneself. If repentance and reform are too late, then there is regret.

■ *4 yang:* Being the source of joy, there is great gain.
Do not doubt. Companions gather.

THE IMAGE: Being the source of joy, there is great gain—
the aspiration is carried out greatly.

This represents the strength that is a source of joy to the weak who are unbalanced. As for those who are weak but balanced, they keep their uprightness, so do not doubt them. If you do not doubt them, then your association will grow stronger.

■ *5 yin:* Chaste in illness, one never dies.

THE IMAGE: Being chaste in illness means riding on firmness.
Never dying means not losing balance.

The second and fifth lines represent balance, so neither gets addicted to joy; therefore they are chaste. However, the second yin is far from the fourth yang, which is correct, so both action and inaction are always appropriate. The fifth yin rides on the strength of the fourth yang, which is not correct, so it produces illness. However, this is better than inwardly losing self-control and seeking joy outside.

■ *Top yin:* Oblivious in joy, what has come about changes.
There is no blame.

THE IMAGE: Oblivion in joy is at the top. What can last?

When joy reaches oblivion, it is time to stop. Any situation that has come
about must inevitably change. Due to the change, you get through it; when
there is oblivion, you stop it. Thus you may avoid error.

In terms of Buddhism, the fourth yang represents the person who teaches
in the Buddha's stead; the other lines represent disciples.

The first yin is not balanced, not correct, depending on the bountiful protection of great people and forgetting the work of spiritual cultivation and
realization. Therefore the outlook is bad.

The second yin represents flexible obedience being balanced and correct,
able to instantly understand phenomena, arrive at principles, and embrace
the concrete and abstract worlds in the mind. The inner reality cannot be
changed. Understanding all at once, observing all at once, one does not need
much time, and so does not procrastinate. This line represents those who
skillfully cultivate the mind and attain a true way of enlightenment, so the
outlook is good.

The third yin also represents one who is unbalanced and incorrect. Although one can look up in joy and have some sense of repentance and reform, because of being near a strict teacher, yet there is a lack of decisiveness
and courage; thus there is the warning that if one is too late, one will have
regrets.

The fourth yang is the master of the hexagram. This represents concentration and insight evenly balanced, accomplishing the enlightenment of oneself and others. Therefore companions firmly trust one, and one's aspiration
is carried out greatly.

The fifth yin represents weak and warped people who nevertheless are in
positions socially above enlightened teachers and good companions; they
are incurable, so they have a "persistent illness." Nevertheless, as long as
they are in a position of balance, there is still some faith in them, and the
roots of goodness in them are not cut off, so they "never die."

The top yin represents people who are flexible yet upright; at the end of
joy, people cannot avoid attaining realization sinking into emptiness, but because of the power of their original vows to help others, they still do not
ultimately enter nirvana. Therefore they are able to turn individual liberation into means of collective liberation, so there is change that is blameless. If
they remained in nirvana, they would become stagnant, so this cannot last.

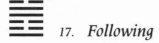

17. Following

thunder below, *lake* above

Following is very successful, beneficial if correct. No fault.

In political terms, when the rulers and ruled are pleased with each other, they will follow each other.

In terms of Buddhist influence, this is when people are pleased with it, and many people accept the influence.

In terms of contemplating mind, once one has attained the joy of truth, one can harmonize with the true character of things.

These are all paths of great success. However, they are only beneficial if correct; only thus can there be no fault. Otherwise, following will produce degeneration.

THE OVERALL JUDGMENT: **Following, firmness comes under flexibility, active and joyful. Following is very successful if it is correct; then there is no fault, and the world follows the time. The meaning of following the time is great indeed.**

In Buddhism it is said that when the right time arrives, the truth is self-evident. The combination of potential and sensitivity is called a time; so the meaning of following the time is said to be great.

THE IMAGE: **Thunder in the lake—following. Leaders go in and rest at sundown.**

In terms of contemplating mind, once one has united with the original source, inherent essence, then one is the same as the enlightened people of the past, so one will inevitably conceal the embodiment of reality, wisdom, and liberation in esoteric storage, and enter great nirvana.

■ *First yang:* **Standards change; it is good to be correct. Interaction outside the gate is successful.**

THE IMAGE: **Standards change, and it is good to follow what is right. Interaction outside the gate is successful in the sense of not losing.**

Standards are what properly direct people. In this hexagram, the fifth yang is the proper master of the second yin, so the second yin is governed by standards. But yin is recessive and weak and cannot reach far, so there is a change in standards, to follow the first yang. In the beginning, it is appropriate to maintain correctness and not let others follow. The reason for this is that if it interacts with the second yin inside the gate, then it will get the second but lose the fifth; it is better to interact with the fifth yang outside the gate, so that there is success in spite of losing the second. A leader would call this not losing.

■ *2 yin:* Involved with the child, one loses the adult.

THE IMAGE: Involved with the child, one is not with both at once.

Getting involved with the second yin, one will lose the fifth yang, so there cannot be completeness of both, so this is a warning for the second.

■ *3 yin:* Involved with the adult, one loses the child.
Following with an aim, one gains. It is good to remain correct.

THE IMAGE: Involved with the adult, one's aspiration leaves the low behind.

The fourth yang is the adult; the second yin is the child. The third place is close to the fourth and far from the first; but there is no proper correspondence. Just follow the high and obey; get closely involved and you will be stabilized.

■ *4 yang:* Following gains, but it bodes ill even if right.
Having faith in the way, thereby understanding,
what fault is there?

THE IMAGE: When following gains, the meaning is inauspicious. Having faith in the way, the understanding is successful.

If the second yin wants to follow the fifth yang, it must pass through the fourth place to get there, and the fourth yang will therefore surely get it. Getting it, the fourth yang will be punished by the fifth, and this bodes ill.
    Only if one has deep faith in the right way is the trail of mind clear and faultless.

■ *5 yang:* Truthfulness in good is auspicious.

THE IMAGE: Truthfulness in good is auspicious because the state is correctly balanced.

The second yin represents recessive flexibility that is balanced and correct, a good partner for the fifth yang, which represents positive firmness that is balanced and correct.

- *Top yin:* **In a binding involvement, the king sacrifices on the western mountain.**

THE IMAGE: **This is the upper impasse of involvement.**

Recessive flexibility that is correct, dwelling at the culmination of following, wholeheartedly trusts the balanced strength represented by the fifth yang, and forms a firm association. Thereby it is possible to get through to spiritual illumination. However, it ultimately comes to an impasse and is not sufficient to act on.

In terms of Buddhism, the three yangs all represent those who are followed by others, so they illustrate the meaning of following potential. The three yins all represent those who follow the strong, so they illustrate ways of following teachers.

The first yang represents strength that is correct but is in a low position. At first it seems as if there is no desire to help people, so there must be a change for there to be a good outlook; there will be accomplishment if one in this state is outgoing.

The fourth yang represents strength that is not correct but is in a superior position. Though one in this state may take on the responsibility of spreading the teaching, there seems to be personal ambition involved, so there is gain, but this bodes ill, even though the teaching may be correct. One must firmly believe in the true way out of the mundane; then the matter of mind can finally be clarified.

The fifth yang represents firm strength that is balanced and correct, helping oneself and helping others. Therefore there is truthfulness in good, which bodes well.

The second yin represents flexible obedience that is balanced and correct, yet has no power of insight; thus it does not escape giving up the universal and taking to the individual.

The third yin is not balanced and not correct, yet there is the power of insight, so it is possible to give up the individual and take to the universal. However, even though one may be said to give up the individual, this does not mean that one can look lightly upon individual self-criticism and fail to remain upright.

The top yin represents recessive flexibility that is correct, but still has no power of insight, concentrating on cultivating the joy of meditation for self-amusement. This is a path that must inevitably come to an impasse. Only by the power of sincere faith, directed toward the west, which in Buddhist terms means the western paradise of Amitabha, the land of ultimate happiness, is it possible for anyone who cultivates this dedication to go there.

18. *Degeneration*

wind below, *mountain* above

From degeneration comes great development.
It is beneficial to cross a great river.
Three days before, three days after.

Degeneration is like when a vessel is not used for a long time and begins to corrode, or like when people indulge in partying for a long time and become sick, or when a country is peaceful for a long time and becomes decadent.

In political terms, this is when rulers and officials gladly go along with each other and there is no salutary protest, thus bringing about corruption.

In Buddhist terms, when the teaching is flourishing and a society gladly goes along with it, there will inevitably be people who join Buddhist organizations for the wrong reasons, with personal ambitions. Because of this the organizations become corrupt.

In terms of the ultimate following of contemplating mind, this is manifestation of unhealthy behavior out of compassion and becoming degenerate because of this.

In terms of the minor following first attained in contemplating mind, this is when one has not yet cut off confusion, or when one develops religious attachment following the path, or when past habits arise in meditation, and one degenerates because of this.

Nevertheless, since order is the start of disorder, disorder can also be used to bring about order; therefore there is reason for great success. But it is impossible to remedy degeneration and decadence without great courage and strength, like that needed to cross a great river.

Therefore one should renew oneself "three days before" and be on the alert "three days after," before one can withdraw accumulated degeneration and eventually preserve good aims.

THE OVERALL JUDGMENT: **In degeneration, strength is above,**
weakness below. Pliancy with stopping; this is degeneration.
In degeneration there is great development, whereby the

world is ordered. It is beneficial to cross a great river; going
forth, there is something to do. Three days before, three days
after—the end thus has a beginning, the activity of heaven.

The trigram *mountain,* which is strong and represents stopping, is above; it
stops above and has no light to help those below. The hexagram *wind,* which
is weak and represents pliancy, is below; it rests below and has no virtue to
go higher. This represents those above and below taking it easy, just enjoying
the leisure of the moment, unaware of the gradual fermentation of troubles
ahead.

Only if people know the gradual process of accumulating degeneration
can they set up means of rescue, so that the world can be set in order; how
can they sit there and do nothing, as though the world will order itself? It is
necessary to go do something, like "crossing a river," as it were. And it
is necessary to understand how the activity of heaven has an end and a
beginning.

This applies to political affairs, to Buddhism, to education, and to contemplating mind.

THE IMAGE: Wind in the mountains—degeneration.
Leaders thus arouse the people to nurture virtue.

Arousing the people is like wind, nurturing virtue is like mountains. The
people cannot be sufficiently aroused without nurturing virtue, and virtue
cannot be sufficiently nurtured without arousing the people. This means the
twin action of compassion and wisdom, seeking to rise higher while educat-
ing those who are lower.

■ *First yin:* Dealing with the degeneration of the father,
if there is a child, the late father has no blame.
It is dangerous but turns out well.

THE IMAGE: Dealing with the degeneration of the father means
consciously taking up after the late father.

Degeneration does not take place all at once; it becomes apparent only with
the passage of generations. Therefore it is expressed in terms of father and
child. The first yin is in the beginning of degeneration, when deterioration is
not yet serious; if there is a wise child, the dead father can escape blame. But
it is necessary to be wary of danger, so that things may turn out well. And
the way to deal with degeneration requires that one consciously take up
after the father, and not take up after the father's deeds.

- *2 yang:* Dealing with the degeneration of the mother,
it will not do to be righteous.

THE IMAGE: Dealing with the degeneration of the mother is
attaining balance.

The yin nature is comfortable when there is nothing to do, and dislikes doing anything, so dealing with the degeneration of the mother is most difficult. If you correct her, you injure love, but if you do not correct her you injure justice. It can only be done by someone who is actually strong but is not adamant.

- *3 yang:* Dealing with the degeneration of the father,
there is a little regret, but no great blame.

THE IMAGE: Dealing with the degeneration of the father,
in the end there is no blame.

The quality represented by the third yang is no different from that of the second yang, but here one does not know how to use it. The second yang uses it flexibly, the third uses it adamantly; therefore there is a little regret but no great blame.

- *4 yin:* Indulging the degeneration of the father,
if you go on you will experience shame.

THE IMAGE: Indulging the degeneration of the father,
if you go on you will not attain anything.

This represents weakness and lack of virtue, whereby one can increase the degeneration of the father by indulging it.

- *5 yin:* Dealing with the degeneration of the father,
the action is praised.

THE IMAGE: Dealing with the father, the action is praised,
because one takes up after him with virtue.

Here flexibility is in balance and one can deal with degeneration well. This is taking up after one's predecessors with reviving virtues.

- *Top yang:* Not serving kings or lords, one makes one's concerns
loftier.

THE IMAGE: **Not serving kings or lords, one's will can serve as a model.**

To discuss the six lines in terms of politics, the first is like a wise citizen, the second is like a cultured official, the third is like a wise general, the fourth is like a scheming official, the fifth is like a wise king, the sixth is like a righteous dissident.

In terms of the promulgation of Buddhism, the bottom three lines are like outside protectors, the top three lines are like inside protectors. The first yin is flexible and in a low position; this represents those who exert generosity to the utmost to obey the Buddha, the Teaching, and the Community. The second yang is strong and balanced; this represents those who protect the true teaching with the teaching of compassion. The third yang is too strong; this represents those who protect Buddhism with overwhelming authority.

The fourth yin is flexible yet correct; this represents those who can only save themselves and cannot guide others. The fifth yin is flexible and balanced; this represents those who can guide everyone. The top yang represents those who practice asceticism and detachment; they seem to have no will to teach others, but Buddhism needs such people as models.

In terms of contemplating mind, the first yin represents those in whom concentration is originally dominant; this is the degeneration of the father. But they are in a yang position, so they have the "child" insight; thus there is no blame. However, it is necessary to go through a crisis before it is possible to equalize insight and concentration so that the end turns out well.

The second yang represents those in whom insight is originally predominant; this is the degeneration of the mother. But they are in a yin position, so they have concentration. However, the reason they attain concentration is only to foster insight; it will not do to maintain this concentration to the end.

The third yang represents excessive strength that is not balanced, so insight turns into degeneration; therefore there is a little regret. But to save the world from decadence it is essential to rely on the power of insight, so there is no great blame.

The fourth yin represents excessive weakness, inability to develop insight; if one goes on this way, one will not avoid becoming conceited about one's meditation experiences, and so should be ashamed.

The fifth yin represents flexibility in balance; concentration has equivalent insight, so one will surely see the way.

The top yang represents insight with equivalent concentration, whereby one immediately enters into effortlessness; so one "does not serve kings or lords" and "makes one's concerns loftier." This means not resting in the ranks of the enlightened; therefore "the will can serve as a model."

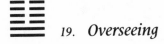

19. *Overseeing*

lake below, *earth* above

**Overseeing is very successful, beneficial if correct.
If you go on until the eighth month, there will be
misfortune.**

In political terms, it is possible to oversee the citizenry after degeneration
has been corrected. In terms of Buddhism, the influence of Buddhism is restored after decadence has been reformed. In terms of contemplating mind,
this means getting rid of meditation illnesses and progressively cutting off
delusions; therefore it is very successful.

Whether it is politics, Buddhism, or contemplating mind, it is necessary
that the method be correct from beginning to end in order for there to be
benefit. If you ride on the momentum of the time and do not know to turn
back, at a certain point deterioration will inevitably set in, after flourishing
has reached its climax, and there will surely be misfortune.

THE OVERALL JUDGMENT: **In overseeing, strength gradually
grows. Joyful and harmonious, strength is balanced and
responsive. Great success in a correct manner is the way of
nature. In the eighth month there will be misfortune because
waning does not take long.**

Strength gradually grows, so it is called overseeing; joyful and harmonious,
strength is balanced and responsive, so it is very successful. A correct manner means one in harmony with the beneficial consummation of creative
development deriving from the original energy of the universe; this is the
original quality of inherent power.

If you let things go too long and do not prevent reversal early on, then
there will surely be misfortune, because whatever grows must wane, as a
natural matter of course. Only those who cultivate themselves to conform to
essence can direct the course of nature and not be caused to wax and wane
by nature.

THE IMAGE: **There is earth above a body of water. Leaders
use inexhaustibility of education and thought to embrace and
protect the people without bound.**

The body of water stands for the oceans; the earth supports beings, the oceans
support the earth. This is the embrace and protection of the inexhaustible.

In terms of Buddhism, inexhaustibility of education and thought is like an ocean, whereby it is possible to be a teacher of the worlds; embracing and protecting without bound is like earth, whereby it is possible to be a compassionate parent of all beings.

■ *First yang:* Sensitive overseeing is good when correct.

THE IMAGE: Sensitive overseeing is good when correct, because the intention and the action are correct.

In political terms, to correct degeneration it is important to be firm and brave; to oversee the populace it is important to be human and flexible.

In Buddhist terms, to get rid of decadence it is appropriate to overwhelm it and break it down; to guide people it is appropriate to be compassionate and accommodating.

In terms of contemplating mind, to get rid of ills it is appropriate to apply the power of insight; to penetrate noumenon it is appropriate to apply the power of concentration.

The first yang represents strength gradually growing, so it is called sensitive overseeing. The warning that it is only good if correct is given lest strength be allowed to become excessive.

■ *2 yang:* Sensitive overseeing is good, beneficial all around.

THE IMAGE: "Sensitive overseeing is good, beneficial all around"—this is addressed to those who are not yet in harmony with the universal order.

The second yang is also in the momentum of gradually increasing strength, but at this point it is best to keep still and not ride on the momentum to try to advance; then it will be good and beneficial all around.

If it is not good, then some will not benefit. This comes about because riding on momentum to try to advance is not in harmony with the universal order, according to which great success comes about through application of proper manner.

■ *3 yin:* Presumptuous overseeing is of no benefit, but if you trouble over it, there will be no blame.

THE IMAGE: Presumptuous overseeing is out of place. Once you trouble over it, blame will not last long.

If you are weak but your will is adamant, you eagerly try to advance, becoming presumptuous in overseeing without realizing there is no benefit in this.

However, if you are flexible and intelligent, you will be able to take stock of yourself and change; then there will be no blame.

■ *4 yin:* Consummate overseeing is impeccable.

THE IMAGE: Consummate overseeing that is impeccable is in the right place.

In Buddhist terms, this represents using correct concentration corresponding to correct insight; therefore it is consummate overseeing.

■ *5 yin:* Knowing overseeing, appropriate for a great leader, bodes well.

THE IMAGE: What is appropriate for a great leader is balance in action.

In Buddhist terms, this is concentration with insight, corresponding to the insight with concentration represented by the first yang; this is what is called the sovereign samadhi. The way of balance comprehends all things, so it is said to be appropriate for a great leader.

■ *Top yin:* Attentive overseeing is good and blameless.

THE IMAGE: The good of attentive overseeing is in the will being within.

This represents flexible harmony that is correctly oriented, at the end of overseeing. In Buddhist terms, once subtle concentration is deep, it naturally awakens genuine insight, realizing that there are no objects outside of mind, so that one does not seek anything outside mind. This is referred to as the will being within, so the will is blameless.

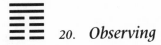

20. *Observing*

earth below, *wind* above

Observing, having washed the hands but not presented the offering, there is sincerity that is reverent.

In political terms, this represents overseeing the people benevolently and being admired by them.

In Buddhist terms, this means helping people by influencing them rightly and being trusted by everyone.

In terms of contemplating mind, this means that progressive cultivation to cut off delusion requires the use of subtle observation.

But when you make your spirit and will always like one who has washed the hands but not presented the offering, then in both social affairs and Buddhist affairs, helping yourself and helping others, "there is sincerity that is reverent," worthy of respect.

THE OVERALL JUDGMENT: **The great observed on high, harmonious, shows the world balance and rectitude. Observing, having washed the hands but not presented the offering, there is sincerity that is reverent. Those below observe it and are transformed. Observing the spiritual way of heaven, the four seasons are orderly. Sages use the spiritual way to establish education, and all the world accepts.**

Positive strength on high shows the world the virtues of balance and rectitude, harmonious and agreeable; therefore it is as in a ceremony when one has washed the hands but not yet presented the offering; sincerity built up within shows outwardly, so that people understand it without anything being said about it.

That which is sacred and unknowable is called spiritual. Heaven does not say anything, but the four seasons go on, unfathomably; therefore it is called the spiritual way. People establish education on this pattern, which all follow without knowing why.

The spirit is truthfulness, truthfulness is sincerity, sincerity is the heart of humanity. The heart of humanity is basically harmonious, docile, balanced, and upright; mind impresses mind, so there is spontaneous acceptance without the need to present an offering.

In Buddhist terms, "the great observed" refers to the subtle observation of the absolute; "on high" refers to transcendence of all unenlightened states of mind. "Harmonious" means not deviating from essential nature, and being omnipresent in all phenomena. "Balance" means not falling into either extreme of samsara or nirvana; "rectitude" means simultaneous awareness of the ultimate truth and the conventional truth, without missing anything.

In politics, the citizens are "those below." In Buddhism, unenlightened states of mind are "those below." In contemplating mind, all auxiliary methods to foster enlightenment are "those below."

The "spiritual way of heaven" is inherent virtue, which includes the four qualities of eternity, happiness, selfhood, and purity; like the four seasons, these are orderly. "Using the spiritual way to establish education" refers to complete teaching that is in accord with essential nature; therefore it is ultimately accepted by those in all realms of consciousness.

THE IMAGE: Wind travels over the earth—observing.
Kings of yore examined the regions and observed the people
to set up education.

In Buddhist terms, the ancient buddhas examined the "regions" of possible experience and observed the people in various states of being, then set up various teachings to accommodate them, just as the wind travels over the earth reaching everywhere.

■ *First yin:* Naive observation is blameless in undeveloped people but shameful in developed people.

THE IMAGE: The naive observation represented by the first yin is the way of underdeveloped people.

Those who are weak and lowly cannot see far, so they are ignorant like children. When undeveloped people are like children, this is not considered bad, but if developed people are like children, there is no way to govern nations and bring peace to earth.

■ *2 yin:* Peeking observation is beneficial for a woman's chastity.

THE IMAGE: Peeking observation and the chastity of a woman can also be shameful.

This refers to observing from within; this may be appropriate for women who stay at home, but not for men in charge of civil affairs.

■ *3 yin:* Observing personal growth, advancing and withdrawing.

THE IMAGE: Observing personal growth, advancing and withdrawing, one has not lost the way.

Advancing to carry out the way, withdrawing to cultivate the way, if one can observe personal growth, then one will not lose the way whether advancing or withdrawing.

■ *4 yin:* Observing the glory of the country, it is beneficial to be a guest of the king.

THE IMAGE: Observing the glory of the country is esteeming guesthood.

Flexible yet upright, secretly approaching the king, one may well carry out the duty of a visiting teacher.

- **5 yang: Observing personal growth, developed people are impeccable.**

  THE IMAGE: **Observing personal growth means observing the people.**

  The path of developed people is to cultivate themselves seriously and to regard the faults of others as their own.

- **Top yang: Observing the growth, developed people are impeccable.**

  THE IMAGE: **Observing the growth, the mind is not yet at peace.**

  In the position of a teacher and protector, one is observed by everyone; only developed people can be impeccable. Once one is observed by everyone, that makes for consciousness of being observed, so that one cannot be lazy; therefore the mind is not yet at peace.

  To interpret the six lines in Buddhist terms, the first represents the naive observation of those pursuing false paths, who have aberrant intellects.

  The second represents ordinary people; theirs is "peeking observation," in that they indulge in meditation to the point of addiction.

  The third represents people with the potential for personal liberation; for them, "advance" means practicing ways of transcendence, "withdrawal" means opting for individual salvation.

  The fourth represents the initiatory phase of the general teaching for collective liberation, which can lead into particularized and complete teachings for collective liberation; therefore "it is beneficial to be a guest of the king."

  The fifth represents people with the potential for the complete teaching; therefore "observing oneself is observing the people." This is what is referred to in Buddhism as the nondifferentiation of mind, Buddha, and all beings.

  The top line represents people with the potential for the particularized teaching. Going beyond both the absolute and the relative by way of central balance, true being-as-is rests high in the state of fruition. Because of focus on the particular rather than the essence that is the same in all phenomena, "the mind is not yet at peace."

  To interpret the six lines in terms of contemplating mind, the first represents ideal buddhahood, which is like being a child, without knowledge.

The second represents intellectual buddhahood, which is like a woman without real wisdom.

The third represents contemplative buddhahood, which is just observing one's own mind.

The fourth represents semblance buddhahood, close to the real state.

The fifth represents partial realization of buddhahood, helping oneself and helping others.

The top line represents ultimate buddhahood, not grasping nirvana, observing all beings in the cosmos, manifesting compassion and innocence.

 21. Biting Through

thunder below, *fire* above

Biting through is successful. It is beneficial to apply justice.

In political terms, this means quelling disruptive influences. In Buddhist terms, this means correcting the immoral. In terms of contemplating mind, this means using subtle observation to overcome afflictions, compulsive habits, sicknesses, delusions, pride in meditation, and opinionated views, as they arise in contemplation. All of these are types of success in which it is beneficial to apply justice.

THE OVERALL JUDGMENT: **There is something between the jaws; this is called biting through. In biting through successfully, the hard and soft are proportionate. Active and clear, thunder and lightning join and stand out. Flexibility attains balance and moves upward; though it is not in place, it beneficially applies justice.**

The way of kings is to use just laws to nurture the country. The method of Buddhism is to use correct education to nurture the community. Contemplating mind uses subtle insight to nurture the spiritual body. All of these are represented by the jaws. When recalcitrant people become set in their ways, they need to be corrected. When Buddhist practitioners are undisciplined, they need to be corrected. When states arise in the practice of stopping and seeing, they need to be examined. All of these are represented by "there is something."

When "the hard and the soft are proportionate," concentration and insight are equal. "Active and clear," one works without the light of wisdom being obscured. "Thunder and lightning join and stand out" in the sense that speech and silence help each other. Thunder is like expounding the teaching; lightning is like going into concentration and radiating light.

In this hexagram, the second and fifth lines, the positions of balance, are both yin, representing flexibility; therefore "flexibility attains balance." This is subtle concentration on the center of all things. As for "moving upward," *thunder* has the image of bursting forth, and *fire* has the image of reaching toward the sky.

"Although not in place" means that the fifth yin is in a yang position, the image of not having entered into the right state of a bodhisattva. But in contemplative practice, concentration and insight are in place, so one can skillfully use nonconceptual observation to control any states that arise.

THE IMAGE: Thunder and lightning—biting through.
Kings of yore used clear punishments to promulgate the law.

Clear punishments are a means of promulgating the law, just as cutting through temporary states is a means of revealing inner qualities.

■ *First yang:* **Wearing stocks stopping the feet, there is no blame.**

THE IMAGE: **"Wearing stocks stopping the feet" means not acting.**

Whether in worldly affairs or Buddhism, "biting through" means biting oneself and others. In either case, it is necessary to establish control early on and not let matters ferment into something serious. Also, it is necessary to use hard and soft control appropriately and not let the serious and the light get out of proportion.

The first yang is at the bottom of the hexagram, representing a condition in which faults are not yet serious. Also, this is a yang position, so yang is correct here; therefore it is only like "wearing stocks stopping the feet," which means being able to criticize what is wrong and not to do it, thus being blameless.

■ *2 yin:* **Biting through the skin, destroying the nose, there is no blame.**

THE IMAGE: **Biting through the skin, destroying the nose, is riding on strength.**

Here flexibility is balanced and correct; faults are easy to correct. Therefore it is like biting through skin. Because it rides on the strength of the first yang, therefore it is like destroying the nose.

■ *3 yin:* Biting dried meat, finding poison, there is a little shame, but no blame.

THE IMAGE: Finding poison means the position is not appropriate.

At the top of the lower trigram, this represents the gradual deepening of faults. Also, as yin is in a yang position, this represents having an aberrant intellect, which is like poison. Obviously this is shameful. However, when biting through, one does not commit further error by being presumptuous, so one can be blameless.

■ *4 yang:* Biting bony dried meat, one finds a metal arrow.
It is beneficial to work hard and be upright.

THE IMAGE: It is beneficial to work hard and be upright;
one is not yet illumined.

An animal is shot on a hunt, and the arrow goes into the bone, so that it cannot be pulled out; now, when biting bony dried meat, one finds it and should beware of it. This represents faults that have accumulated for a long time. However, being strong without excess, one will surely be able to master oneself, so "it is beneficial to work hard and be upright."

■ *5 yin:* Biting dry meat, finding gold, if one is upright and diligent there will be no blame.

THE IMAGE: Upright and diligent, blameless—this is finding what is appropriate.

Though soft as meat, faults are longstanding; this is like meat that has dried out. It is lucky if there is the quality of balance, which is to be valued; this is like finding gold. Keeping this quality of balance correctly, being diligent and careful, one may return to impeccability.

■ *Top yang:* Wearing a cangue destroying the ears is unfortunate.

THE IMAGE: "Wearing a cangue destroying the ears" means not listening clearly.

When faults and evils have developed to the point of being irremediable, this is like wearing a cangue destroying the ears. Generally one comes to this because one does not listen clearly and does not know how to repent of faults and take to the good.

To interpret in terms of contemplating mind, the first yang represents immediately overcoming a mental state that arises, by using true insight; this is like stopping the feet and not allowing them to walk.

The second yin represents using correct concentration to overcome a state that has arisen but is not yet deeply rooted. Though what is "bitten through" is not hard, still one cannot help losing one's grip, which is represented by the word "nose."

The third yin represents states arising with gradually increasing severity, and concentrated insight not being purely correct. One cannot help being disturbed by these states, but does not get to the point of completely falling prey to them.

The fourth yang represents states arising with a mixture of good and bad, and concentrated insight not being purely correct. Even though one gets some small benefit from the teaching, one has not yet realized the profound teaching.

The fifth yin represents pure development of good states, so that the benefit gained from the teaching is also great; but one still has not entered into the absolute, so one must still be upright and diligent in order to be impeccable.

The top yang represents states becoming extremely deep-rooted; there seems to be concentrated insight, but it is not balanced and not correct. One perversely grasps the wrong things and considers them sacred, forever falling into uninterrupted hell.

22. *Adornment*

fire below, *mountain* above

Adornment is successful. It is beneficial to go somewhere in a small way.

In political terms, this means disarming and developing culture after having gotten rid of disruptive elements. In terms of Buddhism, this means setting up more regulations after punishing corrupt practitioners. In terms of contemplating mind, this means adornment with concentration and insight after perfecting observation of the development of mental states. All of these are ways to success, but whether in politics or Buddhism, at this time it is not necessary to do much; it only requires a small application of ordering and adornment.

THE OVERALL JUDGMENT: Adornment is successful. The soft comes and embellishes the hard, hence success. A portion of

the hard rises and embellishes the soft, so it is beneficial to go
somewhere in a small way. This is the adornment of heaven.
Control by civilization is the adornment of humanity. Observe
the adornment of heaven to see the changes of the times;
observe the adornment of humanity to transform and complete
the world.

Adornment must succeed, because the lower trigram is basically *heaven,* but
the second yin comes and embellishes it with softness; so this is substance
with appropriate adornment, or insight with appropriate concentration,
hence success. The upper trigram is basically *earth,* but the top yang embellishes it with a portion of hardness; so this is adornment with appropriate
substance, or concentration with appropriate insight, and therefore it is beneficial to go somewhere in a small way.

Embellishment and substance complement one another; concentration
and insight balance one another. This is inherently so, and not something
forced, so it is called the "adornment of heaven." Embodying insight with
concentration, calm yet ever aware, is "civilization." Embodying concentration with insight, aware yet ever calm, is "control." This means using culture
to unite with nature; this is called the "adornment of humanity."

Inherent qualities create all possible realms of experience, so by observing
them one can see the changes of the times. In terms of cultivated qualities,
all possible realms of experience ultimately rest in one mind; therefore by
observing them one can transform and complete the world.

THE IMAGE: There is fire below a mountain, adorning it.
Leaders clarify governmental affairs without presumptuous
adjudication.

The time of adornment is not the time for adjudication; as long as governmental affairs are clear, it is possible thereby to see to it that the people have
no complaints.

In Buddhist terms, "there is fire below a mountain" stands for outward
stillness with inward illumination, whereby the "governmental affairs" of
the natures and characteristics of all possible realms of human experience
are clarified. Understanding what is right and what is wrong about all
things, one ultimately does not create emotional opinions grasping and re-
jecting by judging one as right and one as wrong; this is like not making
"presumptuous adjudication."

■ *First yang:* Adorn the feet; leave the car and walk.

THE IMAGE: Leave the car and walk—it is right not to ride.

This represents concealing one's virtues and living a simple life in obscurity, walking instead of riding. This is adorning oneself with righteousness.

■ *2 yin:* Adornment is seeking.

THE IMAGE: Adornment is seeking, in the sense of rising with those who are higher.

Flexible docility balanced and correct, one opens one's mind to derive benefit from the wise. This is adorning oneself through the agency of teachers and companions.

■ *3 yang:* Adorned, luxuriant, perpetual uprightness bodes well.

THE IMAGE: The good fortune of perpetual uprightness is that no one can ever slight you.

Strength that is correct, at the peak of illumination, is sufficient to nurture others and enable them to become wise. This is adorning oneself with teacherhood.

■ *4 yin:* Adorned plainly, a white horse runs swiftly. They are not enemies, but partners.

THE IMAGE: The fourth yin, in its place, doubts. They are not enemies but partners, and ultimately bear no grudge.

When flexible and correct, one knows that adornment with plainness is valuable, and so seeks the wise tirelessly. One approaches teachers, corresponds with the righteous, and looks up to the perfected; all of them are one's enlightened teachers and companions. Sincere students and those full of virtue are also helpful associates. Seeing the wise, one thinks of how to be equal to them; seeing the unwise, one reflects on oneself. How can there be enmity? And being in a low position among those on the ascendant, though rising one can still lower oneself, and does not presume to believe in oneself or act arbitrarily. This is adorning oneself with an open mind.

■ *5 yin:* Adornment in the hills and groves. The roll of silk is small. There is regret, but the end is auspicious.

THE IMAGE: What is auspicious about the fifth yin is that there is joy.

When one is flexible but balanced, and has a positive strong will, one is able to know the joys of enlightened virtue and does not pride oneself on power or position. Rather, one looks upon the honor of exalted rank as equal to hills and groves, just like the ancient sage-king who ate poor food, wore poor clothing, and lived in a poor house. This is the image of the regret of the roll of silk being small; but really one has no complaints and comes to an auspicious end. This is adorning oneself with abundant virtue.

■ *Top yang:* Adornment by simplicity is impeccable.

THE IMAGE: Adornment by simplicity is impeccable.
One attains one's aspiration above.

This represents strength under utmost control, growing more illumined as one gets older, one's qualities becoming pure and flawless. This is adorning oneself with ultimate goodness.

In terms of Buddhism, the first yang represents adorning oneself with generosity, the second yin represents adorning oneself with discipline, the third yang represents adorning oneself with patience, the fourth yin represents adorning oneself with perseverance, the fifth yin represents adorning oneself with concentration, the top yang represents adorning oneself with wisdom.

Also, the first yang represents adornment with an ideal, not letting inherent qualities displace cultivated qualities. The second yin represents adornment with intellectual understanding, from this determining to progress to higher development. The third yang represents adornment with contemplation practice, not forgetting it for a moment. The fourth yin represents adornment with conformity, not dwelling on religious attachment. The fifth yin represents adornment with partial realization, not missing the absolute truth, conventional truth, or the center of balance. The top yang represents adornment with ultimate realization, returning to the original essential nature, which has not the slightest flaw.

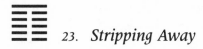

23. *Stripping Away*

earth below, *mountain* above

Stripping away, it is not beneficial to go anywhere.

THE OVERALL JUDGMENT: Stripping away is overthrowing. The weak changes the strong. It is not beneficial to go anywhere,

because petty people are increasing. Accordingly stopping this
is watching the form. Leaders value the process of waxing and
waning, filling and emptying; this is the action of heaven.

In political terms, after disarmament and development of culture, people
tend to indulge in comfort, leading to the inevitable decline of the basic energy of the country.

In Buddhist terms, when there are too many regulations, this inevitably
defeats real practice.

In terms of contemplating mind, there is a positive sense and a negative
sense. The positive sense is that after concentrated insight is developed, the
"skin" of the ego is stripped away and true reality alone remains. The negative sense is that mundane imitation of concentration and insight can develop mundane intellect and ability, but the essential practice of real cultivation will be overcome by this.

Leaving the positive sense aside for the moment, here we are talking
about the negative sense. That is, it is not beneficial to go anywhere, whether
in terms of worldly or transcendental affairs. Now, when it says it is not beneficial to go anywhere, this does not mean taking a laissez-faire attitude toward stripping away; it refers to subtle work toward restoration. To go on
would result in stripping away; not to go is to accordingly stop this. This is
how to restore the full cycle of the process of waxing and waning, filling and
emptying, so as to accord with the action of heaven.

THE IMAGE: Mountains cleave to the earth. Those above secure
their homes by kindness to those below.

In political terms, this means rulers need people; if the people are satisfied,
the rulers should be satisfied. Therefore they can only secure their homes by
kindness to those below. This is the best strategy for saving oneself from
being overthrown.

In terms of contemplating mind, this means that the work of higher development must be understood from right where you stand.

In Buddhist terms, the six lines show how both laypeople and initiates are
caught up in personal ambitions, from which only the wise are aloof.

In terms of contemplating mind, they show how when cultivated good is
completely destroyed, inherent good alone is never destroyed.

■ *First yin:* Stripping a bed of its legs, destroying uprightness
brings misfortune.

THE IMAGE: Stripping a bed of its legs is destroying the
foundation.

Strip a bed of its legs, and there is nowhere to rest the body. The first line is at the bottom, so it is like stripping away the legs. In political terms, this refers to bad citizens. In Buddhism, this refers to bad sanctuary keepers. In contemplating mind, this refers to removing the foundation of discipline.

In a positive sense, this is stripping away the causes of miserable states. But if there were no miserable states, then great compassion would have no object of focus; hence the warning that destroying uprightness brings misfortune.

- *2 yin:* **Stripping a bed of its frame, destroying uprightness brings misfortune.**

THE IMAGE: **Stripping a bed of its frame, there is nothing to work with.**

In political terms, this refers to bad officials. In Buddhism, this refers to bad patrons. In contemplating mind, this refers to eliminating meditation concentration; without concentration, the mind is scattered and cannot deal with truth, so "there is nothing to work with."

In positive terms, this is stripping away unfocused virtue. But if there were no unfocused virtue at all, then there would be no way to accommodate and guide people; hence again the warning that destroying uprightness brings misfortune.

- *3 yin:* **Stripping away without fault.**

THE IMAGE: **Stripping away without fault loses above and below.**

In politics, this refers to a leader who mixes in among the populace, unbeknownst to them. In Buddhism, this refers to outside protectors who have true insight. In contemplating mind, this refers to stripping away knowledge. Stripping away knowledge means not being attached to knowledge, so one can effect accomplishment through this defeat, cutting through dualism and "losing above and below."

In positive terms, this is stripping away addictive meditation and ignorant concentration in the realms of form and formlessness, thereby getting to be without fault.

- *4 yin:* **Stripping a bed to the skin brings misfortune.**

THE IMAGE: **Stripping a bed to the skin is getting very close to disaster.**

The lower trigram is like a bed; the upper trigram is like a body. When stripping away reaches even to the skin on the body, it is irremediable.

In politics, this is when the chief executive is bad. In Buddhism, this is when the initiates are bad. In contemplating mind, this is denying all causality.

In positive terms, this is stripping away the ways that people enter into reality for individual liberation. But if there were no absolute reality, there would be no way to leave samsara and be unaffected by the ills of the world; hence the warning about getting very close to disaster. What this means is that the slightest deviation results in tremendous error.

■ *5 yin:* Leading fish with the favor shown to court ladies, there is all-around benefit.

THE IMAGE: Using the favor shown to court ladies, in the end there is no grudge.

In politics, this represents a weak leader who nevertheless is in a dominant position and also has the balance to be able to learn from the wise how to rescue the country from disorder.

In Buddhism, this represents a virtuous monk acting as the head of a community, leading the other monks to learn from the truly wise.

In contemplating mind, this represents comprehending inherent evil in cultivated evil. When inherent evil is made flexible, one can naturally absorb the inherent virtues of buddhahood, so there is all-around benefit.

Also, in a positive sense, this is going from contemplation of emptiness into contemplation of the conditional, stripping away dualistic extremism and entering into central balance. Therefore it is necessary to arrive at central balance, which comprehends all things, like "leading fish with the favor shown to court ladies," causing everything to become part of the path of universal enlightenment, so there is all-around benefit.

■ *Top yang:* A hard fruit is not eaten. The leader gets a vehicle. The petty person is stripped of a house.

THE IMAGE: The leader gets a vehicle, in the sense of being carried by the people. The small person is stripped of a house, after all unsuitable for employment.

In politics, this refers to taking the advice of outside advisers of advanced wisdom. In Buddhism, this means that highly developed people are fields of blessings for human society. In contemplating mind, this means that inherent good can never be stripped away; therefore it is like a hard fruit that is not eaten.

True leaders realize this, and thus attain enlightenment; petty people presume on this, and thus become so arrogant that they try to displace real sages.

Also, in positive terms, this also points out to the unchangeability and indestructibility of inherent qualities. If you can awaken to inherent qualities, then you will fulfill all Buddhist teachings right then and there; so "the leader gets a vehicle." But if you cling to inherence and neglect cultivation, you will fall into bad tendencies; so "the petty person is stripped of a house."

 ## 24. *Return*

thunder below, *earth* above

Return is successful. Exiting and entering, there is no ill. When a companion comes, there is no fault. Returning back on the path, returning in seven days, it is beneficial to have a place to go.

In politics, after decline there has to be an enlightened ruler to effect restoration; this is return. In Buddhism, after decadence has set in, there has to be a true sage to appear in response and bring about a revival; this is return.

In contemplating mind, again there are two senses; one in terms of loss, one in terms of gain.

In terms of loss, taking up after the preceding hexagram, there must be return after stripping away. This is like one's mood at dawn, having returned to normal.

In terms of gain, taking up after the preceding hexagram, stripping away is removing all emotional clinging and returning to the essence of all things.

In terms of contemplation of the center of all things, going from contemplation of conditionality to contemplation of emptiness is called "stripping away"; going from contemplation of emptiness to contemplation of the conditional is called "return."

In terms of contemplating conditionality, emptiness, and the center all at once, using cultivation to unite with essence is called "stripping away"; reaching out to teach in harmony with essence is called "return."

Return must lead to success; the quality of positive strength is in the lead, so it is possible to "exit and enter without ill." Using good to transform evil, therefore, "when a companion comes there is no fault." Once you have returned, you should cause the return to be permanent, so "returning back on the path," this comes to last a long time, here represented by "seven days." Then there is a beginning and an end, whereby you can help yourself and help others, "having a place to go."

THE OVERALL JUDGMENT: **Return is successful. Strength comes
back, moving with harmonious action, therefore exiting and
entering without ill; when a companion comes there is no
fault. Returning back on the path, returning in seven days,
is the action of heaven. It is beneficial to have a place to go,
because strength is growing. To return is to see the heart of
heaven and earth.**

To interpret this in terms of contemplating mind, the essence of enlightenment is called the heart of heaven and earth; not even incorrigible criminals
can ever destroy it, but as long as it is covered by evil, we cannot see it ourselves. The ocean of suffering is boundless, but the shore is near at hand; a
moment of inspiration for enlightenment can move the boundless ocean of
samsara.

The reason why return is successful is that the quality of strength emerges
in harmony with essential nature, so that there is the power to turn back
from samsara. Once this inspiration for enlightenment becomes active, this
is working in harmony with it; if you proceed on this basis, then you can go
out and in without ill, and company can come without fault.

But the reason why it is necessary to return back on the path, returning in
seven days, is that the work of embodying the strength of the action of
heaven and strengthening oneself unceasingly should be like this.

Fulfill this one thought of enlightenment, and then it is beneficial to have
a place to go, because even though strength is very faint, the momentum of
its growth cannot be stopped. Therefore from this we can see our inherent
enlightened essence.

Also, "exiting" means going from emptiness into the conditional; "entering" means going from the conditional into emptiness. Once we harmonize
with the essence of reality at the center of all things, we dwell neither in
samsara nor in nirvana, but can roam freely in samsara and nirvana, so
there is no ill. The "companion" means the nature and characteristics of all
possible realms of experience, which when opened up become the nature
and characteristics of the realm of enlightenment; therefore there is no fault.

THE IMAGE: **Thunder in the earth—return. On the winter
solstice, the ancient kings shut the gates; the caravans did not
travel; the ruler did not inspect the regions.**

In terms of contemplating mind, even though there is momentum in the
growth of strength and it is beneficial to have a place to go, nevertheless it is
necessary to nurture potential with serenity. So the buddhahood in contemplative practices, the "ancient kings," have awakened to the "winter solstice" of the latent essence, "shut the gates" of the senses, shed attachments,
and mastered themselves inwardly, temporarily halting the "caravans" of

myriad practices of the six transcendent ways, and just observed the mind of the present moment, without "inspecting the regions" of the mental and physical elements.

■ *First yang:* **Returning not far, no regret. Very auspicious.**

THE IMAGE: **Returning that is not far is done by cultivating oneself.**

In Buddhist terms, when true insight is perfectly clear, one sees the essence of enlightenment all at once and is immediately imbued with all practices; therefore it is very auspicious. This is like the first station of the complete teaching. Also, in terms of the six transcendent ways, this is the correct path of transcendent wisdom.

■ *2 yin:* **Good return is auspicious.**

THE IMAGE: **What is auspicious about good return comes through humble benevolence.**

In Buddhist terms, when correct concentration is balanced, one is near to reality, close to sagehood, as in the stages of faith in the complete teaching. Also, in terms of the six transcendent ways, this is correct concentration combining with insight.

■ *3 yin:* **Repeated return is diligence. There is no fault.**

THE IMAGE: **The diligence of repeated return is faultless if right.**

In Buddhist terms, this is having concentration and insight, but not being balanced correctly; therefore one must first contemplate emptiness, then the conditional, then the center—this is called repeated return. By diligent work in practice and experience one can get to be without fault. Also, in terms of the six transcendent ways, this is the continual urging of perseverance.

■ *4 yin:* **Traveling in the center, returning alone.**

THE IMAGE: **Traveling in the center, returning alone, is done by following the path.**

In Buddhist terms, this represents correct concentration, corresponding to true insight. This is like people of sharp faculties in the general teaching being initiated into the complete teaching. Also, in terms of the six transcendent ways, this is patience. By combining this with insight, one can attain tolerance of people and things, which turns into tolerance of the ultimate truth.

■ *5 yin:* Attentive return, without regret.

THE IMAGE: Attentive return without regret
is balanced reflection on oneself.

In Buddhist terms, this is equilibration of concentration and insight, and temporary attainment of balance. However, this is quite far from positive strength, so after cutting through confusion and witnessing reality, it is necessary to await the revelation of the complete teaching before entering into the state of completeness, like those who follow the teaching for individual emancipation or the general teaching for collective emancipation. Also, in terms of the six transcendent ways, this is discipline; though far from the beginning, one just reflects on one's thoughts, words, and deeds, to make them faultless, thus naturally conforming to truth and becoming free from regret.

■ *Top yin:* Straying return is unfortunate; there is trouble.
Use this for a military expedition, and eventually there will be
a great defeat, unfortunate even for the leader of the nation.
Even in ten years there is no victory.

THE IMAGE: The misfortune of straying return is turning back
on the path of a leader.

In Buddhist terms, this means being unbalanced and awry, relying on a little worldly concentration and insight as the ultimate, straying through return. Therefore not only is it unfortunate, but there is also trouble. If you use this to set up teachings and try to instruct people, you will defeat the purpose of the Buddhist teaching and ruin the accurate methodology of the Buddha. Even in ten years there will be no success, because imitation Buddhism is not real Buddhism, and goes against the path of leadership of the great vehicle of complete all-at-once enlightenment.

Also, in terms of the six ways of transcendence, this is giving; but it is far from wisdom, so it is attached to forms, attached to rewards, giving rise to pride and emotion, and also potentially giving rise to opinionated views. Therefore, even though it may be a good cause, it will bring about bad results. This is because of not realizing the path of leadership of the teaching of Buddha.

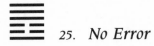

25. *No Error*

thunder below, *heaven* above

Freedom from error is very successful, beneficial for the upright. Denial of what is correct is mistaken, so it will not be beneficial to go anywhere.

In politics, a government that restores well-being accords with the way of heaven and is free from error. In Buddhism, a teaching that restores the true way is the same as the orthodox teaching and is free from error. In contemplating mind, on returning to original essence, truth is found and confusion is ended, so one is free from error. All of these are very successful, and beneficial for the upright.

But whether in worldly affairs or transcendental affairs, helping oneself and helping others, it is necessary to look deeply into oneself to be sure one's mind is free from aberration and one's words and deeds are not mistaken. If inwardly one denies what is correct, outwardly one will make mistakes; then one should certainly not go anywhere or do anything in this way.

THE OVERALL JUDGMENT: **No error—strength comes from outside and becomes the master of the inside. Active and healthy, strength is balanced and responsive. Great success in what is right is the celestial command. Denial of what is correct is mistaken, so it will not be beneficial to go anywhere. Where does one go without error? How could one go anywhere without the assistance of the celestial command?**

Although inherent virtues are in everyone, in terms of confused feelings they become on the contrary external. Now, if we initiate cultivation from essence, we will understand that inherent virtues are our own—so this is called becoming the master of the inside.

Once we have initiated cultivation in accord with essence, everything we do has to accord with the essence of reality. If our thoughts, words, or deeds are not yet pure, even if we have sublime understanding, we cannot help ourselves or others. As long as we do not conform to our inherent virtues, the buddhas of the universe will not watch over us—so how could we go anywhere?

THE IMAGE: **Thunder travels under the sky; things accompany with no error. Ancient kings promoted flourishing appropriate to the time and nurtured myriad beings.**

In Buddhist terms, the full projection of the scope of complete enlightenment benefits people in all times; this is called promoting flourishing appropriate to the time. Planting and ripening the seeds of liberation, causing all
sorts of people to naturally grow and eventually wind up at the unique reality is called nurturing myriad beings.

■ *First yang:* **Going without error leads to good results.**

THE IMAGE: **Going without error, one attains one's aspiration.**

This means going to respond to events based on truly genuine freedom from
error. Thereby one attains one's aspiration, which leads to good results.

■ *2 yin:* **Not plowing for the harvest, it is beneficial to go
somewhere.**

THE IMAGE: **Not plowing for the harvest, one is not enriched.**

This means aspiring only to attain enlightenment, not thinking of riches or
rank. Then it is beneficial to go somewhere.

■ *3 yin:* **The misfortune of no error—a tethered cow is a gain for
a traveler, a misfortune for the local people.**

THE IMAGE: **When a traveler finds the cow, it is a misfortune
for the local people.**

This represents the unbalanced and aberrant who cling to a principle that is
without error and make it into a misfortune. When a traveler finds the cow,
why then cling to principle and seek a reward from the local people? Is this
not misfortune extending to the innocent?

■ *4 yang:* **One should be correct; then there is no error.**

THE IMAGE: **One should be correct; then there is no error—
this is inherent.**

This means not being disposed to act arbitrarily just because one is strong;
the reason is that inherent virtue is thus.

■ *5 yang:* **For sickness without error, do not use medicine—
there will be joy.**

THE IMAGE: **Medicine should not be tried when nothing is wrong.**

This represents sane strength balanced correctly, the epitome of freedom from error. But those who are without error themselves may blame others too much for their faults; this is called clinging to the medicine so much that it becomes a disease instead. Therefore "do not use medicine—there will be joy." If you try to order people based on your own standards, who in the world can follow you?

■ *Top yang:* **Even if there is no error, action involves misfortune, so no benefit is gained.**

THE IMAGE: **Action without error involves misfortune when it comes to an impasse.**

This refers to clinging to a constant and not knowing how to change adaptively; without temporary expedients, how can one carry anything out?

In Buddhist terms, all six lines represent those who understand principle that is without error and make it their practice and realization.

The first yang is accurate insight advancing directly, whereby one gets results in the present life and attains one's aspiration.

The second yin is correct concentration overcoming habits; therefore it is necessary not to grasp meditation methods or take them as final realization, so that one can just use them as a way back home.

The third yin is not balanced and not correct. Though one has a little concentrated insight and can show people how to find the way and attain results, that is like a traveler finding a cow and is instead a loss to oneself, as one lingers in an ordinary state—like the "misfortune of the local people."

The fourth yang is insight with concentration, more than enough to help oneself. This is finding inherent concentration and insight; it is not attained after practice.

The fifth yang is sane strength balanced correctly. Self-help is already complete, so one acts compassionately for the benefit of others. It is no longer necessary to use "medicine" to cure oneself. Even a beginner's practice of contemplation is like this—all mental objects are inherent qualities, so when you comprehend obstacles, they are virtues, and there is nothing to "cure."

The top yang is not balanced and not correct; this is relying on inherent virtues and not working on cultivated virtues. If one's own actions are full of mistakes, what benefit can there be? It is because of only talking loftily about transcendence that one comes to an impasse, so that it becomes a misfortune.

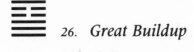

26. *Great Buildup*

heaven below, *mountain* above

**Great buildup is beneficial if correct. It is good not
to eat at home. It is beneficial to cross a great river.**

This means building up a way free from error to nurture the world. In politics, this refers to a leader who returns to a way free from error and builds up the healthy energy of the nation. In Buddhism this refers to great people returning to the true teaching and developing adepts. In contemplating mind this refers to attaining enlightenment, returning to essence without error, and building up provisions for enlightenment on a large scale. All of these may be called great buildup.

Whether in worldly or transcendental affairs, to spread beneficial influence and promote development, it is necessary to be correct for there to be any real benefit. To develop others and self equally is impartiality; to refine the mind through experience is essential; therefore "it is good not to eat at home" and "it is beneficial to cross a great river."

THE OVERALL JUDGMENT: **In great buildup, strength and honesty shine, daily renewing their virtues. Strength rises and esteems the wise. Ability to control power is great rectitude. Not eating at home is good—this is developing the wise. It is beneficial to cross a great river—this is responding to heaven.**

The strength represented by *heaven* and the honesty represented by *mountain* both have the sense of shining light. Using this to renew virtues daily, the buildup will be great in depth and breadth—so it is called great buildup.

But what the expressions "beneficial if correct," "it is good not to eat at home," and "it is beneficial to cross a great river" refer to is not setting up cultivated virtues outside of essential nature; this is cultivation initiated in conformity with essential nature, the completion of which cultivation is in essential nature.

Now observe the quality of strength of *heaven;* it rises to the top end of the hexagram, and the fifth yin is able to honor and esteem it. Furthermore, the body of the hexagram is still outside and powerful inside. Is this not the way whose basic nature is great rectitude?

The fifth yin represents the quality of flexibility in balance, able to nurture wise teachers above to influence the world, and to nurture wise citizens below to serve the nation; is this not the right way in which "it is good not to eat at home"? It corresponds with the strength of celestial qualities represented by the second yang, so that strength and flexibility balance each other, able to reach any distance. Is this not the right way in which "it is beneficial to cross a great river"?

THE IMAGE: **Heaven is in the mountain—great buildup.
Leaders build up their virtues by abundant knowledge of past
words and deeds.**

In one mountain there is the whole body of heaven; on one mental moment there are the past and present of all worlds. Taking up the "past words" of the whole range of Buddhist teachings, comprehending the "deeds" of the myriad virtues of the six transcendent ways, one thereby develops the qualities of one's own mind, thereby building oneself up and using this to build up the world.

■ *First yang:* **There is danger; help yourself.**

THE IMAGE: **There is danger; help yourself—do not get into trouble.**

All six lines have the sense of the shining light of strength and honesty, through which one renews oneself and renews other people. In the first yang, positive strength is in a low position; at such a time it is appropriate to live in obscurity and pursue one's aspiration. This involves the effort to be wary of danger and first help oneself. Once self-help is complete, then one can help others according to circumstances. If one tries to liberate others before having completed work on oneself, then one will get into trouble.

■ *2 yang:* **The car has its axles removed.**

THE IMAGE: **The car has its axles removed, but there is no resentment in the heart.**

Strength in balance, one focuses on cultivating concentrated insight. It seems as if one has no interest in taking advantage of the time to carry out the way, but since self-help is properly the basis on which to help others, therefore there is no resentment in the heart.

■ *3 yang:* **A good horse gives chase. It is beneficial to struggle for right. Daily practicing charioteering and defense, it is beneficial to have somewhere to go.**

THE IMAGE: **It is beneficial to have somewhere to go, in the sense of joining in the aims of those above.**

Strength correctly oriented, at the top of *heaven*, one does not worry about not being able to liberate people, but rather worries about being too eager to advance quickly and thereby slipping up in defense against carelessness. Therefore it is beneficial to struggle for right. "Daily practicing charioteering and defense, it is beneficial to have somewhere to go" because above there are good companions, as represented by the fourth yin, wise leaders, as represented by the fifth yin, and enlightened teachers, as represented by the top yang. Joining in their aims, it will be possible to alert and encourage one another, thus facilitating progress.

■ *4 yin:* The horn-guard of a young ox is very auspicious.

THE IMAGE: What is very auspicious about the fourth yin
is that there is joy.

This represents flexibility that is correctly oriented, corresponding below with strong, upright, good companions, represented by the first yang, associating with strong, upright, awesome companions, represented by the third yang, and approaching flexible, balanced, wise leaders, represented by the fifth yin. Faults have not yet begun to appear, and in fact dissolve unawares and transform silently. This is like putting a horn-guard on a young ox before its horns have grown, so that there is no worry that it will gore anyone. When one develops oneself in this way, and thereby is a model for the world, this is very good and auspicious, joyful and happy.

■ *5 yin:* The tusks of a gelded boar are auspicious.

THE IMAGE: What is auspicious about the fifth yin
is that there is celebration.

A gelded boar is not violent, but its tusks are still hard and sharp. When flexibility is in a position of balance, one honors the wise above and responds to creativity below. Since inherent virtues are not lopsided, what is developed is also comprehensive. When self-help is completed, one can then rule, and all the good and bad people come under one's rule; therefore one is like the tusks of a gelded boar.

■ *Top yang:* Carrying the crossroads of heaven is successful.

THE IMAGE: Carrying the crossroads of heaven, the way is
carried out on a grand scale.

Bearing the responsibility of a leader and guide with strength and flexibility in balance, the aim one sought in private life is now carried out on a grand scale, without obstruction.

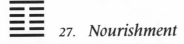

27. *Nourishment*

thunder below, *mountain* above

Nourishment is good if correct. Observe nourishment, and seek food by yourself.

In politics, this is building up virtue to nurture the country. In Buddhism, this is building up virtue to benefit all beings. In contemplating mind, this is nurturing embryonic sagehood once the provisions for enlightenment have been accumulated.

Self-help and helping others are beneficial if correct. In either case it is necessary to see how the sages of the past accomplished nourishment, and to see how you feed yourself.

THE OVERALL JUDGMENT: Nourishment is good if correct. Observing nourishment is observing what is nourished. Seeking food by yourself is observing your own nourishment. Heaven and earth nurture myriad beings, sages nurture the wise, for the effect this has on the general population. The time of nourishment is great indeed.

Nourishment is good if correct; clearly if what is nourished is not correct, or if what is correct is not nourished, then this is not the way to good fortune.

Unless you observe what sages nourish, you have no way to find an example to hope to emulate. If you do not observe the fulfillment of your own nourishment, you have no way to be the peer of those who are good.

If you nourish yourself with the qualities of the absolute, which completely embodies heaven and earth, then you can nourish all beings. Sages nurture wise assistants to complete their own qualities, and thus can extend the effect to the general population.

Who could say that there is any way to benefit people other than to nourish what is right? Therefore when one corrects one's own nourishment, one thereby includes the totality of position, upbringing, achievement, and ability; so this is called "great."

THE IMAGE: There is thunder beneath the mountain. Leaders are prudent in speech, moderate in consumption.

Speech and consumption are both representations of action; to be prudent and moderate is not to lose control. Therefore to nourish what is right, it is best to know when to stop.

■ *First yang:* To give up your sacred tortoise and watch me greedily
leads to misfortune.

THE IMAGE: To watch me greedily is not worthy of respect.

Positive strength is a tool to nourish oneself and others as well; knowing
when to stop is the right way to nourish oneself and others. The first yang
represents positive strength that is sufficient to nourish oneself, like a sacred
tortoise that ingests the energy in the air and so does not need food. To give
this up and watch another's food is greed; thus you lose what is valuable and
suffer misfortune. This is like a leader who proceeds too rapidly; in Buddhist
terms it is like an ordinary externalist with merely theoretical knowledge
that cannot help people.

■ *2 yin:* Perverting nourishment brushes aside the constant.
Feeding on high ground, an expedition bodes ill.

THE IMAGE: An expedition bodes ill for the second yin,
because the action loses companionship.

For those above to nourish those below is the rational constant. Here one in
a higher position is recessive and weak, and relies on strength from below
for nourishment; so this "brushes aside the constant."

Also, this line is in the body of movement; one may not be willing to rest
content in one's own lot, and so may seek to feed on the "high ground" of
the fifth yin. The fifth yin may respond, but it is also weak and unable to
nourish itself, so how can it nourish others? So to go on the expedition will
only bring misfortune. Both the second and the fifth are yin, without any
ability to balance each other, so this is "losing companionship."

This is like a useless official. In Buddhist terms, it is like those who experience blind meditation and lose their bearings.

■ *3 yin:* Going against nourishment is inauspicious even if there
is rectitude. Do not act on this for ten years; there is nothing
to be gained.

THE IMAGE: Do not act on this for ten years, for the way is
greatly confused.

The weak cannot nourish themselves; if they are also not balanced correctly
and dwell on the climax of action in this state, this is going against nourishment. Even though there is a correct correspondence with the top yang, this
cannot save them, and they wind up useless.

This is like crooked executives and officials. In Buddhism, it is like the
senses deranging people so that they lose their standards.

■ *4 yin:* Reverse nourishment is auspicious. The tiger watches intently, about to give chase. No fault.

THE IMAGE: What is auspicious about reverse nourishment is giving out light from above.

When flexibility is correctly oriented and is under control, even if one has no means of nourishment, one has found the right way to nourish. This line corresponds with the first yang, depending on that nourishment for self-nourishment and nourishment of others. This is like an easygoing, tolerant official. This is a way to good results.

In the first yang, you watch me greedily, and I deal politely with your intent watching, about to give chase. This is not worthy of esteem at first, but as far as I am concerned, it is a way to nurture the wise for the effect this extends to the populace. This can be called "giving out light from above."

In Buddhism, this is like when wise and good people manage affairs and skillfully act as outside protectors of the teaching.

■ *5 yin:* Brushing aside the constant, it is good to remain upright, but it will not do to cross a great river.

THE IMAGE: What is good about remaining upright is following those above docilely.

When one is weak and has no means to nourish people, one is in a position of leadership in vain; therefore it is called "brushing aside the constant." But if one is in control of oneself and obediently follows those who are more highly developed, this also nourishes the wise, the effects of which reach the populace; this is finding what is right.

However, in this case one can only deal with what is normal, and cannot deal with change; it is better to preserve what is established and not try to start any new works. This is like wise leaders who make naught of themselves. In Buddhism, this is like flexible and harmonious fellow practitioners who urge each other on.

■ *Top yang:* At the source of nourishment, it is good to be diligent, beneficial to cross a great river.

THE IMAGE: At the source of nourishment, it is good to be diligent. There will be great celebration.

Here positive strength is at the peak of control; this is why the hexagram is called nourishment. This is like being the tutor of an up-and-coming ruler, thus able to help the whole country. In Buddhism, this is like a teacher who has realized enlightenment and is in charge of the mystic order.

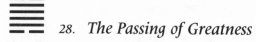

28. The Passing of Greatness

wind below, *lake* above

When greatness passes, the ridgepole bends.
It is beneficial to have somewhere to go, for you will
succeed.

In politics, this is when a wise leader nurtures the country and there has been peace for a long time. In Buddhism, this is when the path transforms people and Buddhism flourishes. In contemplating mind, this is when the work progresses and is about to break through ignorance.

When there has been peace for a long time, the beginnings of disorder inevitably sprout. It is best to prevent it when it is still weak, to stop it from creeping up. When the transformative path is flourishing, contaminations easily arise; it is best to set up guidelines and regulations. When meditation work is advanced, ignorance is about to dissolve; it is best to exercise the mind skillfully.

THE OVERALL JUDGMENT: "The passing of greatness" means the great passes. "The ridgepole bends" means that root and branch are weak. Strength is predominant yet balanced; it is docile and acts joyfully. It is beneficial to have somewhere to go, for you will then succeed. The time of the passing of greatness is great indeed.

When the great has passed, it is therefore time to think about problems and prevent them. In this hexagram, the first and top lines are both weak, so strength is balanced. It is not good to rely on force and cause disturbance; though strength is predominant, yet it is balanced, and it is docile and acts joyfully, so there is still a way to restore order and equilibrium. Then success is attained. This time is critical for the preservation of tranquillity, and it is also critical for sudden decline at the climax of flourishing; so is the relationship not great?

THE IMAGE: Moisture destroys wood—the passing of greatness. Developed people stand alone without fear, avoid society without distress.

Moisture originally nourishes wood, but also can destroy it; this is the image of the passing of greatness. Only when sustained by the power to stand alone without fear and avoid society without distress can learning be firmly rooted and development have a proper basis; then it is possible to refine and support the mediocre.

■ *First yin:* **Spreading a mat of white reeds, there is no blame.**

THE IMAGE: **Spreading a mat of white reeds means flexibility in a low position.**

Whether in worldly affairs or in Buddhism, at the time of the passing of the great, a balance of firmness and flexibility makes for success, while being too firm or too flexible makes for failure. This first yin represents flexibility in a low position, remaining docile, yet in a positive position. Here there is no fame, wealth, or honor to burden the mind, only ordinary qualities and ordinary speech; studying humbly to attain higher things is one's work here. In Buddhist terms, concentration has matching insight and is also refined by the virtues of discipline; therefore there is no blame.

■ *2 yang:* **A withered willow produces sprouts, an old man gets a girl for a wife; none do not benefit.**

THE IMAGE: **An old man getting a girl for a wife has her for a companion in spite of being older.**

This represents strength in balance, and also in a recessive position. Yang getting help from yin is like a withered willow producing sprouts, like an old man getting a girl for a wife. In terms of Buddhism, this is insight together with concentration, like first seeing the way, then afterward practicing meditation on phenomena; therefore none do not benefit.

■ *3 yang:* **The ridgepole bending is foreboding.**

THE IMAGE: **The foreboding of the ridgepole bending is that there is no way to help.**

When too obstinate and unbalanced, indulging in stubbornness, if one cultivates oneself in this way, one's virtues will surely be ruined, and if one governs society in this way, disturbances will surely arise. Therefore the ridgepole bends, and this is foreboding. In terms of Buddhism, this is only using misguided intelligence, so there is no way to help.

■ *4 yang:* **The ridgepole is raised. This is auspicious, but there is another shame.**

THE IMAGE: What is auspicious about the ridgepole being raised
is that it does not bend down.

When strong but not excessively so, one can establish oneself and others as
well. But if one likes greatness and enjoys achievement, one may not keep
calm; hence the warning that there is another shame.

In Buddhist terms, this too is insight along with concentration. But one
may have some personal ambition, in which case self-help and helping
others will not necessarily be fulfilled; hence the warning that there is another shame.

■ *5 yang:* A withered willow bears flowers, an old woman gets a
young man for a husband. No blame, no praise.

THE IMAGE: When a withered willow bears flowers, how can
they last? An old woman getting a young man for a husband
can also be embarrassing.

Although here positive strength is balanced correctly, nevertheless in a time
when greatness has passed, this is relying on intellectual talents; enjoying
peace, one does not know the problems of the people, and does not know
enough to employ wise officials who are in lower positions, only consorting
with weak and useless old officials, as represented by the top yin. How can
this last?

In Buddhist terms, when the power of insight is too much and there is no
meditation concentration to sustain it, how is it possible to produce superior
results?

■ *Top yin:* Going too far, passing away at the peak,
there is misfortune, but no blame.

THE IMAGE: The misfortune of going too far cannot be blamed.

Here there are only the virtues of flexibility and uprightness, without the
ability to solve difficulties, so misfortune cannot be avoided; but one is really
not to blame. In Buddhist terms, this is when correct concentration has no
insight, winding up as a fall at the peak.

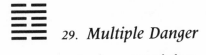 *29. Multiple Danger*

water above, *water* below

In multiple danger, if there is sincerity, the mind gets through and action has value.

In society, when there is peace for a long time, carelessness arises; when carelessness arises, trouble comes again and again.

In Buddhism, when many people follow the influence of the teaching, contamination arises; when contamination arises, destructive activity takes place.

In contemplating mind, when the power of intellect is dominant, past habits become active; when past habits become active, mental states emerge powerfully.

All of these are represented as multiple danger. But in both mundane and transmundane affairs, the problem is not that there is danger; the problem is when there is no good strategy for getting out of danger. If one can be truly sincere within, deeply believing that all objects are only projections of mind, then you will get through and your action will have value; so what danger cannot be overcome?

THE OVERALL JUDGMENT: **Multiple danger is repeated peril. As water flows and does not fill, act in danger without losing faith. The mind gets through because strength is in balance; action has value in proceeding to success. The danger of heaven is that we cannot ascend to it; the danger of earth is its mountains, rivers, and hills. Rulers set up dangers to preserve their countries. The timely use of danger is great indeed.**

Those who are skilled in observing mind can always make an impasse into a way through. Though multiple danger is repeated peril, if one lets it flow and does not become overwhelmed, it will be like the ocean tide, which keeps to its limits—this is the essential art for our cultivation of enlightenment.

What is important is to deeply believe that the mind can get through, with strength in balance as represented by the center yang of the water trigram. To proceed in this way will surely lead to success.

Furthermore, the word "danger" may sound bad, but the meaning of danger really is never bad. We cannot ascend to heaven, so isn't heaven "dangerous"? The danger of walls and moats can be used to protect a country, so when have rulers ever refrained from using danger? It is all a matter of using danger skillfully, and not being used by danger; then it can be used to govern society, and on the transmundane plane it can be used to observe the mind.

THE IMAGE: Water comes repeatedly—multiple danger.
Developed people practice teaching by constant
virtuous action.

Constant virtuous action is indefatigable study. Practicing teaching is instructing people tirelessly. The image of multiple danger is that of the mental method of the sages of all time; danger is not to be feared. This is in perfect accord with the Tiantai Buddhist teaching of knowing how to get through an impasse, the method of making an impasse itself into a way through; this is also the method of skillfully using natural ills.

■ *First yin:* Multiple danger, going into a hole in a pit,
leads to misfortune.

THE IMAGE: Going from danger into danger is the misfortune
of losing the way.

When in danger, whether it is a matter of self-help or helping others, all that is important is that there be true sincerity and that concentration and wisdom balance each other. Now the first yin is negative and in a low position, symbolizing absence of even the slightest sincerity or truthfulness. This represents sinking into bad habits and being unable to extricate oneself from them.

■ *2 yang:* There is danger in a pitfall; one seeks a small gain.

THE IMAGE: Seeking a small gain, one has not yet
gotten out of the middle.

Here strength is balanced, and there is sincerity, but one is still in a low position, meaning that ingrained habits are still deeply rooted; one cannot yet arrive all at once at the realm of the sages, and can only realize a small gain.

■ *3 yin:* Coming and going, pitfall upon pitfall, endangered and
obstructed, gone into a hole in a pit—do not act this way.

THE IMAGE: Coming and going, pitfall upon pitfall, in the end
there is no accomplishment.

Unbalanced and awry, weak yet stubborn, one thinks one has gotten out of danger, but is not aware of the coming of the danger ahead. This is like someone with false views and conceit, who therefore ultimately accomplishes nothing.

■ *4 yin:* **A jug of wine, with a ceremonial vessel of grain alongside. Use a plain cup; take in a pledge through the window. In the end there is no fault.**

THE IMAGE: **A jug of wine with a ceremonial vessel of grain alongside stands for the border of hard and soft.**

Here flexibility is correctly oriented, coupled with the quality of correctly balanced strength represented by the fifth yang. This is what is called developing insight by way of concentration, and is indeed a wonderful way to get out of danger.

Accurate observation is like a jug of wine, auxiliary practices are like a ceremonial vessel of grain. Sincere simplicity is like a plain cup, expedient means are like a window, through which one can discover reality and be faultless.

■ *5 yang:* **The pit is not filled, only leveled. No blame.**

THE IMAGE: **"The pit is not filled" means the center is not yet great.**

Here positive strength is balanced correctly; one has already attained manifestation of transmundane true insight. This is like when a pit is not filled to overflowing with water; the wind is still, and the ripples settle. But this is only the initial breakthrough of ignorance; remaining illusions are not yet ended, so "the center is not yet great." This just urges us to quickly head for consummate sagehood.

■ *Top yin:* **Bound with rope, put in a briar patch, helpless for three years—misfortune.**

THE IMAGE: **The top yin loses the way, unfortunate for three years.**

This is weakness in extreme danger, having concentration without insight. This is like the ordinary externalist who practices ignorant concentration and may reach even to the state where there are no mental images, but ultimately cannot get out of bondage to the world. Attachment to views is now profound, like being in a briar patch and never being able to get out.

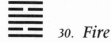 *30. Fire*

fire below, *fire* above

**Fire is beneficial if correct; then there is success.
Raising a cow brings good fortune.**

Fire has no nature of its own; it only appears cleaving to fuel—therefore it is called clinging. In politics, this means that in times of multiple danger it is necessary to cleave to just law to control society. In Buddhism, when demons cause disturbance, it is necessary to cleave to true teaching to get rid of aberrations. In contemplating mind, when mental states arise, it is necessary to cleave to correct observation to dissolve obscurity. Therefore in each case the benefit is in being correct; then there is success.

A cow is gentle and docile, yet very strong; it can also give birth to calves. This symbolizes correct concentration being able to produce subtle insight.

THE OVERALL JUDGMENT: **Fire is clinging—the sun and moon cling to the sky, plants cling to the earth. Clinging to what is correct with twofold illumination transforms and perfects the world. Flexibility clings to balance and correctness, and so is successful. Therefore raising a cow brings good fortune.**

Just as the sun and moon must cling to the sky and plants must cling to the earth, our twofold illumination, knowledge and wisdom, also must cling to the correctness of inherent virtues; then, self-help completed, we can thereby transform the world.

Now, the light of knowledge and wisdom needs meditation concentration to emerge; and meditation concentration also depends on essence for perfection. In this hexagram, the fifth yin and second yin cling to the position of balance and correctness, so there is a way to success, just as a cow can give birth to the calves of knowledge and wisdom, bringing good fortune.

THE IMAGE: **Illumination doubled makes fire. Great people illumine the four quarters with continuing illumination.**

Illumination upon illumination, continuing unending, once one has personally illumined one's qualities, then one can thereby illumine the four quarters.

■ *First yang:* **The steps are awry. Be heedful of this, and there will be no fault.**

THE IMAGE: Be heedful when the steps are awry, to avoid fault.

In the beginning of the exercise of contemplation, even though one has accurate insight, still the practice is not yet pure; so it is like being awry. Only by intent struggle, not daring to be complacent, can virtue progress day by day and habits be removed day by day, so as to avoid fault. Do not wait for faults to arise before getting rid of them.

- *2 yin:* Yellow fire is very auspicious.

THE IMAGE: Yellow fire is very auspicious,
attaining the middle way.

Subtle concentration balanced correctly is developed in harmony with essence; using this to illumine all things causes all things to become the middle way. This is subtle cessation of confused thought by means of the complete fluidity of the absolute.

- *3 yang:* In the fire of the afternoon sun, you either drum on a
jug and sing, or lament as in old age. This bodes ill.

THE IMAGE: The fire of the afternoon sun cannot last long.

When you use insight too much without concentration to balance it, sometimes you will be extremely joyful, drumming and singing, and sometimes you will be extremely anxious, lamenting as in old age. Sadness and joy disturb the song of your heart; intellectual insight cannot sustain itself—backsliding and loss are inevitable.

- *4 yang:* Coming forth abruptly, burning, dying, abandoned.

THE IMAGE: Coming forth abruptly, there is no
accommodation.

Here, though it seems that one has insight and concentration, in reality one is not balanced and not correct, unable to harmonize the elements of the path to enlightenment. Therefore sometimes one pushes forward too quickly, "coming forth abruptly," and sometimes one slacks off heedlessly, "burning, dying, abandoned."

   Those whose advance is too keen will surely regress quickly; if the coming forth is abrupt, there will certainly be no accommodation. Why wait until burning out to realize that this is not the way to a good end?

■ *5 yin:* **Weeping and lamenting, there is good fortune.**

THE IMAGE: The good fortune of the fifth yin is cleaving to rulers.

This represents concentration in balance, which can bring forth genuine insight; therefore progress is certain. "Weeping and lamenting" refers to abstention from complacency and presumption; this is always characteristic of the study of sages.

■ *Top yang:* **The king goes on an expedition, has good luck, and overcomes the leader, taking captives, but not because they are repugnant. No fault.**

THE IMAGE: The king goes on an expedition to bring correct order to the country.

Strong without excess, at the peak of illumination, self-help has already been completed, so there is a way to transform others; people spontaneously seek allegiance, humbling themselves—it is not that they are repugnant or evil and need to be attacked. When people are upright, the country is upright; when it is said that the king goes on an expedition, this does not mean the exercise of force or authority.

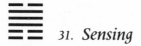

31. *Sensing*

mountain below, *lake* above

Sensing gets through, beneficial if correct.
Marriage is auspicious.

The trigram *mountain* has the top line of *heaven* and is represented as the youngest son in a family; this is like a beginner's insight with concentration, insight not losing concentration.

The trigram *lake* has the top line of *earth,* and is represented as the youngest daughter in a family; this is like a beginner's concentration with insight, concentration not losing insight.

These two are subject and object to one another, sensitively responding to one another; hence the name *sensing.*

In politics, this is the communication of rulers and ruled. In Buddhism, this is the interaction of the enlightened and the unenlightened. In contemplating mind, this is the mutual activation of objects and knowledge.

When there is sensitive response, there must be communication getting through. But sense and response have to be correct, just as in social terms marriage has to be done properly to be correct and auspicious.

THE OVERALL JUDGMENT: **Sensing is sensitive; the flexible above, the firm below, the two energies sense and respond so as to form a couple. Calm and joyful, this man is below the woman; therefore they get through to each other beneficially in the right way, in an auspicious marriage. When heaven and earth sense, myriad beings are born; sages sense people's minds, and the world is at peace. Observe what is sensed, and the feelings of heaven, earth, and myriad beings can be seen.**

What makes sensing sensitive? The flexibility of the body of *earth* in the lower trigram goes up to the sixth line, making *lake*; the firmness of the body of *heaven* in the upper trigram goes down to the third line, making *mountain*: this is the sense and response of the two energies of heaven and earth forming a couple.

Also, *mountain* represents calm, *lake* represents joy. The man is below the woman; this is the correct manner of sense and response, and this is why it is auspicious.

In Buddhist terms, *mountain* represents the unenlightened, *lake* represents the enlightened; once the unenlightened have focused on sensing the enlightened, then the enlightened respond to them with explanations of truth.

In terms of contemplating mind, *mountain* represents observation, *lake* represents mental states; once observing knowledge focuses on investigating mental states, the truth of the states becomes obvious, and one attains joy.

Whether in worldly or transmundane matters, things are accomplished by sensing; so it is thereby possible to see the feelings of heaven and earth and myriad beings.

THE IMAGE: **There is a lake atop a mountain—sensing. Developed people accept others with openness.**

Pride is like a high mountain, where the water of truth cannot remain; here there is a lake atop a mountain, symbolizing receptivity through openness.

■ *First yin:* **Sensing in the big toe.**

THE IMAGE: **Sensing in the big toe means the aspiration is outside.**

Though sensing may lead to effectiveness, it should not stray from tranquil imperturbability. It is also necessary to really know what is appropriate for the time and situation; if sensing disturbs inner autonomy, then one loses the basis for responsiveness.

In this hexagram, the bottom three lines are in the body of stopping, represented by *mountain,* and are in a low position, so it is not appropriate that they should respond arbitrarily to others. The top three lines are in the body of joy, represented by *lake,* and are in a high position, so they all may respond well to others.

Now, this first yin is recessive and in the lowest position, but it is moved by the sense of the fourth yang, with which it corresponds; so it unavoidably becomes active—this is represented by the toes moving first.

There are no fixed times for action and inaction. When it is time to stop, then stop, and when it is time to go, then go. If action is appropriate, then it leads to good results, and if action is inappropriate, then it leads to bad results. Therefore it cannot be judged as right or wrong a priori. So when it is said that the aspiration is outside, this too has its own differences. If the aspiration is on the whole world, without selfish concern for one's person or family, then it bodes well; if the aspiration is toward fame and fortune, without concern for the essence of mind, then it is shameful.

■ *2 yin:* Sensing in the calf bodes ill. To stay put bodes well.

THE IMAGE: To stay put in spite of foreboding leads to good results, because obedience does no harm.

Here flexibility is balanced correctly, and is moved by the sense of the fifth yang. If you try to advance in haste arbitrarily, this bodes ill, but if you stay put and keep to yourself, this bodes well. This is because staying put and keeping to oneself is obeying the path of flexible balance and does no harm.

■ *3 yang:* Sensing in the thighs, when clinging to following, to go on brings shame.

THE IMAGE: Sensing in the thighs is also not staying put; the aim is in following others; what is clung to is low.

At the end of calmness, with a strong sense of rectitude, moved by the top yin, one hastily tries to liberate others without realizing that to liberate others requires that self-liberation be accomplished first. Once bound by pleasant circumstances, one immediately loses what one has cultivated hitherto, and this is shameful.

■ *4 yang:* Correctness brings good fortune, and regret disappears. Coming and going ceaselessly, companions follow your thoughts.

THE IMAGE: **Correctness brings good fortune, and regret disappears; one has not yet sensed danger. Coming and going ceaselessly, one is not yet great.**

Strong but not excessive, concentration and wisdom in balance, one attains the right way of sensitive response; so one is fortunate and regret disappears.

Seeing the mutual embrace and inclusion of one's own mind and others' minds, there is the image of coming and going ceaselessly.

Since the mind is made the basis of sensitive response, mettlesome people will all honor you and draw near to you, as in the image of companions following your thoughts.

Because one has attained the correct way of sensitive response, one may sense all day without deviating from tranquil imperturbability; therefore one has not yet sensed danger.

Because one is aware of the comings and goings of the mind, though one knows basically what one is thinking, it is still necessary to enter into the spirit thoroughly to bring out its function. Efficient functioning calms the person and allows one to pursue virtue. By thoroughly examining the spirit and knowing its transformations, one can go deeply into the realm of the unknown. Therefore one is not willing to hastily regard one's present realization as great.

■ *5 yang:* **Sensing in the flesh of the back, there is no regret.**

THE IMAGE: **Sensing in the flesh of the back, the aim is concluded.**

Here positive strength is balanced correctly and is in the body of joy. This is like the image of "stopping at the back, not finding the body, walking in the garden, not seeing the person." This is full accord with the subtlety of being "tranquil and imperturbable yet sensitive and effective." Therefore one has no faults to regret and carries a good beginning to a good end, realizing the ultimate. This is called the conclusion of one's aim.

■ *Top yin:* **Sensing in the jaws and tongue.**

THE IMAGE: **Sensing in the jaws and tongue is speaking a lot.**

Here flexibility is correctly oriented; this is the key to joy. Inwardly based on calmness, one outwardly exercises intelligent eloquence; this is the image of sensing in the jaws and tongue. Expounding the truth inexhaustibly, teaching people tirelessly, it is therefore called "speaking a lot."

The reason that the first "sensing in the big toe" and the top "sensing in the jaws and tongue" do not say whether they are good or bad is that for beginners, in the first steps, there are both wrong and right, about which it is impossible to generalize, and in teaching people there are also wrong and right, which are not on the same track. This is a question to be pondered in connection with the admonitions in the sayings about "getting through" and "beneficial if correct."

 *32. Constancy*

wind below, *thunder* above

Constancy comes through without fault, beneficial insofar as it is correct. It is beneficial to have a place to go.

The mechanism of sense and response does not allow any discrepancy, while the principle of sense and response is eternally unchanging. Sense and response are based on the principle which is always thus, so *lake* and *mountain* can be called *sensing.* The constant principle is explained based on the subtlety of meeting potential, so *thunder* and *wind* can be called *constancy.*

   Lake and *mountain* are called *sensing,* so the eternal is identical to impermanence; *thunder* and *wind* are called *constancy,* so impermanence is eternal. Also, *sensing* is *lake* and *mountain,* so impermanence is fundamentally eternal; *constancy* is *thunder* and *wind,* so the eternal is fundamental impermanence.

   Since the principle is eternal, eternity must come through and must be without fault. But eternity does not mean the permanence of fixation; one must know that there is both substance and function. The substance is neither eternal nor impermanent; the function illumines both eternity and impermanence.

   To understand the substance that is neither eternal nor impermanent is called the benefit in being correct. To activate the function that can be both eternal and impermanent is called the benefit in having a place to go.

THE OVERALL JUDGMENT: **Constancy is enduring. Firmness is above, flexibility below. Thunder and wind pair up, moving along harmoniously; the hard and the soft correspond constantly. Constancy comes through without fault, beneficial insofar as it is correct, in the sense of enduring on the path. The path of heaven and earth is constant and enduring, never ending. It is beneficial to have a place to go, in the sense that the end has a beginning. As long as there is the sky, sun and moon can shine forever; the four seasons change, yet can go on forever. Sages endure on the path, and the world develops.**

Observe what they are constant in, and the conditions of heaven, earth, and all beings can be seen.

Why is constancy called enduring? Because the path can endure forever. The body of *thunder* is basically *earth*, but firmness comes up to direct it; the body of *wind* is basically *heaven*, but flexibility goes down to direct it: this is the constant path of mutual balance of firmness and flexibility. *Thunder* moves, *wind* drums; this is the constant path of creation of beings, growth and development. Inwardly harmonious, outwardly active; this is the constant path of human affairs and physical principles. Firmness and flexibility corresponding is the constant path of structural complementarity.

Enduring on the path is called being correct; thus one can come through without fault. So also is the path of heaven and earth. Since a beginning necessitates an end, an end must also necessitate a beginning. Beginning and ending alternate, so they are impermanent, but since beginning and ending continue, they are not final. Neither final nor permanent, the facts of eternity and impermanence are both established: so heaven and earth have becoming, subsistence, decay and emptiness; sun and moon rise and set by day and night; the four seasons supersede one another; the path of sages has substance and function of beginning and ending. In all of these, the facts of eternity and impermanence reside together, but the essence is neither eternal nor impermanent—the name of constancy is imposed on it.

THE IMAGE: **Thunder and wind are constant; so do developed people stand without changing place.**

"Place" means that which is completely fixed yet completely fluid, completely fluid yet completely fixed. Look from the east and it is west; look from the south and it is north—is this not fluid? South is not north, east is not west—is this not fixed? To "stand without changing place" simply means to stand on the path which is completely fixed yet completely flexible, completely flexible yet completely fixed.

■ *First yin:* **In deep constancy, fidelity brings misfortune; there is no gain.**

THE IMAGE: **The misfortune of deep constancy is from seeking depth to start with.**

In *sensing*, there is a problem when one lacks the discipline to keep controlled calm; in *constancy*, there is a problem when one lacks the learning to change adaptively. This first yin, being passive and in a low position, represents one who knows how to persist to the death but does not know how to change adaptively; thus the deeper the seeking, the more the loss of the benefits of coming through correctly with a place to go—therefore it brings misfortune.

■ *2 yang:* Regret disappears.

THE IMAGE: Regret disappears, as one can remain balanced.

Strong yet flexible, and in a position of balance, not biased or partial, neither eager nor averse, one remains on the path of balance, not fixated on un-adaptive constancy; therefore regret disappears.

■ *3 yang:* Not being constant in virtue may be taken as a disgrace. Even if one is right, one is humiliated.

THE IMAGE: Not being constant in virtue, there is no accommodation.

Excessive strength unbalanced, one is unwilling to persist in what one should persist in. Too much is as bad as not enough; positive strength that is not constant is most disgraceful.

■ *4 yang:* No game in the fields.

THE IMAGE: This is not the place for persistence. How can one catch game?

This line represents one who is constantly on the move; but being on the move is not something that can endure forever, so how can one catch the game? Only by stillness can one get anything.

■ *5 yin:* The fidelity of constancy in virtue bodes well for a woman, bodes ill for a man.

THE IMAGE: What bodes well in fidelity for a woman is consistency from start to finish. For a man doing his duty, to follow a woman bodes ill.

This represents flexibility in balance, and also in correspondence with the wise; it seems to be correct constancy, but a leader in charge of guiding the people is acting like a housewife if he has no ability to adapt successfully to changes.

■ *Top yin:* Constant excitement bodes ill.

THE IMAGE: Constant excitement in those on top is utterly unsuccessful.

Weak at the climax of action, one's aspirations are great but one's talents are small; one's position is high but one's qualities are meager. What is more, one is in league with inconstant friends. How then is it possible to help the world?

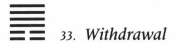 *33. Withdrawal*

mountain below, *heaven* above

Withdrawal is successful. Small benefit is correct.

In the course of the development of a society, after a time there must be change for further development to take place; after moving forward, it is necessary to take a step back in order to last. This hexagram represents strength with the ability to stop. This does not take advance to be progress, but takes withdrawal for progress. Therefore there is success.

But when we talk about withdrawing, it seems to be like the small path of self-help. If we fulfill this small path, is this not close to losing the universal rule that we should help others? This is the reason for the statement that "small benefit is correct," meaning that even though this seems to be the same as a small path, it ultimately is beneficial for the righteousness of a great person.

THE OVERALL JUDGMENT: **Withdrawal is successful, in that by withdrawing you get through successfully. Strength is in its proper place and is responsive, acting in accord with the time. Small benefit is correct, in that it gradually grows. The meaning of the time of withdrawal is great indeed.**

In the study of higher development, those who wish to help themselves and others attain success by withdrawal. Strength in a position of leadership, coupled with wisdom, is the way to act in accord with the time, and thus is successful. The statement that "small benefit is correct" is made in consideration of the fact that the will for self-discipline on the part of the weak gradually grows. Those who withdraw properly actually progress through their withdrawal, while those who withdraw improperly ultimately do not progress. So the consideration involved is very important.

THE IMAGE: **There are mountains under heaven, which is inaccessible. Developed people keep petty people at a distance, being strict without ill will.**

If you are outwardly strong and inwardly stable, even though you never even think of keeping petty people at a distance, petty people naturally will be unable to flatter you. Petty people can be useful, so there is no ill will, but their pettiness cannot wield authority, so be strict. In terms of learning to be a sage, the celestial ruler is the master, and the physical body takes orders from it, so that the desires of the various parts of the body cannot cause disturbance.

■ *First yin:* Withdrawing the tail is dangerous. Do not go anywhere with this.

THE IMAGE: With the danger of withdrawing the tail, if you do not go anywhere, what trouble will there be?

In withdrawing, one must accord with one's qualities and state in making this a way of advance or retreat; only thus can one avoid losing the way to success in the correct manner. This first yin, weak and lowly, represents lowliness in both ability and position. Strict conservatism alone is appropriate, and one should not go forth arbitrarily, for that will lead to trouble.

■ *2 yin:* Fasten this with the hide of a yellow ox; no one can loosen it.

THE IMAGE: Fastening with the hide of a yellow ox means making the will firm.

When flexible docility is balanced and correctly oriented, it cannot be influenced by fame or fortune. When those in this condition carry out their aspirations in cooperation with leaders who are firm, strong, and balanced correctly, then the country is on the right track and will not become deviated or stagnant.

■ *3 yang:* Entangled in withdrawal, there is affliction and danger, but feeding servants and concubines leads to good results.

THE IMAGE: The danger of entanglement in withdrawal is that there is affliction and exhaustion. The good results of feeding servants and concubines is not suitable for great works.

When one is strong and upright, one may thereby work actively, but if one abides in ultimate stillness, one will then not escape entanglement in withdrawal. This is the path of detachment from humanity, forgetting society; this is the affliction of those with leadership potential.

But even if one cannot do anything great, one should still urge on one's spirit to "feed servants and concubines," for that will lead to good results. What this means is that if one cannot govern a nation, one should still take care of one's family, as a model for the world.

■ *4 yang:* Developed people who withdraw in the right way are fortunate; petty people are not.

THE IMAGE: Developed people withdraw well; petty people do not.

This is being strong but remaining flexible, receiving the favor of the ruler and seeing to the comfort of the people, being tolerant and accommodating. This is a way to good fortune for developed people, something that petty people cannot learn.

■ *5 yang:* Excellent withdrawal, correct and auspicious.

THE IMAGE: Excellent withdrawal, correct and auspicious, is so because of right aspiration.

Firm and strong, balanced and upright, cooperating with wise people whose flexibility is balanced correctly, this withdrawal means that even if one has heroic brilliance and extraordinary strategy, one does not reveal one's own abilities. This is excellence in withdrawal, correct and auspicious.

■ *Top yang:* Withdrawal of the rich is beneficial to all.

THE IMAGE: Withdrawal of the rich is beneficial to all, as there is no suspicion.

This represents being strong but not excessively so, and being in the exalted position of tutor of future leaders, yet not being presumptuous. Therefore it is "withdrawal of the rich" and it is "beneficial to all."

34. *The Power of the Great*

heaven below, *thunder* above

The power of the great is beneficial if correct.

The more thorough the work of withdrawal for self-development, the more powerful one's spiritual qualities. But once the great are powerful, the problem is not one of inability to function effectively; the problem is when they act arbitrarily with their power. The warning that the power of the great is beneficial if correct is important for those who are at the point of fulfillment.

THE OVERALL JUDGMENT: The power of the great means that the great are powerful. Strong and active, they are therefore powerful. "The power of the great is beneficial if correct" means that the great should be upright. With correct greatness, the conditions of heaven and earth can be seen.

In the human being, there is that which is great and that which is small. Follow the great and you will be a great person; follow the small and you will be a small person. Now when the text speaks of the power of the great, it means that the great is powerful.

Here, being strong means not being subject to disturbance by emotions; being active means not being imprisoned by past habits. This is what is meant by power. When it says this power is beneficial if correct, this is because that which is great is basically inherently correct. Were it not correct, how could it be called great? Therefore, with correct greatness the conditions of heaven and earth can be seen.

In Buddhist terms, heaven and earth represent principle and knowledge; they also represent concentration and insight.

THE IMAGE: Thunder is up in the sky, with great power. Developed people do not do what is improper.

Not doing what is improper, in the context of Buddhism, is what is known as compassion regulating action.

■ *First yang:* **With power in the feet, an expedition bodes ill, having certainty.**

THE IMAGE: With power in the feet, that certainty comes to an impasse.

Although we say that the great must be correct, we must realize that it is the correct who are great. If you presume upon greatness as being correct, then correctness turns into aberration. If you presume upon power as being great, that greatness cannot last long. If you presume upon correctness as being powerful, that power will surely deteriorate. This is why ancient political guidelines teach the gentle mastery of high illuminates.

Now this first yang represents excessive strength that is not balanced. To proceed in an adamant and unbalanced way will surely lead to bad results.

This is because of being too sure of oneself; this is certain to lead to an impasse.

■ *2 yang:* Correctness is auspicious.

THE IMAGE: For the second yang, correctness is auspicious because of balance.

When the positive remains in a recessive position, strength is not excessive, and gains balance. Gaining balance, it therefore becomes correct.

■ *3 yang:* Petty people use power; superior people use nothingness, chaste in danger. When a ram butts a fence, it gets its horns stuck.

THE IMAGE: Petty people use power; superior people disappear.

Even if one is originally a superior person, if one likes power and indulges in it, one will be the same as petty adventurers. This will only lead to exhaustion, and one will not be able to break through the impasses of the time. If one is really a superior person, even if one is full of power, one will not be too sure of oneself and will be content to be as though naught.

■ *4 yang:* Being correct leads to good results; regret vanishes. Fences opened up, one does not get exhausted. Power is in the axle of a great vehicle.

THE IMAGE: Fences opened up, one does not get exhausted—it is valuable to go.

This represents using flexibility to balance firmness, achieving correctness of great power. This is how to get rid of troubles without injuring the spirit. Using this to bear the world, there is gain wherever one goes.

■ *5 yin:* Losing the ram in ease, there is no regret.

THE IMAGE: Losing the ram in ease, the position is not appropriate.

When one is flexible and balanced, there is no attitude of rambunctious strength, so there is no regret. "The position is not appropriate" means that one is as though master of the world but does not have anything to do with it.

■ *Top yin:* The ram butting the fence cannot retreat, cannot go ahead. There is no benefit. Work hard and there will be good results.

THE IMAGE: Inability to retreat or go ahead is due to carelessness. Work hard and there will be good results, because error will not increase.

This represents weakness of both character and position; there is only the name of power, without real meaning. Therefore there is no benefit.

However, those who use weakness skillfully need not seek an empty reputation of great power; let them just work hard to keep to the way of gentle mastery, and weakness can overcome strength, thus leading to good results. This exhorts those who cannot go forward to retreat.

35. *Advance*

earth below, *fire* above

Advancing, a securely established lord is presented with horses in abundance and grants audience three times a day.

If one is very powerful and upright, then one can advance to the realm of self-help and helping others. In this peaceful and secure time, a wise lord gains the favor of a sage ruler and is given many horses as a rich reward. "Granting audience three times a day" signifies diligence in dealing with the people.

In terms of contemplating mind, subtle observing knowledge is the "securely established lord," and increasing virtues in conformity with essence is being "presented with horses in abundance." Witnessing the noumenal body of reality is "granting audience three times a day."

THE OVERALL JUDGMENT: Advance is progress. Light emerges over the ground, following and cleaving to great illumination. Flexibility progresses and moves upward; therefore a securely established lord is presented with horses in abundance and grants audience three times a day.

In terms of contemplating mind, the light of fundamental real knowledge emerges by breaking through the ground of ignorance; therefore it is called "light emerging over the ground." Concentration and insight are together, stopping confusion and seeing truth are not two; therefore it is called "following and cleaving to great illumination." The real nature of ignorance is none other than the buddha-nature. When ignorance is overturned, it transforms into enlightenment, so "flexibility progresses and moves upward." Because of this virtue and knowledge grow and improve over and over.

THE IMAGE: **Light emerges over the ground, advancing. Developed people illumine the quality of enlightenment by themselves.**

The essence of fundamental awareness is called "the quality of enlightenment." The accomplishment of awakening to this is called "illumination." The nonexistence of objects outside mind is called "by oneself." When you illumine the quality of enlightenment by yourself, then renewal of the people and resting in ultimate good are therein.

■ *First yin:* **Advancing, impeded, it bodes well to be correct. If there is no trust, be easygoing, and there will be no blame.**

THE IMAGE: **Advancing, impeded, one carries out what is right alone. Being easygoing, without blame, is not accepting fate.**

All six lines of *Advance* correspond to those who illumine the quality of enlightenment by themselves and thus renew the people, but the times and positions are not the same, and what is developed is also different, so good and bad, regret and shame, are differentiated.

The first yin represents concentration that has matching insight and is also pliable; therefore it is possible to make progress and advance. However, it is at the bottom of the hexagram, and in correspondence with the "squirrels" of the fourth yang, who are not good companions; so it is certainly not appropriate to progress quickly. Hence there is obstruction and one is impeded.

But advancement and impediment are both externals—what have they to do with one's self? Just remain correct, and it will turn out well. Even if this is temporarily insufficient to gain trust, just deal with it in an easygoing manner, and in the end there will be no blame.

When it says that "one carries out what is right alone," this means one has self-confidence and does not seek to be acknowledged by others. When it speaks of "not accepting fate," this is what the philosopher Mencius was referring to when he said, "Fate has its own nature; developed people do not speak of fate."

■ *2 yin:* Advancing, grieving, it is good to be correct.
One receives this great blessing from one's grandmother.

THE IMAGE: One receives this great blessing because of balance
and rectitude.

Here flexible docility is balanced and correct; one illumines the quality of
enlightenment by oneself, constantly feeling the grief of not yet seeing reality. This is one who is correct and has good luck. Sharing in the virtues of
the "grandmother" of the fifth yin above, one receives the blessings that are
one's basic right; therefore it is called "great blessing."

■ *3 yin:* The group approves; regret vanishes.

THE IMAGE: The group approves; the aim is upward progress.

This represents concentration with matching insight, at the time for advancing, with optimum pliability. Whereas in the first yin there was a lack of
trust, when easygoing development reaches this point, everyone approves
and regret vanishes. Living in obscurity to seek one's aim, carrying out one's
duty to arrive on the right path, thus "the aim is upward progress."

■ *4 yang:* Advancing like a squirrel is dangerous even if
determined.

THE IMAGE: Advancing like a squirrel is dangerous even if
determined, because the position is not appropriate.

When developed people illumine the quality of enlightenment by themselves, they should be dark on the outside and light on the inside—that is,
they should be outwardly unnoticeable while inwardly illumined. But this
fourth yang represents outward strength with inner weakness, outward light
with inward darkness—it is like a squirrel, which can run and jump, but not
very fast and not very far. Its capabilities are limited, and it is in danger. This
is the case of people who are in high positions without any real virtue.

■ *5 yin:* Regret vanishes. Do not worry about loss of gains. To go
leads to good results, beneficial all around.

THE IMAGE: Do not worry about loss of gains. If you go, there
will be joy.

This represents concentration with insight, in command of the intellect,
having attained the way of balance, occupying the position of leadership.

This is what is called self-renewal and renewal of the people, using everything to the best advantage. This is a government that "follows and cleaves to great illumination," so it has "good results, beneficial to all." The whole world reaps the blessings, so what loss of gains is there to worry about?

■ *Top yang:* **Advancing the horns; this requires conquering one's domain. Hard work leads to good results, without blame; but even though correct, one is humiliated.**

THE IMAGE: **This requires conquering one's domain, because the way is not yet illumined.**

The top yang also represents outer strength with inner weakness, outer light with inner darkness; and it is at the culmination of advance, so it is like the horns of an animal: goring people with horns is bad for them. This calls for self-mastery, which may be likened to "conquering one's domain." So "hard work leads to good results, without blame." However, since one was unable to govern oneself early on, and only now has been capable of self-mastery, even though it is correct, it is still humiliating.

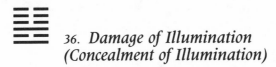

36. *Damage of Illumination (Concealment of Illumination)*

fire below, *earth* above

When illumination is damaged, it is beneficial to be upright in difficulty.

If one knows how to advance but not how to withdraw, there will surely be damage. When illumination goes underground, its light does not shine. If you know that being upright in difficulty is beneficial, this is illumination through use of darkness.

THE OVERALL JUDGMENT: **Illumination goes underground; illumination is damaged or concealed. Inwardly civilized, outwardly pliable, one thus suffers great difficulties. It is beneficial to be upright in difficulty, in the sense of obscuring one's illumination. Be able to make your aims upright in spite of internal difficulties.**

In terms of contemplating mind, this means that afflictions, bad habits, illnesses, bedevilments, conceits, and false views are all excellent objects for the exercise of complete all-at-once cessation of confusion and seeing of truth.

THE IMAGE: **Illumination goes underground, in concealment of illumination. In dealing with the masses, true leaders act unobtrusively while in fact being illumined.**

This means using stillness to control movement, using darkness to peer into the light. These are functions of concealment of illumination. What sages learn is to become daily more illumined unbeknownst to others.

■ *First yang:* **Illumination concealed in flight, letting the wings droop, superior people on a journey, not eating for three days, have a place to go. The ruler has something to say.**

THE IMAGE: **When superior people are on a journey, it is right that they do not eat.**

This is like just people fleeing a vicious tyrant: letting the wings droop means not revealing the flying form; and such is the speed of travel that they do not have the leisure to eat for three days. This is because it is right to flee far away; they do not wish the tyrannical ruler to know and speak against them.

■ *2 yin:* **Illumination concealed, injured in the left leg, going to the rescue, it is lucky if the horse is strong.**

THE IMAGE: **The luck of the second yin is in model obedience.**

This represents the virtues of cultured intelligence, balance, and uprightness. In this time when illumination is concealed, even though the work of the left leg is injured, one still goes to the rescue; only because the horse is strong is there luck. This is like leading people to work for the good of the country, in spite of having been mistreated by ignorant people in authority, obeying temporal authority and not overtly rebelling; this is truly a timeless model.

■ *3 yang:* **Illumination concealed, hunting in the south, catching the big chief, hasty correction will not do.**

THE IMAGE: **The aim of hunting in the south is a big catch.**

This is the end of the night, just before dawn. This is like when the enlightened who have been in concealment overthrow the reign of ignorance.

But since ignorance has been a ruling force for so long, it is impossible to accomplish this overthrow hastily; it must be sustained by rectitude.

■ *4 yin:* **Entering the left belly, finding the heart of illumination in concealment and going out of the house.**

THE IMAGE: **Entering the left belly is finding the heart's intent.**

This is flexibility that is correctly oriented. This is like one who recognizes an illuminate in concealment and withdraws allegiance from the ignorant.

■ *5 yin:* **The concealment of illumination on the part of a just scion of an evil ruling house is beneficial and upright.**

THE IMAGE: **The uprightness of a just scion of an evil ruling house is that his understanding cannot be suppressed.**

This represents being outwardly flexible while inwardly strong, remaining balanced in the middle, appearing to be ignorant while actually being illumined. That illumination shines throughout all ages.

■ *Top yin:* **In the darkness of ignorance, first ascending to heaven, later going underground.**

THE IMAGE: **First ascending to heaven is lighting up the nations; later going underground is losing guidance.**

This is the extreme of damage of illumination, like one who was once an emperor and then later became an isolated individual. The first five lines all represent being illumined but appearing to be ignorant, thus being able to use apparent ignorance in an enlightened way. This line represents the ignorance of not understanding, whereby one loses guidance and so goes underground.

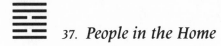

37. *People in the Home*

fire below, *wind* above

For people in the home, it is beneficial for the women to be chaste.

If we want to heal the wounds of the nation, nothing compares to turning our attention to the home. And if we want to rectify family life, nothing compares to strictness about the chastity of the women.

In Buddhist terms, when contemplation practice is disturbed by demons, one should just remember that it is only mind. Only mind is the "home" of Buddhism. And it is necessary to sustain insight by concentration, to assist knowledge by virtue, and to reveal essence by cultivation; this is called the benefit of female chastity.

THE OVERALL JUDGMENT: **For people in the home, the woman's proper position is inside, the man's proper position is outside. For men and women to be in their proper positions is universally important. The people in the home have a strict rulership, which is the father and mother. When a parent behaves like a parent, a child like a child, an elder like an elder, a youth like a youth, a husband like a husband, and a wife like a wife, then the conduct of the household is correct. Make the home correct, and the country will be stable.**

In Buddhist terms, when meditation concentration supports the mind, then inwardly one merges with the substance of reality; when knowledge understands external objects, then outwardly one carries on transformative functions.

When cultivated concentration and insight are equally correct, they are based on the nonduality of inherent tranquillity and awareness. In the causal state they are called man and woman; in the resulting state they are called father and mother. Once one has realized the qualities of fruition, all possible realms of consciousness are subject to one's mastery; this is called a "strict rulership."

When essence and cultivation are not mixed up, this is called a parent behaving like a parent and a child like a child. When the absolute truth and conventional truth are simultaneously illumined, this is called an elder behaving like an elder and a youth like a youth. When virtue and wisdom sustain each other, this is called a husband behaving like a husband and a wife like a wife.

When one world is pure, then all worlds are pure; this is called making the home correct, so that the country is stable.

THE IMAGE: **Wind emerges from fire, members of a family. Developed people are factual in speech, consistent in action.**

Fire is fanned by wind, but now "wind emerges from fire"—this is like the way a family is transformed by virtue, and now virtue is spread from the family.

When there is factuality in speech, it is not untrue; when there is consistency in action, it is not mere display. Thereby it is possible to regulate the family and nation.

So it is also in Buddhism: when behavior is pure, it is then possible to absorb virtue and help people.

■ *First yang:* Guarding the home, regret vanishes.

THE IMAGE: **Guarding the home, the aim does not change.**

Beginning a home with firm rectitude, speaking factually and acting consistently to guard it, one can thus ensure that it will not break up. In terms of Buddhism, this refers to learning discipline.

■ *2 yin:* Not concentrating on anything but household duties, it bodes well to be chaste.

THE IMAGE: **What bodes well in the second yin is docile obedience.**

Here flexibility is balanced and correct, and is in charge of the inner situation. Therefore one does not dare to be self-centered or willful in anything, but only concentrate on household duties. In Buddhist terms, this refers to learning concentration.

■ *3 yang:* When people in the home are strict, conscientious diligence leads to good results. When the women and children are frivolous, it will end in humiliation.

THE IMAGE: **It is not a mistake for the people in the home to be strict. When the women and children are frivolous, the order of the household is lost.**

Excessive firmness that is not balanced seems to make the mistake of being too strict and demanding, but from the point of view of the correct way of ordering the home, it is not a mistake and in fact leads to good results. If you fear conscientious diligence and give yourself over to frivolity, it may seem comfortable at first, but ultimately you will lose order in the home and suffer humiliation. In Buddhist terms, this is learning wisdom.

■ *4 yin:* **A rich home is very fortunate.**

THE IMAGE: **A rich home is very fortunate, docilely occupying its position.**

Here flexibility is correctly oriented and acts as the director of docility. This is what is called producing wealth in the right way. In Buddhist terms, this is when a good state of mind arises through enlightening practices, richly embued with myriad virtues; this is called liberation.

■ *5 yang:* **The king has a great home. Do not worry; it is auspicious.**

THE IMAGE: **The king has a great home, with communication and mutual love.**

This represents positive strength balanced correctly and in the position of leadership, in which all the world is one's home. The great way is impartial; what worry is there? When the leaders find happiness in the happiness of the people, then the people will also find happiness in the happiness of the leaders. Therefore there is communication and mutual love.

In Buddhist terms, this means discovery of the essential mind that is the true basis of enlightenment; essence and cultivation interpenetrate, revealing the qualities of the real spiritual being.

■ *Top yang:* **There is truthfulness, which is impressive. The end is auspicious.**

THE IMAGE: **What is auspicious about his impressiveness is that it calls for personal transformation.**

Strong but not excessive, one's virtue can be trusted, so it is impressive without force. In Buddhist terms, this is when the knowledge on which enlightenment is based emerges, worthy and important in that it is in accord with the design of reality; this is called the quality of transcendent wisdom.

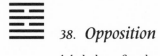 ## 38. *Opposition*

lake below, *fire* above

Opposition; a small matter will turn out all right.

For those who skillfully cultivate themselves and thereby harmonize their families, the whole world can be one home. If the ordering of the family is not correct, however, then opposition and alienation arise in the family. This is represented by the juxtaposition of a body of water and fire; water tends to go downward, fire tends to go upward. If the aims of people in a group are not the same, how can anything great be accomplished? So it is also with contemplating mind: there is transmundane meditation and mundane meditation; one is higher, one is lower—they proceed in different ways. Before one understands how to harmonize them completely, one can only attain small realization.

THE OVERALL JUDGMENT: Opposition—when fire moves, it goes upward; when water moves, it goes downward; two women live together, but their aims are not the same. Joyfully cleaving to illumination, flexibility goes forward and moves upward, attains balance and responds to firmness. Therefore a small matter will turn out all right. Heaven and earth are opposite, but their work is the same; man and woman are opposite, but their aim is in common; myriad beings are disparate, but their affairs are of a kind. The timely use of opposition is great indeed.

To interpret this in Buddhist terms, when tranquillity and awareness are one, this is called heaven and earth being opposite while their work is the same. When stopping confusion and seeing truth are practiced together, this is called man and woman being opposite but having an aim in common. Myriad practices are all of two kinds—main practices and auxiliary practices. These two kinds of practice are not apart from what is inherent, just as myriad beings are not apart from positive and negative energies, positive and negative energies are not apart from the absolute. This is called myriad things being disparate while their affairs are of a kind.

THE IMAGE: Above is fire, below is a lake—opposite. Developed people are the same yet different.

When you look at appearances, which are basically unreal, the appearances are different, so it seems that essence is also differentiated. When you look at essence, which is basically real, since essence is the same, appearances are also fundamentally the same.

Only developed people know how to be the same yet different, so they do not obscure sameness by difference. They know that differences are based on sameness, so they know that different stages of spiritual development are based on a fundamental identity of enlightenment, and do not shrink from going through the stages. They know that there are differences in the stages in spite of fundamental sameness, so even though they realize this identity of mind and Buddha, they also understand the need for the stages and do not become conceited.

They know the different stages are based on the same enlightenment, so they merge with the real source; they know the sameness of enlightenment does not abridge the differences in the stages, so they carry on all necessary practices.

They know that differences are based on sameness, so there is no buddha-hood above to attain and no unenlightened people below to liberate. They know there are differences in spite of sameness, so they perpetually adorn pure lands and teach people to transform them.

They know that differences are based on sameness, so neither samsara nor nirvana can be grasped. They know there are differences in spite of sameness, so they sometimes roam at play in samsara and sometimes appear to enter nirvana.

■ *First yang:* **Regret vanishes. Having lost the horse, do not chase it—it will come back by itself. Seeing evil people, there is no blame.**

THE IMAGE: **Seeing evil people, one avoids blame.**

This represents being firm and upright, without correspondents, in the beginning of opposition. Proceed trusting in this, and there will be no error and so regret vanishes.

Even if you have "lost the horse," there is no need to chase it, for "it will come back by itself"—this is an exhortation not to let gain and loss disturb your spirit.

Even if you meet evil people, there is no harm in seeing them, for you can be blameless—this is an exhortation not to let good and bad divide your mind.

Whenever thoughts of gain and loss become serious, or the idea of good and bad is too defined, then what is the same will be differentiated, and what is different cannot be made the same. Only when we follow firm and upright celestial virtue do gain and loss disappear, good and bad merge. Then even if we are in a time of oppositions, we can be free of regret.

■ *2 yang:* Meeting the ruler in an alley, there is no blame.

THE IMAGE: Meeting the ruler in an alley does not deviate from the right way.

It is imperative to thoroughly understand the affairs of the mind in every detail; this is like meeting the ruler in an alley. The meeting of ruler and minister is the constant way of all time; how could it be said to be lost because it is "in an alley"?

■ *3 yin:* Having the vehicle dragged back, the ox halted, the person is punished by heaven. There is no beginning, but there is an end.

THE IMAGE: Having the vehicle dragged back means being out of place. Having an end without a beginning means encountering firmness.

This represents having no balance or proper orientation and doubting oneself, therefore arbitrarily having one's "vehicle dragged back" and "ox halted," meaning that one does not dare to proceed to follow those who are more highly developed. Yet one still thinks one is going to work for the benefit of others. Sure to be punished by those above, one cannot communicate one's honest feelings, so there is no beginning.

But when opposition culminates, there must be reconciliation, so one's intentions will eventually become clear in the end. Luckily one encounters the firmness of the highly developed and in the end can meet without hostilities. Therefore there is an end.

■ *4 yang:* The solitude of opposition. Meeting good people, associate sincerely, work hard, and there will be no blame.

THE IMAGE: Associate sincerely, and there will be no blame, for the aim will be carried out.

Opposition can only be resolved when there is communication. The fourth yang has no partner, so it is called the solitude of opposition. However, the firm uprightness represented by the first yang is below, and this can resolve opposition. At this time, people of similar qualities trust one another and their interaction refines one another. This is how to carry out the aim of resolving opposition, so that there is no blame.

■ *5 yin:* Regret vanishes. With the ally in close cooperation, what is wrong with proceeding?

THE IMAGE: With the ally in close cooperation, to proceed will result in celebration.

This represents the alliance of a flexible leader with a strong administrator; when leader and adminstrator are in harmony, in the end opposition can be resolved.

■ *Top yang:* Isolated in opposition, seeing a pig covered with mire, a wagonload of devils, first drawing a bow, later putting the bow down, not enemies but partners, going on, encountering rain, then there is good fortune.

THE IMAGE: The good fortune of encountering rain is that doubts disappear.

The top yang corresponds with the third yin, so basically it is not isolated, but opposition is not yet reconciled, so it seems isolated. The third yin is basically not influenced by the second and fourth yangs, but it seems to be despoiled, so this is "seeing a pig covered with mire." The second and fourth each have a spontaneous meeting and have no intention of despoiling the third, but falsely give rise to doubt; so this is "a wagonload of devils." First there was serious doubt, resulting in "first drawing a bow" to shoot; later the doubt is lessened, resulting in "later putting the bow down" and going to see it. When the top yang sees that the third yin is after all not an enemy, they marry, and the relief is like clouds bursting into rain, resulting in good fortune. Not doubting the third, it therefore does not doubt the second and fourth, so "doubts disappear."

To discuss the six lines overall, only the firm rectitude of the first yang is the very best at resolving opposition; the others are not really correct, so it is necessary to cooperate in order to achieve resolution. In Buddhist terms, it means that only fundamental true wisdom can arrive at difference based on sameness, thereby always being the same in the midst of differences. Otherwise, it is necessary to rely on the mutual assistance of concentration and insight, the twin operation of stopping confusion and seeing truth, in order to be able to give up personality differences to enter into universal essence.

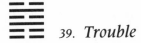

39. *Trouble*

mountain below, *water* above

**When in trouble, it is beneficial to go southwest;
it is not beneficial to go northeast. It is beneficial to
see a great person. Correctness leads to good results.**

Whenever unharmonized differences are not reconciled, whatever you do
there will be many obstacles and difficulties. However, when you are at an
impasse, is there is no good strategy for getting out of difficulty? Go southwest—this means joyfulness, harmony, clarity; this is the essential way of
getting out of difficulty. To go northeast means halting and danger, only increasing trouble. Only great people can solve trouble; only the correct way
can lead out of trouble. Trouble therefore can stir the forebearance of the
mind to increase your ability to do what you could not do before, thus leading to good results.

THE OVERALL JUDGMENT: **Trouble is difficulty; danger lies
ahead. Being able to stop on seeing danger is knowledge. In
trouble, it is beneficial to go southwest, in the sense of
achieving balance; it is not beneficial to go northeast, for that
path comes to an end. It is beneficial to see a great person, in
that there is merit in going. Correctness in the right place
leads to good results, whereby it is possible to rectify the
country. Timely action in trouble is great indeed.**

Foolish people are so absorbed in the subjectivity of emotions and desires
that even when unexpected danger looms before them, they are blind to it.
Because they do not see it, of course they cannot stop in time. If you are able
to stop, not only will you avoid falling into danger, but you will seek from it
a good strategy for getting out of danger—is this not knowledge?

Starting from a situation of danger and halting (symbolized by "northeast"), going to clarity, joyfulness, and harmony (symbolized by "southwest"), one can thereby combine firmness and flexibility and so attain balance. If one keeps to the northeast, one will wind up in danger and
ultimately be stopped.

Only in the fifth yang in the hexagram is positive strength balanced correctly; this is the state of a great person, where one can save the country
from trouble. Therefore those who go to see such a one will have the merit
of helping the country out of danger.

But among the six lines, only the top yin illustrates the benefit in seeing a great person; the others do not speak of it, because seeing a great person is also a matter of proper timing. When it is time to stop, then stop, and when it is time to go, then go. Timely action when in trouble completely embodies timely action in the universal process of transformation expounded in the *I Ching*. All of the sixty-four hexagrams are like this, but I just bring it up here because it is commonly neglected.

THE IMAGE: **Water on a mountain—trouble. Developed people examine themselves to cultivate virtue.**

Mountains nurture springs, which should provide moisture but not flood; here water flows over the top, so that people cannot get a foothold. This means there is a cleft in the mountain; it is not a fault of the water.

Developed people know that all dangerous and difficult situations are made and manifested by their own minds, so they do not dare to resent heaven or bear a grudge against people; they just examine themselves to cultivate their virtues, just as people might fix a mountain by filling in a cleft so that water will flow back into a valley and not run off to the side.

■ *First yin:* **Going means trouble; coming is praised.**

THE IMAGE: **Going means trouble; coming is praised. It is best to wait.**

In troublesome situations, knowledge is to see the danger and be able to stop. Therefore the lines all warn about going and allow coming. Here, "coming" means turning around to examine oneself and cultivate inner qualities.

The first yin represents seeing danger and immediately stopping, knowing the situation and not getting into difficulty. The achievement of self-examination and cultivation of virtue is earliest, so it can win praise. It is not shilly-shallying and shrinking back in fear. The reasonable thing to do is just to cultivate one's inner qualities and await the right time.

■ *2 yin:* **King and minister recognize trouble as trouble, not for personal reasons.**

THE IMAGE: **King and minister recognize trouble as trouble, so in the end there is no bitterness.**

This represents flexibility balanced correctly, examining oneself without shame, cooperating with a leader having positive strength balanced correctly, as represented by the fifth yang. When in trouble, how can they not recognize trouble as trouble and so work together?

All the lines but this one represent knowledge as the ability to stop. This one does not becaue it represents what is called working for a leader with all one has in the public interest, forgetting about oneself. Therefore it may seem adventurous, but in the end there is no bitterness.

Not acting selfishly is based on having examined oneself. If one can comprehend trouble by daily self-examination, only then can one solve troubles impersonally when the time comes.

■ *3 yang:* Going means trouble; come back.

THE IMAGE: Going means trouble; come back, and those inside will rejoice at this.

The third yang is the master of the *mountain* trigram, which represents stopping; it stands for one who is strong and upright, and can stop on seeing danger. Since one knows that to go would surely mean trouble, one comes back to examine oneself and cultivate virtue; then those represented by the inside two lines will both rejoice.

■ *4 yin:* Going means trouble; coming back brings company.

THE IMAGE: Going means trouble, coming back brings company; one's position is solidified.

Here we are now in the body of the *water* trigram, which symbolizes danger; the trouble is extreme. However, if one can come back to examine oneself and cultivate virtue, then one can still bring along the three lines of the *mountain* trigram and be able to stop. Yin is basically not solid, so bringing back company to one's position solidifies it. This refers to the third yang, which stands for mastery of stopping.

■ *5 yang:* In great trouble, companions come.

THE IMAGE: In great trouble, companions come, because of balance and moderation.

In the middle of *water* is great trouble. Here firm strength is balanced and correct, and the flexibility represented by the second yin cooperates, so it gets a "companion" to come, and together they solve the trouble.

However, it is not that a companion comes to help one here; it is actually because of one's fulfillment of the way of balance, as a moderating guideline for getting out of trouble, that those represented by the lines above and below take one as an example. This is like Shakyamuni Buddha appearing in a corrupt world, attaining supreme enlightenment, and explaining to all the truth, so hard to believe. This is truly one who can do what is very difficult and rarely accomplished.

■ *Top yin:* Going means trouble; coming means great good fortune. It is beneficial to see a great person.

THE IMAGE: Going means trouble; coming means great good fortune. The aim is within. It is beneficial to see a great person, by following what is valuable.

Here one is weak and in extreme danger; how could one go anywhere? Only if one comes to examine oneself and cultivate inner qualities will one have great good fortune. The reason this good fortune can be truly great is through the benefit of seeing a great person, as represented by the fifth yang.

Superior people seek this in themselves, so "the aim is within," and thus there is good fortune. To help society and cause the people to grow, nothing is as good as virtue, so the benefit of seeing the great is that of following what is valuable. Here, "what is valuable" refers to spiritual values, not just ordinary human values; "great good fortune" refers to something like that of the saint Subhadra, who saw the Buddha at the end and attained liberation.

40. Solution

water below, *thunder* above

For solution, the southwest is beneficial. Going nowhere, coming back is fortunate. Going somewhere, promptness is fortunate.

In worldly situations, there are never troublesome obstacles that last forever without resolution. On the verge of the solution, it is important that firmness and flexibility balance each other, so "the southwest is beneficial." Once the solution has been achieved, the general situation is settled, so where else is there to go? It is just a matter of coming back to the perennial Way, that is all.

But even if there is somewhere to go, in every case one should examine the matter thoroughly right away. If one goes precipitately without due consideration, misfortune will follow along—how can one be fortunate?

When good generals mobilize armies, they only expect the soldiers to be obedient. When good physicians use medicine, they only hope to get rid of the disease. In the practice and realization of contemplating mind, the only aim is to return to essence; there is nothing else to grasp.

THE OVERALL JUDGMENT: For a solution, one acts because of
danger, and through action escapes from danger; hence the
solution. For solution, the southwest is beneficial, as to go
there wins the masses. Coming back is fortunate, in that one
attains balance. Going somewhere, promptness is fortunate, in
that going is successful. Heaven and earth dissolve, and there
is thunder and rain. When it thunders and rains, the sprouts of
the fruitful plants and trees shed their sheaths. The time of
solution is great indeed.

When danger lies ahead, it is best to stop; when danger is below, one should
act to avoid it. Both of these are matters of the conditions of the time, and
cannot be forced.

The southwest stands for *earth*, so to go there wins the masses. Coming
back to the northeast means not being too soft, so that one attains balance.

By perceiving the onset of events early on, one can proceed successfully.
This is like the thunder and rain of heaven and earth; when it is prompt and
timely, the sprouts of the fruitful plants and trees shed their sheaths.

To interpret in terms of contemplating mind, full cultivation of meditation
concentration is the benefit of the southwest. The manifest activation of
myriad practices is "going there wins the masses." Not abandoning accurate
observation is called "coming back." Witnessing the body of reality is "attaining balance."

Going somewhere to help people, it is necessary to be able to perceive
their potentials from the start; then it will be fortunate. By explaining the
truth usefully, "going is successful."

The merging of essential nature and cultivation is "heaven and earth dis-
solving." Compassion regulates the activity of thunder and showers the rain
of liberative teaching, so the fruits of realization, mundane and transmundane, each attain timely growth, maturity, and release. Who but buddhas
and bodhisattvas can use this time of solution?

THE IMAGE: Thunder and rain—solution. Thus do leaders
forgive errors and pardon crimes.

This means directly forgiving transgressions made by mistake, getting
people to renew themselves, and also generously pardoning crimes to minimize their ramifications.

In Buddhist terms, this refers to using the three kinds of repentance—by
confession, by visualization, and by contemplation of nonorigination—to
enable people to solve doubts and get away from guilt.

In terms of contemplating mind, this is sitting upright and meditating on
reality so as to melt away all wrongdoing.

■ *First yin:* No blame.

THE IMAGE: At the border of hard and soft, it is right that there should be no blame.

Solution means that yin and yang are in harmony. This line represents being yin at the beginning, while cooperating with the fourth yang above, being right on the borderline of yin and yang; so it is right that there should be no blame.

■ *2 yang:* Catching the third fox on a hunt, finding a yellow arrow, correctness brings good fortune.

THE IMAGE: The good fortune of correctness of the second yang is attaining the way of balance.

Here, because firmness is balanced and cooperates with the flexibility of the fifth yin, there is naturally nothing to be suspicious of. The third yin is not balanced, not correct, but wants to take one over; this is represented as "the third fox." One goes on a "hunt," "catches" it, and gets rid of it, thus getting to join with the flexible balance of the fifth yin; this is correct and leads to good fortune.

Yellow is the color associated with the center; an arrow represents a straight path. By gaining the path of balance and straightforwardness, one gets rid of doubts and cooperates with what is right.

■ *3 yin:* Carrying and riding brings on enemies. It is right to be humiliated.

THE IMAGE: Carrying and riding are both disgraceful. One brings on attack by oneself—who else is to blame?

This line represents weakness, not balanced and not correct, without a partner, wanting to carry the fourth above and ride the second below, unaware that this is not the right way to go. Therefore the second regards this as "foxy" and hunts it, the fourth regards it as a "big toe" and removes it, the fifth regards it as a "petty person" and repels it, the top regards it as a "hawk" and shoots it. Is this not the epitome of humiliation?

■ *4 yang:* Remove your big toe. When a companion comes, then you trust.

THE IMAGE: Removing your big toe, you are not yet in the right position.

The third is below the fourth and wishes to carry the fourth, so the fourth regards the third as a toe. The fourth is not yet in the right position and is not as good as the second yang, in which firm strength is balanced. The second yang can hunt and catch the "fox" of the third, thereby following the fifth yin to balance yin and yang. The fourth must await the arrival of the second before it can believe that the toe should be removed. The second and fourth are both yang, so they are called companions.

■ *5 yin:* The developed person here has a solution, which is fortunate. There is sincerity toward a petty person.

THE IMAGE: The developed person has a solution.
The petty person withdraws.

The fifth and the second are proper correspondents, but the third wants to ride on the second, so the fifth cannot but have doubts about the second. Luckily the "developed person" represented by the second yang is firm and balanced, certainly able to achieve a solution, getting rid of the third yin and going up to follow the fifth yin, which is fortunate. Just observe the withdrawal of the third yin, and you will believe that the second yang has a solution.

■ *Top yin:* The lord shoots a hawk on a high wall and gets it, to the benefit of all.

THE IMAGE: The lord shoots the hawk to solve the conflict.

A hawk flies high and attacks skillfully; this represents the third yin, which "carries and rides." At the time of solution, everyone happily acts as developed people do, all except the third yin, who flies to the attack, in conflict with reason. Though the second "hunts" it, and though the fourth "removes" it, this is because both of them have proper correspondents; they are not the same as the top yin, which is outside the situation. Also, yang and yin feelings must have each other, so one considers it a "fox," the other considers it a "toe"—this is not as good as the top yin, who has no emotional involvement at all, and just considers it a "hawk." Furthermore, the top yin is at the end of the hexagram, the position of the lord. It is flexible, yet correctly oriented, so it hides its weapon, waiting for the right time to act, thus getting the hawk, to everyone's benefit.

Interpreting the six lines in terms of contemplating mind, the third yin represents the confusion that is to be cured, and the other five lines represent curative methods.

The first uses insightful concentration, in cooperation with the concentrated insight represented by the fourth yang above. Confusion cannot burden one then, so "there is no blame."

The second yang uses insight into the center of all things, in cooperation with concentration on the center of all things, as represented by the fifth yin above; but the third yin uses trifling mundane concentration and insight to take over before realization, hoping to confuse it. Therefore it is necessary to hunt down and repel foxy doubts, so as to attain the true way that is balanced and straightforward.

The third yin relies on worldly meditation to foster worldly knowledge, producing arrogance and opinionated views, falsely pretending to enlightenment; therefore it is to be overcome by the right path.

The fourth yang represents concentrated insight, which can certainly cure confusion; but because it is borne by the opinionated conceit of the third yin and has not yet attained the way of balance, it must await the insight into the center of all things represented by the second yang before it can remove this inner confusion.

The fifth yin uses concentration on the way of balance at the center of all things to cooperate with the second yang's insight into the center of all things; insight can cut through confusion, so concentration then accords with essential reality.

The top yin uses correct transmundane concentration to overcome the false pride and false views of worldly meditation and worldly knowledge, so it is to the benefit of all.

 41. Reduction

lake below, *mountain* above

Reduction with sincerity is very auspicious and impeccable. It should be correct. It is beneficial to have somewhere to go. What is the use of the two bowls? They can be used for presentation.

Once confusion is cured, from this point on one increases enlightenment and reduces mundanity. This is reduction in terms of contemplating mind. Those who contemplate mind believe that the realm of enlightenment is none other than all possible realms of experience; therefore "reduction with sincerity is very auspicious and impeccable." They know that all possible realms of experience are none other than the realm of enlightenment, so they benefit from going to the realm of enlightenment without displacing any other realm of experience. Without destroying the two truths, absolute and relative, they present the middle way.

THE OVERALL JUDGMENT: **Reduction reduces the lower to increase the higher; the path goes upward. "Reduction with sincerity is very auspicious and impeccable. It should be correct. It is beneficial to have somewhere to go. What is the use of the two bowls? They can be used for presentation." The two bowls must have their times; reducing hardness and increasing softness must have their times; reduction and increase, filling and emptying, go along with the time.**

Helping those below is "increase," going upward is "reduction." Sages established this term observing the way of the world, which never changes. There must be sincerity in higher things before it is possible to reduce lower things in a way that is very auspicious and impeccable. There must be correctness in lower things before it is beneficial to have a place to go and increase higher things. Even though there are two bowls, they can still be used for presentation; it is only a matter of the right timing of each, it being important to go along with the time.

THE IMAGE: **Lake below a mountain—reducing. Thus do developed people eliminate anger and greed.**

When there is a body of water below a mountain, the mountain will be reduced day by day. Developed people consider anger and greed to be most in need of reduction from the mind; therefore they eliminate anger as they would blast a mountain to smithereens, and eliminate greed as they would fill in a ravine, restoring a level ground surface.

■ *First yang:* **Ending one's affairs and going quickly, there is no fault. Assess the reduction of this.**

THE IMAGE: **Ending one's affairs and going quickly is because of valuing unification of aims.**

The first yang is a proper correspondent of the fourth yin; here one should reduce oneself to enhance the fourth. The fourth yin is weak and ailing, so one should end one's own affairs and quickly go to help; then there is no fault. However, when using strength to help the weak, assess carefully so as to obtain balance; do not allow excess. Because strength that is correctly oriented responds to one who is weak but correctly oriented, therefore proceeding in this way results in unification of aims.

■ *2 yang:* It is beneficial to be correct. An expedition would lead to misfortune. Increase it without reduction.

THE IMAGE: The benefit of correctness in the second yang is the balance that characterizes its aim.

The second yang is strong and balanced, not too adamant. The fifth yin, with which it corresponds, is flexible and balanced, not too weak. It is enough for each to preserve its correctness, so why still go and increase one in a way that would result in the misfortune of excess that is as bad as insufficiency? When increasing without reduction, that increase is then great; therefore the fifth yin "is given a profit of ten tortoise shells."

■ *3 yin:* Three people traveling are reduced by one person. One person traveling gets companionship.

THE IMAGE: When one person travels, three then doubt.

The third yin and the two lines below both represent reducing the lower to increase the higher. The first two lines are yang, the third alone shifts to yin; so "three people traveling are reduced by one person." Now, since one yin travels upward to enhance the top yang, for oneself this is "losing one's home in working for the country," but since the top yang is strong, instead it can enhance one by "increase without reduction"—is that not "getting companionship"? So whatever one does, it is best to be single-minded.

■ *4 yin:* Reducing the ailment causes there to be joy soon. No blame.

THE IMAGE: Reducing the ailment is a matter for joy.

Weakness and imbalance are an ailment. The first yang has already come quickly to help one in this situation, so one just assists the first yang in reducing one's own ailment; thus the first yang is joyful, and the one in this situation is blameless.

■ *5 yin:* One is given a profit of ten pairs of tortoise shells. None can oppose. This is very auspicious.

THE IMAGE: What is auspicious about the fifth yin is help from above.

In this state of flexible balance, one sets oneself at naught to respond to the second yang. The second yang, maintaining propriety, does not increase one's material goods, and therefore one can attract the admiration of the world, so all come bringing treasure. In general, when leaders can employ administrators in an open-minded way, then they are in accord with the celestial and receive help from above.

■ *Top yang:* **Increase without reduction, and there will be no blame. Correctness leads to good results. There is somewhere to go. Getting an administrator without a house.**

THE IMAGE: **Increase without reduction is great attainment of the objective.**

The top yang receives the enhancement of the third yin to the ultimate degree. If there is nothing to requite this, the third yin will not be resentful, but other people will not accept—then how can there be no blame, how can there be correctness with good results, how can there be somewhere to go? But to increase the third yin, it is necessary not to reduce the top yang. This is because the third yin as an administrator is in the position of "losing one's home in the service of the country," but the top yang perceives the sincerity of this lone journey, so this is "great attainment of the objective," and the third yin considers this "getting companionship." This is called "increase without reduction."

 42. Increase

thunder below, *wind* above

For increase, it is beneficial to go somewhere.
It is beneficial to cross great rivers.

Increasing enlightenment, reducing mundanity, one progresses daily toward the realm of self-help and helping others; this is contemplating mind accomplishing increase. "Going somewhere" to deal with the ordinary, "crossing great rivers" to deal with changes, if one attains the path of increase, there is all-around benefit.

THE OVERALL JUDGMENT: **Increase is reducing the higher to enhance the lower; the people rejoice boundlessly. Descending from above to below, that path is great and brilliant. "It is beneficial to go somewhere"—balance and rectitude are felicitous. "It is beneficial to cross great rivers"—the path of**

harmony is then carried out. Increase moves and tames,
progressing daily, without bound. Heaven disburses, earth
produces; that increase is not localized. The path of increase
always goes along with the time.

In terms of Buddhism, this means bringing the realm of enlightenment down
to benefit those in other states of mind; therefore the people "rejoice boundlessly." Enlightenment, which is basically transcendental, is manifested on a
lower plane, so it "descends from above to below," and "that path is great
and brilliant."

Celestial action and the action of sages are called "balance and rectitude."
Pure conduct initiates innocent and compassionate action; this is called "the
path of harmony then being carried out."

Emanating illumination and manifesting wonders move people; explaining the truth intelligently tames them.

Opening up complete understanding to reveal inherent qualities is called
the disbursal of heaven. Establishing rounded behavior to complete cultivated qualities is called the production of earth.

Seeding, maturing, liberating, teaching in terms of the world, or to cure
specific ills, or to develop individuals, or in terms of ultimate truth, is called
"going along with the time."

THE IMAGE: Wind and thunder increase. Thus do developed
people take to good when they see it, and correct whatever
faults they have.

The drumming of the wind represents the swiftness of taking to good; the
stirring of thunder represents the courage to correct faults.

■ *First yang:* It is beneficial to undertake to do great work.
If it turns out very well, there is no blame.

THE IMAGE: Only if it turns out well is there no blame,
because it is not for those in low positions to be deeply
concerned with affairs.

At the beginning of increase is when one receives benefit from those above
most richly. Because one receives this rich benefit while in a low position,
one can relax and do nothing; but as long as one is strong and upright, and
is also in charge of action, one will surely be able to do great work that will
turn out very auspiciously, so one thus avoids blame.

- *2 yin:* One is given ten sets of tortoise shells; none can oppose. It bodes well to be always correct. It bodes well for the king to make offerings to God.

THE IMAGE: What one is given comes from outside.

Here flexibility is balanced correctly, thus receiving benefit from the correct balance of positive strength of the fifth yang. One is blessed psychologically, not materially, so one can cause everyone to believe in one and bring precious gifts. As an administrator, it is good to be always correct and not let help from heaven or from other people change one's attitude. As a ruler, it is good to make offerings to God, renewing oneself and renewing the people, so that the mandate of rulership is thereby refreshed. When the image says that what one is given comes from outside, this means that it is not anticipated, because there is no calculating selfishness.

- *3 yin:* Enhancement through unfortunate events is blameless. Sincere and balanced in action, one presents impartial use of authority.

THE IMAGE: There has always been such a thing as enhancement through unfortunate events.

This represents being unbalanced and awry, at the top of the lower echelon, and being subjected to the attack of the highest power. Being subjected to this attack is what benefits one. If one knows that unfortunate events truly can benefit one, then one will be blameless.

Although one is not in a state of balance, if one is sincere one can act in a balanced way and thus can present impartial use of authority. Impartiality is characteristic of the highest power, and authority is used to get a message through. Once the message goes through, the authority is returned to the public domain and not used for personal gain. The only personal gain one receives is through being subjected to impartial criticism.

Ordinarily people always think that unfortunate events are not beneficial; it is sages who realize that there has always been such a thing as benefit from unfortunate events. If one can believe that misfortune is beneficial, then it is no longer unfortunate.

- *4 yin:* Balanced action openly expressed is followed impartially. It is beneficial to use this as a basis to move the center of operations.

THE IMAGE: Open expression of impartial following is because of the beneficial aim.

The fourth yin and the two lines above it all represent reduction of the higher to augment the lower. The fifth and top lines are both yang, the fourth alone has shifted to yin; this represents sacrificing oneself for the people, which is symbolized by moving the center of operations, and is the path of balanced action.

Since the first line has already received one's help, and is strong and upright, it has a great impartial attitude, with which it now is going to repay one with great work, so one can rely on this. Because the aim is to benefit the people, the people will follow impartially.

■ *5 yang:* There is sincerity to benefit the mind. Do not ask—it is very auspicious. There is sincerity granting one rewards.

THE IMAGE: There is sincerity to benefit the mind—do not question it. Granting one rewards is because of great achievement of what is intended.

Here positive strength is balanced correctly and corresponds with the second yin. This represents one who truly wishes to benefit those below. Benefiting them mentally, the benefit requires no expenditure, and all receive the blessing. What need is there to question that great good fortune? So one here can feel the good fortune of the constant uprightness of the second yin, greatly achieving what is intended, and it repays one with fine rewards.

■ *Top yang:* None benefit one here; they may attack one. Do not persist in this attitude, for that would lead to misfortune.

THE IMAGE: "None benefit one here" expresses partiality; "they may attack one" refers to what comes from without.

In the position of the top yang, basically one should reduce oneself to enhance the third yin, but since the third yin is not balanced and not correct, therefore one does not grant benefit and instead attacks. The third yin, of course, does receive benefit from the stimulus of this unfortunate event; but the top yang should not persist in this attitude. If one at the top persists in this attitude, then none of those below will benefit one, and indeed those below may attack one. Therefore it warns that to persist in this attitude will lead to misfortune.

The top yang is not balanced, not correct; this is one who is not benevolent yet is in a high position. Only thinking of benefiting oneself, one is unexpectedly attacked; hoping for benefit, one does not get it—hence this "expresses partiality." Because the attack is unexpected, it "comes from without."

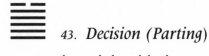

43. Decision (Parting)

heaven below, *lake* above

Decision is brought up in the royal court. A sincere statement involves danger. Addressing one's own domain, it is not beneficial to go right to war, but it is beneficial to go somewhere.

In worldly terms, this is when the people rejoice without bounds, and enjoy prosperity and happiness without effort, so action must be decisive.

In terms of Buddhism, this is when one has reduced oneself for the benefit of others, is successful in teaching, and should decisively progress to cut through residual confusion and realize the ultimate attainment.

Now there cannot be yang without yin, but in this hexagram yin rests on top of yang. This is like undeveloped people being above developed people—it is imperative to cooperate to get rid of this situation, to "bring it up in court," to trust one another to state the error. These are courses of action that involve danger.

Here it is appropriate to examine oneself and cultivate virtue, thus "addressing one's own domain." It is not appropriate to contend forcefully or "go right to war." Just exert the influence of virtue, and all will benefit.

In Buddhist terms, when we comprehend the reality of confusion, then confusion becomes knowledge; this is called "addressing one's own domain." Opposing it to get rid of it is called "going to war."

THE OVERALL JUDGMENT: **Decision is removal; strength removes weakness. Robust and joyous, there is harmony is spite of the decision to part. What is brought up in the royal court is the weak riding on five of the strong. A sincere statement involves danger, but that peril is then illuminating. Addressing one's own domain, it is not beneficial to go to war; otherwise the preferred course will come to an impasse. It is beneficial to go somewhere; the growth of strength then ends.**

Robust and joyous, harmonious in spite of the decision to part, correct illumination should use the influence of virtue and should not fight with force.

If you know what is perilous, that will enlighten you. If you prefer force, you will come to an impasse.

It is beneficial to have a place to go, which is to transform undeveloped people by virtue. When undeveloped people are all developed, the growth of strength then ends.

■ *The Image:* Moisture rises to the sky, which then parts with
it. Thus do developed people distribute wealth to those below.
If they presumed on their virtue, they would be resented.

Wealth should be distributed; virtue should be accumulated. If wealth is not
distributed, then blessings dry up; if virtue is not accumulated, then the
basis is lost. When wealth is distributed to those below, it is possible to educate people thereby; but if this virtue is presumed upon, it will lead to complacency, and people will resent it.

■ *First yang:* Vigorous in the advancing feet, going but
not prevailing is faulty.

THE IMAGE: To go without prevailing is faulty.

When strength is not balanced, one should not go forward; if one still
goes forward vigorously, this will only be self-defeating. Then how can one
prevail?

■ *2 yang:* When there is a cry of alert, even if there are attackers
in the night, there is no worry.

THE IMAGE: There is no worry when there are attackers,
because one has attained balance.

Here strength is in balance, and one knows enough to be wary and alert.
Once accumulated virtue is complete, one can be untroubled even when
there are attackers.

■ *3 yang:* Vigor in the face involves misfortune. Developed
people part decisively and travel alone. Encountering rain, if
they get wet there is irritation but no fault.

THE IMAGE: Developed people part decisively and are faultless
in the end.

When excessively adamant and unbalanced, anger shows in the face; excessive strength inevitably breaks down, and leads to misfortune. In view of
these facts, developed people have no reason not to take upon themselves
the decision to part, leaving the other four yangs above and below them,
going on alone to pursue the reasonable course of correspondence with the
top yin. Then yin and yang influence each other by their qualities and harmonize with each other. One in this position soon encounters rain and gets
wet; but even though the other yangs do not know one's intention and do

not understand one's actions, though one may be irritated, nevertheless the way to influence undeveloped people must be like this, so in the end there is no fault.

- *4 yang:* With no flesh on the buttocks, one walks haltingly. Leading the sheep, regret disappears. The words heard are not believed.

THE IMAGE: One walks haltingly, being out of place. The words heard are not believed, because of not hearing clearly.

For the fourth yang, the lines below are "buttocks." The lines below are pure hardness, without softness, like bones without flesh. Since there is no flesh on the buttocks, one will walk haltingly and not make progress. If one has the sheep be in front and follows up behind, one is still leading the sheep, but regret can disappear. But because strength is not balanced properly, on hearing these fine words one will certainly not believe. The "sheep" here is the top yin, which is the director of the trigram *lake,* representing joy; the fourth yang should lead this and not part from it, and also should not compete with it for precedence.

- *5 yang:* A hill of amaranth; parting with what is to be parted with, balanced action is faultless.

THE IMAGE: Balanced action is faultless, but balance is not yet obvious.

The top yin is soft and weak, like the amaranth plant; but it is on top of five yangs, like amaranth on a hill. Everyone can walk over it; does this alone not indicate the quality of submissiveness? Is this alone not "what is made by the whole body of the absolute containing the whole body of the absolute"? Here it is appropriate to part with what the other yangs part with, but still preserve and nurture it; this is the path of balanced action, whereby it is possible to be faultless. However, when parting, after all one does not avoid distinguishing between developed and undeveloped people, though one still does not forget what is universally the same in everyone—therefore "balance is not yet obvious." In *Return* (number 24), sages carefully preserve the faint yang; in *Decision/Parting,* they carefully preserve the remaining yin—neither yin nor yang can be wholly abandoned.

- *Top yin:* No call; in the end there is misfortune.

THE IMAGE: The misfortune of no call is that there cannot be growth at the end.

The five lines below epitomize the exhortations and admonitions of sages to the strong who gather together. Here one who is weak is at the top and even though correct is unable to call forth caution for preparedness, so in the end cannot grow.

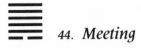

44. *Meeting*

wind below, *heaven* above

In meeting, the woman is strong. Do not marry the woman.

In ordinary terms, after you have dismissed something from your mind, when you do encounter it, it will be unexpected.

In Buddhist terms, those who decisively cut through residual confusion and become the same as the buddhas on a higher plane must then make skillful use of inherent evil to meet with unenlightened people on a lower plane.

In terms of the ultimate, *Decision* (hexagram 43) represents the path where there is no obstruction by confusion, while *Meeting* represents the path of liberation.

In terms of beginner's mind, *Decision* represents intellectual knowledge and *Meeting* represents noumenon. Because the yin "without call" (at the top of *Decision*) suddenly descends to the bottom (of *Meeting*) and finds a place to rest, its strength gradually grows; therefore the second yang should embrace and encompass it, and not let a stranger take it.

In buddhas, this is using inherent evil as a means of entry into truth. In unenlightened people, who do not understand, this is cultivated evil. The second yang, practicing the path of the bodhisattva, can appear to assimilate to cultivated evil and not let others to do evil.

Also, the path of liberation, once attained, is attained forever; hence "the woman is strong." There is no attachment; hence "do not marry the woman." This also applies to noumenon.

THE OVERALL JUDGMENT: **Meeting is encounter; the flexible encounters the firm. "Do not marry the woman" means that it will not do to associate for long. When heaven and earth meet, all things become manifest. When the firm meets balance and uprightness, the whole world works well. The significance of the time of meeting is great indeed.**

In Buddhist terms, the firm is inherent virtue and the flexible is cultivated virtue. Using cultivation to manifest what is inherent is called the flexible encountering the firm.

The firm is subtle perception of reality; the flexible is subtle cessation of confusion. Producing this perception from this cessation is called the flexible encountering the firm.

The firm is knowledge; the flexible is meditation concentration. Awakening knowledge by means of concentration is called the flexible encountering the firm.

Cultivation basically adds nothing to inherent essence. Stopping the mind should not be totally overwhelming, and concentration should not be excessive. Therefore "it won't do to associate for long."

When heaven and earth meet, heaven gets the first line of earth to form the trigram *wind*. Nothing stirs things as rapidly as wind. Make the wind even, and all things are cleanly leveled—therefore "all things become manifest."

The firmness of the second yang encounters the first yin below, and encounters the balance and uprightness of the fifth yang above. In political terms, this is an administrator who gets a leader that enables him to help the people. In Buddhist terms, this is knowledge in accord with essence, able thereby to achieve well-being. Hence the text says, "the world works well."

THE IMAGE: Wind under heaven—meeting. Thus do rulers announce their directives to the four quarters.

When what is "stripped away" from the top (in hexagram 23) goes back to the bottom, this is called *Return* (hexagram 24): this represents inherent virtue, perceptive insight; it cannot be used right away, so it is like thunder being in the earth, and "the ruler does not inspect the regions." When what is "parted" from the top (hexagram 43) goes back to the bottom, this is called *Meeting* (hexagram 44): this represents cultivated virtue, concentration to stop confusion; this can be used effectively, so it is like "wind under heaven" and "rulers announcing their directives."

By return, you see the heart of heaven and earth; by meeting, you see the greatness of the significance of the time. "Return" is creative recognition of a great beginning; "meeting" is receptive action forming beings. "Return" is skill through knowledge; "meeting" is power through enlightenment.

■ *First yin:* Arrested by a metal brake, it is good to be correct. If you go anywhere, you will see misfortune, an emaciated pig leaping in earnest.

THE IMAGE: Being arrested by a metal brake means the reining of the course of flexibility.

But for essential nature, there is no way to produce cultivation; without cultivation, it is impossible to reveal essential nature. Meditation without knowledge is not meditation; knowledge without meditation is not knowledge. In Buddhism, these are complementary and must be linked to one another.

Here, one yin arises at the bottom and is arrested by the metal brake of the second yang; this is the correct course, which leads to good fortune. If it is not arrested, then it will go somewhere, and if it goes it will run into misfortune, like an emaciated pig that will be able to leap as long as it has not been tamed already. The course of flexibility should be linked with the quality of firmness; then they form a partnership and can accomplish something.

■ *2 yang:* **There is a fish in the bag. There is no blame. It is not beneficial to visitors.**

THE IMAGE: **When there is a fish in the bag, duty does not extend to visitors.**

When cultivation reveals essential nature, essential nature then has cultivation; when concentration activates insight, insight then has concentration. When essential nature and cultivation are perfected through interaction with each other, and concentration and insight are equal, this is the blameless path. But it can only be realized within oneself—it cannot be expressed to others.

■ *3 yang:* **With no flesh on the buttocks, the walk is halting. There is danger, but no great fault.**

THE IMAGE: **The walk is halting because it is unconnected.**

The second yang is near the first yin, so "there is a fish in the bag." The third yang is far from the first yin, so there is "no flesh on the buttocks." If there is no flesh, one's walk will be halting. But even though it is dangerous, there is no great fault, because the third yang is together with the first yin in the body of *wind,* which represents harmony; it is just that its progress is not yet linked up with the course of flexibility.

■ *4 yang:* **No fish in the bag; this causes misfortune.**

THE IMAGE: **The misfortune of having no fish is that of alienating the people.**

When strength is not balanced correctly, one clings to essential nature and neglects cultivation, relies on intellect and neglects concentration. This is like a top executive dwelling in a high position and alienating the people.

When one is talking loftily about essence and flaunting uncontrolled intellectualism, one does not know that this causes misfortune. Then, when one is about to die and sees hellish visions, one will regret one's insufficiency, just like one who only finds out there is no fish in the bag after having left the river.

■ *5 yang:* **Wrapping a melon in river willows, containing brilliance, there is a descent from heaven.**

THE IMAGE: **The fifth yang contains brilliance, being balanced correctly. There is a descent from heaven, aspiration not disregarding destiny.**

Willow branches are supple and long; use these to wrap a melon, and the branches and vine intertwine inextricably. This represents the meeting of the second yang and the first yin. The fifth yang is the director of *Meeting* and dwells on high, distant and unreachable. However, since here one's firm strength is balanced correctly, one's inherent qualities form seeds after long development and are about to burst forth in glory; so the text speaks of "containing brilliance."

Because one's aspiration does not disregard destiny, one is not willing to be reckless. So even though there is no meeting with the first yin, there surely will be "a descent from heaven" to meet one. Discovery of what is inherent is called "from heaven," and spontaneous accord is called "a descent."

■ *Top yang:* **Meeting horn is humiliating, but there is no blame.**

THE IMAGE: **Meeting horn is the humiliation of coming to an impasse above.**

At the end of meeting, one does not meet with flexibility; this is called "meeting horn." This is like those devoted to individual liberation, who are biased toward insight into absolute emptiness. Nevertheless, they do escape the misfortune of having no fish in the bag, yet they do not avoid the humiliation of stunted potential.

45. *Gathering*

earth below, *lake* above

Gathering is successful. The king goes to his shrine. It is beneficial to see a great person; this leads to success. It is beneficial to be correct. It is good to make a great sacrifice. It is beneficial to go somewhere.

Meeting and thus gathering is normal in both mundane and transmundane matters. How can gathering not lead to success? Because of the gathering of the feelings of the unseen and the apparent, there is a shrine to go to; because of the gathering of the feelings of the higher and the lower, a great person can be seen. Making a great sacrifice to go to the shrine, it is beneficial to go somewhere to see a great person. These are all matters of course when obeying the duties of the time; this is what is meant by being correct.

THE OVERALL JUDGMENT: **Gathering is assembly. Obeying joyfully, firmness balanced and responsive, hence there is gathering. The king goes to his shrine, practicing piety successfully. It is beneficial to see a great person, leading to success; this is gathering correctly. It is good to make a sacrifice, beneficial to go somewhere; this is obeying the mandate of heaven. Observe what is gathered, and the conditions of heaven, earth, and myriad beings can be seen.**

Various expressions are used in the *I Ching* to express the successful carrying through of pious behavior; in this case it says, "making a great sacrifice." Various expressions are also used to express going to see great people; in this case it says, "it is beneficial to go somewhere." There is nothing personal about it. When it is appropriate to be abstemious, then be abstemious; when it is appropriate to be lavish, then be lavish. When it is appropriate to go, then go; when it is appropriate to come back, then come. All of these are ways of obeying the mandate of heaven and observing the conditions of people and things.

THE IMAGE: **Moisture rises onto the earth—gathering. Thus do leaders prepare weapons to guard against the unexpected.**

One commentator says, "Moisture can gather into a body of water on the surface of the earth if there are retaining walls; people can live in peace and assemble as long as they are armed and able to defend themselves." In Buddhist terms, this refers to the inner prohibitions of the disciplinary code. In terms of contemplating mind, this refers to esoteric spells for overcoming habits.

■ *First yin:* There is trust, but it does not last to the end. There is disorder and mobbing. If you cry, laughter is mixed in. Do not worry; it is blameless to go.

THE IMAGE: "Disorder and mobbing" means confusion of mind.

When it is time to gather, everyone wants to gather. The two yangs in the hexagram represent the leaders of the gathering, and the four yins represent those who gather around them. The first yin and fourth yang are proper correspondents; they are basically to be trusted, but since they are not balanced correctly, they cannot take their trust to its proper conclusion, so there is "disorder and mobbing." Because there is disorder, you may cry; because there is mobbing, laughter is mixed in. But since they are proper correspondents, why doubt or worry? It is better for the first yin to go follow the fourth yang; this is blameless. It is because of confusion of mind that crying and laughter are mixed; this means that the principle of correspondence itself has never been confused.

■ *2 yin:* Drawing out is good and blameless. If trusted it is beneficial to perform a ceremony.

THE IMAGE: Drawing out is good and blameless, as balance has not changed.

Here flexible docility is balanced and correct, corresponding with the leadership of positive strength in correct balance represented by the fifth yang above; basically there is nothing suspicious. But the first yin and the third yin both go to gather around the fourth yang, and one is in between these two yins; if one does not draw oneself out, how can one get the confidence of the fifth yang? If one draws oneself out and wins trust, then it is not necessary to make a great sacrifice; just to perform a ceremony will still be beneficial. Leaving the two yins behind and going alone to follow one's correspondent is like performing a ceremony; it requires very little. But this is only because the second yin has the virtue of balance. Such a one does not change his discipline to follow others who are weak, as represented by the two surrounding yins.

■ *3 yin:* Gathering, lamenting; there is nothing gained.
To go involves no blame, but there is a little shame.

THE IMAGE: To go involves no blame—the one above is
willing.

Above there is no correspondent, no partner. One wants to gather, but there
is no one to go along with; therefore one laments and gains nothing. However, when it is time to gather, if one goes to follow the fourth yang, one can
still escape blame. But since it is not a proper correspondent, one is shamed
a little, though the fourth agrees to accept this.

■ *4 yang:* If there is great good fortune, then there is no blame.

THE IMAGE: There is no blame only if there is great good
fortune, because one is out of place.

When it is time to gather, the first yin responds to this one, the third yin
pledges allegiance to this one; is this not close to regarding an administrator
as a ruler? This is why one in this position can only be blameless if there is
great good fortune. This is like the case of ancient wise men who never became leaders but spent their whole lives fulfilling the duties of administrators.

■ *5 yang:* Gathering around the position, there is no blame.
If those who are not loyal remain ever-faithful to their original
commitment, regret vanishes.

THE IMAGE: When there is gathering around the position, one's
aspiration is not yet glorious.

Here positive strength is balanced and correct; this is one in the position of
the leader, around whom others gather. But it is only the second yin that
really responds and the top yin that really cleaves to one here. The first and
third have already gathered around the fourth yang, so one can achieve no
more than being without blame. If one can forget one's position and delegate
responsibility to the fourth yang, allowing those two yins not to be loyal to
oneself, and if those who originally gathered around the fourth are always
faithful, then since the fourth yang is one's own minister, those two yins are
one's own subjects; therefore regret vanishes. Then again, if one just relies
on one's position and expects others to gather around, one's aspiration is not
yet glorious.

■ *Top yin:* Sighing and weeping, there is no blame.

THE IMAGE: Sighing and weeping is because of not being comfortable at the top.

Here one is weak but in a high position, and is uncomfortable and uneasy; so one sighs and weeps, cleaving to the fifth yang, so as to be without blame.

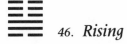 *46. Rising*

wind below, *earth* above

Rising is very successful. It calls for seeing a great person, so there will be no grief. An expedition south brings good fortune.

When energy amasses, it rises upward, like a tree growing upward from the earth; great success is sure. But since docile receptivity, as symbolized by the *wind* and *earth* trigrams, is not of itself fruitful in action, there is the exhortation to "see a great person, so there will be no grief." The south is associated with fire, symbol of illumination; an expedition south brings good fortune insofar as people turn toward illumination to carry out their aim.

THE OVERALL JUDGMENT: Flexibility rises in accord with the time. When there is docile receptivity, strength in balance responds; hence there is great success. It is useful to see a great person, so there will be no grief, but rather celebration. An expedition south brings good fortune, in the sense that the aim is carried out.

By flexibility one rises in accord with the time. This rising depends on receptivity, and is an achievement of receptivity. When strength in balance responds to docile receptivity, that is the aim of docility and receptivity.

THE IMAGE: Trees grow in the earth—rising. By following virtue, developed people accumulate the small into lofty greatness.

The body of the Tao is fundamentally not great or small, but when developed people accumulate virtue, they do so by following the Tao receptively, always proceeding from smallness to greatness, just as a huge tree starts out as a small sprout. The thing to remember is that one should neither damage the sprout nor try to force it to grow.

■ *First yin:* Truthful rising is very auspicious.

THE IMAGE: Truthful rising is very auspicious in that
there is accord with a higher aim.

Obediently according with a higher positive aim, truthfulness can ascend in
a way that is very auspicious.

■ *2 yang:* If there is sincerity, it is beneficial to perform
a ceremony. There is no blame.

THE IMAGE: The sincerity of the second yang is joyful.

The second yang seeking sincerity in the fifth yin of the hexagram *Rising* is
not as good as the second yin's sincerity toward the fifth yang in the hexagram *Gathering*, because in *Rising* yang is below yin in the relationship of the
second and the fifth, meaning that they are not correct in their respective
positions. However, the second yin in *Gathering* has neighbors of the same
character but different aims, so though its balance is not changed, it must
withdraw itself for things to turn out well. Now the second yang of *Rising* has
neighbors of different character but a united aim, so it not only is blameless,
but even joyful.

■ *3 yang:* Rising in an empty domain.

THE IMAGE: Rising in an empty domain, there is no hesitation.

When firm strength rises from a basis of flexible receptivity, what hesitation
or obstacle could there be?

■ *4 yin:* The king makes offerings on the mountain.
This is auspicious and blameless.

THE IMAGE: The king making offerings on the mountain
performs services accordingly.

The rising of people is like making offerings to heaven, earth, mountains,
rivers, ghosts, and spirits; the services are not the same, but the basis of accord is one. This is like adapting to the local situation wherever one goes;
the situations are different, but the principle of adaptation is the same.

■ *5 yin:* Correctness is good in raising one up the steps.

THE IMAGE: Correctness is good in raising one up the steps,
in that the aim is fully attained.

When there are enlightened people at court, the aim of a wise ruler is attained. The second yang, representing the enlightened person, is strong and balanced, so the fifth yin, representing the wise ruler, responds to this. This illustrates presenting a path on which to rise, as a wise ruler sets up steps to raise enlightened people to high positions. The only worry is that a less enlightened ruler will be overbearing toward a more enlightened person, like yin sitting on top of yang, and will not be able to perceive the sincerity of the latter; hence the special admonition to be correct, intending that the ruler have the correct attitude toward the enlightened person.

■ *Top yin:* **Rising into the unknown, it is beneficial to be unceasingly correct.**

THE IMAGE: **Rising into the unknown on high dissolves poverty.**

When one rises into the unknown, one can stop; but if one is unceasingly correct, then one should rise yet further into the unknown. This is what is called spiritual rank. If they cultivate spiritual rank, people of low social status are not really poor and lowly—their poverty can disappear.

 47. Exhaustion

water below, *lake* above

Exhausted but coming through successfully, upright great people are fortunate and impeccable. Mere words are not believed.

If you rise without stopping, you will inevitably get exhausted; this is part of the normal cycle of filling and emptying, waxing and waning. When the exhausted mind balances its thoughts, this is actually the way to come through successfully. However, if this is not sustained in the right way and not dealt with in the manner of a great person, how could it be possible to be fortunate and impeccable? If one does not personally practice real virtue and only has empty talk, this will surely not be enough to win confidence.

THE OVERALL JUDGMENT: **In exhaustion, strength is covered over. Only developed people can be joyful even in danger and come through successfully in spite of exhaustion. Upright great people are fortunate, because their strength is in balance.**

Mere words are not believed, because if you value talk you will come to an impasse.

In this hexagram, the strength in the *water* trigram is below, covered over by the weakness in the *lake* trigram; since the strength is covered over, the water leaks out and the lake dries up—this is the image of exhaustion.

To be joyful even in danger, to adapt to difficulty and carry through in difficulty, to avoid society without anguish, remaining happy—who but developed people can do this?

The second yang and fifth yang both represent strength in balance; this is the uprightness of great people, the way to good fortune. If you do not maintain this uprightness and merely value talk, you will only come to an impasse.

THE IMAGE: **The lake has no water—exhausted. Developed people accomplish their will by living out their destiny.**

In this hexagram, water is below the lake, which has no water; it is dried up, exhausted—this is its established fate. Developed people only live out their destiny; they do not willingly try to avoid following and accepting it. Being strong and balanced, they are able to be joyful even in danger; this is the will that is up to oneself. Developed people intend to accomplish their will and do not vacillate just because they run into problems.

■ *First yin:* **Sitting exhausted on a tree stump, gone into a dark ravine, not to be seen for three years.**

THE IMAGE: **Gone into a dark ravine, it is obscure and unclear.**

The six lines of the hexagram all represent dealing with exhaustion; only strong, balanced great people can avoid losing the way to come through successfully. The first yin is at the bottom; hence the image of sitting. It corresponds with the "tree stump" of the fourth yang above, which cannot give it protection in a state of exhaustion. Furthermore, the first yin is at the beginning of danger, which is like having gone into a dark ravine, unable to appear for "three years."

■ *2 yang:* **Exhausted, but with food and drink. When the regal robe comes, it is beneficial to make a ceremonial offering. An expedition leads to misfortune, but there is no blame.**

THE IMAGE: **Exhausted, but with food and drink, there is celebration within.**

This represents those who can nurture themselves with strength and balance when exhausted; so it is called being exhausted, but with food and drink. The fifth yang, with which the second corresponds, represents the leader with positive strength balanced correctly, who will surely reward one with a regal robe, enabling one to cooperate in solving the impasse of the time. One should just silently respond with sincerity, like making a ceremonial offering. If one proceeds abruptly, there will be misfortune; yet the aim is to rescue the age, so there is no blame. Celebration within is the fortune of upright great people.

- *3 yin:* **Exhausted on a rock, resting on thorns, going into a house but not seeing the wife—this is inauspicious.**

THE IMAGE: **Resting on thorns is riding on the unyielding. Going into a house but not seeing the wife is not a good sign.**

This represents negativity, weakness, imbalance, deviation. It is between two yangs: the fourth yang is like a rock, the second like thorns. The top yin does not correspond; this is like going into a house but not seeing the wife. Because one lacks auspicious virtue, one brings misfortune on oneself.

- *4 yang:* **Coming slowly, exhausted in a gold car, there is shame, but there is a conclusion.**

THE IMAGE: **"Coming slowly" is because the mind is on something lower. Though one is out of place, there is a partner.**

To deal with exhaustion and come through successfully is something that no one can do without strength and balance. The fourth yang represents one who, when exhausted, still cannot forget his feelings about the first yin, and so comes along slowly. Since his mind is on the first yin, not only does he not share the virtues of the second yang, he instead gets exhausted in the "gold car" of the second yang and is shamed. However, the second yang is strong and balanced, and will surely be able to cooperate in solving the impasse of the time, not abandoning him just because he is out of place; therefore there can be a conclusion.

- *5 yang:* **Nose and feet cut off, exhausted in a regal robe, gradually there is joy. It is beneficial to make ceremonial offerings.**

THE IMAGE: **"Nose and feet cut off" means that the aim is not yet attained. Gradually there is joy because of taking a** balanced course. It is beneficial to make ceremonial offerings because one receives blessings.

The fifth yang represents positive strength that is balanced and correct, in the honored position, looking upon the whole world as one being. The top yin is "exhausted in difficulty"—this is like cutting off one's nose; the bottom yin is "exhausted on a tree stump"—this is like cutting off one's feet. One then relies on the second yang for cooperation in solving the impasse of the time; this is like a regal robe, but the second yang is at this moment "exhausted in the midst of food and drink," so this fifth yang is "exhausted in a regal robe." Nevertheless, the second yang is balanced and straightforward, and will surely respond gradually, so that there is joy; one should react to this with utmost sincerity, as in making a ceremonial offering, in order to receive blessings.

■ *Top yin:* Exhausted in difficulty, in distress, thinking there will be regret if one acts, one does regret. Going forth leads to good fortune.

THE IMAGE: Exhausted in difficulty, one has not hit the mark. There is regret because of regretting action; good fortune is to go.

At the extreme of exhaustion, one should go on actively. If one is negative, weak, and feeble in ability, one doubts whether one's ideas are right; this is like being all tangled up and ill at ease. Fearing that if one acts one will regret it, one always shrinks back, regrettably. Therefore sages go directly forth to good fortune, resolving this.

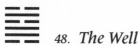

48. *The Well*

wind below, *water* above

Changing the village, not changing the well, there is no loss, no gain. People come and go, but the well remains a well. Lowering the bucket to the water, if you overturn the bucket before drawing it up from the well, this is unlucky.

A well is something that stays in its place in spite of movement. If you know how a well stays in place in spite of movement, you will know how to get through the impasse of exhaustion; therefore *The Well* is explained after *Exhaustion.*

A village can be changed, but a well cannot be changed. When change is possible, there is loss and there is gain; if change is not possible, how can there be any loss or gain?

Those who have drunk water go; those who are yet to drink come. People come and go, but the well does not come and go.

When you draw water up from the well, then you have achieved your purpose; if you overturn the bucket before drawing it up from the well, this is unlucky. This is gain and loss for the person; it is not the gain or loss of the well.

If you know how a well has no gain or loss, then you will know how inherent virtues can be different yet always identical. If you know how people have gain and loss, then you will know how cultivated virtues can be identical yet always different.

THE OVERALL JUDGMENT: **The well nourishes inexhaustibly. Changing the village without changing the well is because of strength and balance. Before the water is drawn up from the well, the purpose is not yet achieved. Overturning the bucket is the cause of bad luck.**

There is water in the earth, so if you dig into the earth, you will find water. This is symbolic of the potential for enlightenment being inherent in all elements of experience; so if you examine the elements of experience, you will realize the potential for enlightenment. But it is important to use the power of extremely calm observation to penetrate deeply and bring it out in the open. Once this hidden essence is revealed, it nourishes oneself and nourishes others inexhaustibly.

In *Exhaustion,* the "fortune of the upright great person" is due to strength and balance; here, "changing the village without changing the well" is also said to be due to strength and balance. *Exhaustion* seems to point solely to cultivated qualities, but really it makes it clear that the completion of cultivation lies in essential nature. The present hexagram seems to point solely to inherent qualities, but really it calls for people to develop cultivation with the whole essential nature. Therefore it explains that it is unlucky to upset the bucket before anything is achieved, laying great emphasis on cultivated qualities.

THE IMAGE: **Water above wood—a well. Leaders comfort the people and encourage reciprocity.**

Carrying water to give to others can only reach a few; digging a well and letting them draw from it will benefit many. "Carrying water" is contrived good, "digging a well" is uncontrived good. The way leaders comfort the

people is to encourage them to take care of each other; thereby they are
nourished inexhaustibly.

- *First yin:* Mud in the well is not drunk. There are no animals at
  an abandoned well.

  THE IMAGE: Mud in the well is not drunk; it is below. There
  are no animals at an abandoned well, because its time is gone.

Of the six lines of *The Well,* the three yin lines are the well, the three yang
lines are the spring. The first line is at the very bottom, so it is likened to
mud; not only do people not drink it, but even animals pay no attention.
This is buddhahood as a mere ideal.

- *2 yang:* The depths of the well water a minnow. The jar is
  broken and leaks.

  THE IMAGE: The depths of the well water a minnow;
  it has no partner.

This is the middle of the bottom trigram, so it is called the depths of the well;
there is a spring there which can water a minnow, but it has no corresponding partner above, so this is like the jar being broken and leaking, so that it
cannot be used to draw water. A minnow is the smallest of fish; this indicates the first yin. This second yang is intellectual buddhahood, where one
has been influenced somewhat by learning but has not yet become a vessel
of truth.

- *3 yang:* The well is cleared, but not drunk from; this is the
  concern of one's heart. It is worth drawing from. When the
  king is enlightened, all receive the blessings.

  THE IMAGE: When the well is cleared but not drunk from,
  travelers are concerned; they seek enlightenment in the king,
  to receive blessings.

Here positivity is in a positive position; the spring is pure. But it is still in the
lower trigram, and not drunk by people—this is something to be concerned
about. The top yin corresponds, so it can be used to draw from the well.
Since the king is enlightened and employs wise people, the blessings of the
wise are not received alone. This is buddhahood in contemplative practice;
because it subdues the basic afflictions of the mind, the well is cleared, but
because it does not yet realize essence, it is not drunk from. Here one should
seek the aid of the buddhas; then one can help oneself and help others.

■ *4 yin:* When the well is tiled, there is no fault.

THE IMAGE: When the well is tiled, there is no fault—
this means fixing the well.

A well is tiled to keep impurities out of it, in order to keep the spring clean; therefore it is called "fixing the well." This is conformative buddhahood, going from wisdom through thought into wisdom through practice, warding off the impurities of dualistic extremism and keeping the spring of the middle way pure.

■ *5 yang:* The cold spring in the well is drunk from.

THE IMAGE: The drinking of the cold spring is balance and correctness.

Positive strength balanced and correct is the utter purity and coolness of the spring. Its merit extends to others, so they can "drink" it. This is partially realized buddhahood; the water of the essence of the middle way benefits oneself and benefits others.

■ *Top yin:* Do not cover the well enclosure. There is nurturance, which is very fortunate.

THE IMAGE: Great fortune at the top is great fulfillment.

Yin at the top is like the well enclosure; if this is kept open and not covered, then everyone can draw from the well, and it will nourish them inexhaustibly. This is ultimate realization of buddhahood, in which worthy qualities are completely fulfilled, always bringing benefits to people throughout the entire future.

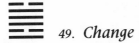 *49. Change*

fire below, *lake* above

Change is believed in on the day it is completed.
It is very successful, beneficial if correct.
Regret vanishes.

When the village is changed but not the well, this refers to the place. When the well is used up, there are no animals there and it is muddy; it has to be changed.

The first priority of learners is to change their character. This is like fire refining gold: during the process of refinement, the gold finds it painful; only after the refinement is done and the gold is made into a vessel does it believe in the merit of the fire.

This path of change is the path of creativity and receptivity; it is very successful for those who do it correctly. Before believing in it, there is regret; once it proves trustworthy, regret vanishes.

THE OVERALL JUDGMENT: In change, water and fire cancel each other. Two women live together, but their aims are not complementary; this is called change. The day it is finished, then it is believed in. When change is believed in, rejoiced in because it is civilized, very successful because it is correct, as the change is appropriate, regret vanishes. As heaven and earth change, the four seasons take place. When ancient leaders changed the social order, they obeyed nature and responded to humanity. The time of change is great indeed.

"When change is believed in" means that before change, people do not believe in it. When the change is appropriate, this makes people believe in it, and their regret vanishes; this makes it clear that if the change is not appropriate, regret does not disappear. Change must come about the way nature changes the seasons or the way ancient sages changed the social order for the better; only then can it win people's confidence. So change is not an easy matter.

THE IMAGE: Fire in a lake—changing. Leaders make calendars to define the seasons.

There is no actual reality in time; it is artificially defined by distinguishing positions based on matter and mind. Mind is formless and is represented through the medium of matter. Matter has collective forms and individual forms.

Collective forms of matter above us are the sun, moon, and constellations of stars. As the sun, moon, and stars course through the sky, based on the degrees of their passage we define the seasons of spring, summer, fall, and winter.

In spring, it is spring for everyone; in winter, it is winter for everyone. So we know that time is just a manifestation of mind; it is nowhere, yet there is nowhere that it is not. This is like fire, which essentially has no self; it is even inherent in bodies of water; evidence of this is the way fiery light always rises from the ocean.

■ *First yang:* Use yellow ox hide for wrapping.

THE IMAGE: Using yellow ox hide means that it will not do to use contrivance.

Fire is that which changes; *Lake* is that which is changed. The first yang is on the bottom and has no corresponding partner above; this represents one who should not use contrivance. Just use the hide of a yellow ox to wrap yourself, in the sense of making yourself firm and secure.

■ *2 yin:* On the day of completion, the change has taken place. An expedition leads to good fortune, without blame.

THE IMAGE: Change having taken place on the day of completion, there is felicity in going.

Here flexibility is balanced and correct; this is the master of *fire,* which represents illumination, one who attains the complete ability to change things. Change will be believed in on the day of completion, and above there is a correspondence with the fifth yang, which represents great people; so to go on will lead to a felicitous partnership.

■ *3 yang:* An expedition leads to misfortune, dangerous even if correct. Change, then speak; on the third presentation, there will be trust.

THE IMAGE: Change, then speak. Make three presentations. Where are you going?

Here one is too adamant and unbalanced; but one is in correspondence with the top yin, which is flexible but upright, representing a leader that is like a spotted leopard and cannot be changed forcibly. So to "go on an expedition" would surely lead to misfortune; even if one is right, it is still dangerous. One can only change oneself so as to go along with the leader; when one has spoken up three times, one may win confidence.

■ *4 yang:* Regret vanishes; there is trust. Changing one's fate, there is good fortune.

THE IMAGE: The good fortune of changing one's fate is belief in the aim.

The trigram *lake* is associated with metal, which must be refined before it can be made into a vessel. But the fourth yang has no correspondent below, which means that there is not one who will develop you; so obviously there is regret. However, being strong but not excessive, and also being close to the top of *fire,* which represents illumination, your aim can be believed in, so regret vanishes and there is trust. You can thereby change your fate and progress daily toward the realm where you can benefit yourself and others as well.

■ *5 yang:* **Great people change like tigers. There is certainty without augury.**

THE IMAGE: **When great people change like tigers, their stripes are clear.**

Great people with positive strength balanced and correct, who also have the assistance of those who are flexible, balanced, and correct, as represented by the corresponding second yin, are therefore like tigers miraculously transforming, their stripes clearly evident. They can win people's trust without any need for auguries.

■ *Top yin:* **Developed people transform like leopards; undeveloped people change their faces. To go on an expedition leads to misfortune. To remain upright leads to good fortune.**

THE IMAGE: **Developed people transform like leopards—their spots are dense. Undeveloped people change their faces—they follow the leader docilely.**

Leopards are born with spots, but they only show them at specific times, as if they were transformed. The third yang represents undeveloped people who are adamant and impulsive; when they see the transformation of their leaders, they too change and speak up repeatedly in such a way as to follow along. However, they only change their faces, not their hearts; so leaders should not expect too much of them. If leaders want the people's hearts to change, and go after them aggressively, they will not avoid misfortune; they will only be fortunate if they themselves remain upright so as to influence the people silently.

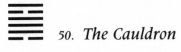

50. *The Cauldron*

wind below, *fire* above

The cauldron is very auspiciously developmental.

To change things, nothing compares to the cauldron; this is the vessel used to refine the wise, forge sages, cook buddhas, and purify adepts. How could it not be very auspicious and developmental?

THE OVERALL JUDGMENT: **The cauldron is an image, using wood, wind, and fire to cook to perfection. Sages cook offerings to present to God, which is the great development whereby sages are nurtured. Obedient and brilliantly clear of eye and ear, flexibly progressing upward, balanced and responsive to strength, therefore it is greatly developmental.**

The first yin is the legs; the second, third, and fourth yangs are the belly; the fifth yin is the knobs; and the top yang is the handle. Is this not the image of a cauldron? Using wood, wind, and fire to cook to perfection; is this not the function of a cauldron?

Do not say the way of the cauldron is small; what sages use to cook offerings to God is just this cauldron. This is to say that the great development used to nurture the sages of the world is just this cauldron. Why seek the principle outside the phenomenon?

Speaking in terms of the qualities of the hexagram, inside is the trigram *wind,* which stands for obedience; outside is the trigram *fire,* which stands for brilliant clarity of eye and ear. The fifth yin is the master of *fire,* progressing upward, gaining the state of balance, and responding to the strength of the second yang. Is this not the path whereby sages, wise people, buddhas, and adepts refine themselves, forge themselves, cook themselves, and purify themselves? That great development is good indeed.

■ *The Image:* **Fire over wood—the cauldron. Leaders stabilize their mandate by correcting their position.**

The cauldron is the treasure of the state, that in which the position of the leader resides. When the right way is found by correcting the position, then the mandate can be stabilized; if one's qualities are not in conformity with one's position, then one's mandate departs, and the cauldron goes along with it.

To explain this in terms of the image, virtuous qualities are like wood, the mandate is like fire. As long as there is wood, there is fire; when the wood is exhausted, the fire dies out. If one makes one's position correct by having virtuous qualities, then one's mandate will be stabilized. When virtue is lost, the mandate is lost. Therefore it is said, "This mandate is not permanent."

■ *First yin:* When the cauldron overturns on its base, it is beneficial to take out what is wrong. When one has a concubine, because of her child there is no blame.

THE IMAGE: When the cauldron overturns on its base, that is not bad. It is beneficial to take out what is wrong, to go along with what is valuable.

The first line is the base of the cauldron; it overturns because it correponds with the fourth line. When you overturn it along with the uncooked stuff in it, then the unhealthy things that have accumulated there can be taken out.

Overturning the base is like taking a concubine; taking out what is wrong is like having a child. The mother is valued because of the child; because of the child it is known that having a concubine is not bad. Through taking out what is wrong, it is known that "overturning the base" has merit.

■ *2 yang:* The cauldron has content. My enemy is afflicted, but luckily it cannot get to me.

THE IMAGE: The cauldron having content is being careful about where one goes. While my enemy is afflicted, after all there is no resentment.

The second line is the bottom of the belly of the cauldron; as yang is strong, this is construed as having content. The line corresponds with the fifth yin of "yellow knobs and gold handle," and is able to preserve this.

Though the first line "overturns the base" and "is afflicted," after all the harm does not reach one here. However, for the second position, this means it is best to be careful where one goes.

■ *3 yang:* The knobs of the cauldron are removed, so its use is impeded. Pheasant fat is not eaten. When it rains, regret is removed and all is well in the end.

THE IMAGE: When the knobs of the cauldron are removed, it loses its meaning.

The third line is the middle of the belly of the cauldron; the contents are rich, and there is pheasant fat to be eaten. But there is no corresponding partner above; this is like the knobs of the cauldron being removed, so that it cannot be moved. Luckily, there are the "yellow knobs" of the flexible balance of the fifth yin, coupled with the "jade handle" of the strength without excess of the top yang, which can be used to lift the second and third. This is like yin and yang combining so as to produce rain; thereby regret is removed and all turns out well.

If one takes the Tao to heart but does not think about putting it to effective use, it therefore loses its meaning. This is like the saying that there is no meaning, duty, or justice if it is not put to work. This is to inspire us to practice the Tao in a way that is effective for the time.

- *4 yang:* **The cauldron breaks its legs, spilling your food; your face drips. This is unfortunate.**

THE IMAGE: **Now that you have spilled your food, what happened to your confidence?**

The fourth line is the top of the belly of the cauldron. Its content fill it, and it weighs so heavily on the corresponding first yin below that its legs break under the strain. Your face then drips with sweat and embarrassment. To begin with, you did not know that your virtue was slight, your knowledge small, and your power little. Since you wrongly depended on your noble position, your plans were great and your responsibility heavy. Now you cannot bear that responsibility—what happened to your self-confidence?

- *5 yin:* **The cauldron has yellow knobs and a gold handle. It is beneficial to be correct.**

THE IMAGE: **The knobs of the cauldron are filled through the center.**

The fifth line is the knobs of the cauldron; it has the quality of centered balance, so the color is yellow, which is the color associated with the center. It receives fulfillment through openness, so it has a golden handle; the golden handle refers to the top yang. The handle is fitted through the knobs; the knobs are used to lift the cauldron. To nurture the wise people throughout the land is the right path of great service of sages.

But the fifth yin originally has no fulfillment of its own; it is fulfilled through its correspondence with the centered balance of the strength of the second yang below. Using this to nurture the world is what is called finding people for the benefit of the world.

- *Top yang:* **The jade handle of the cauldron is very auspicious, beneficial to all.**

THE IMAGE: **The jade handle is above. Hard and soft join.**

The top line is the handle of the cauldron. From the point of view of the fifth yin, it is hard as metal, but since the virtue of its hardness is not excessive, it is like the luster of jade. When metal is subjected to a fierce fire it melts, but jade cannot be destroyed by fire. When you use this to lift the cauldron, it is very auspicious, beneficial to all.

 51. Thunder

thunder below, *thunder* above

Thunder comes through. When thunder comes, there is alarm, then laughter. Thunder startles for a hundred miles, but one does not lose spoon and wine.

In Buddhist terms, as soon as a single thought begins to stir, you examine it in terms of four phases—before the arising of the thought, on the verge of arising, during the thought, and after the thought; this is called alarm. Then you realize it has no essence and no origin; this is called laughter.

The random arising of various bedeviling phenomena, such as objectifications of afflictive habits, is called "thunder startling for a hundred miles." Not losing the techniques of concentration and insight is called "not losing spoon and wine."

THE OVERALL JUDGMENT: **Thunder comes through. When thunder comes, there is alarm—fear brings fortune. Then there is laughter—afterward there is an example. Startling for a hundred miles, it startles those far away and terrifies those nearby. If you come out, you can thus preserve the ancestral shrine and the earth and grain shrines, and so be the master of ceremonies.**

When you are afraid, you can bring about good fortune; you cannot expect gratuitous fortune. As it is said, fortune is born of worry and trouble. When you are not careless even as you laugh, then you do not lose your standards.

Only by virtue of a lifetime of this sort of development can you go forth alone in emergencies that "startle those afar and terrify those nearby," from which other people all flee, and stand up to them with a steady mind.

Thus you can preserve the ancestral shrine and the earth and grain shrines, and be master of ceremonies, meaning that you can protect the people and the land, and fulfill the role of leadership. This is "not losing spoon and wine."

THE IMAGE: Repeated thunder reverberates. Developed people practice introspection with caution.

Developed people do not worry or fear. Why would they need repeated peals of thunder before they practice introspection cautiously? Cautious introspection actually refers to their daily practice of being careful by themselves of what they might not notice. This daily effort ca foster what is good and diminish what is bad. Because they are accustomed to cautious introspection in daily life, therefore even when they run into "repeated thunder," they no longer worry or fear.

■ *First yang:* When thunder comes, there is alarm, afterward laughter. This is auspicious.

THE IMAGE: When thunder comes, there is alarm—fear brings fortune. There is laughter—afterward there is a model.

All six lines illustrate the way to cautiously practice introspection, but there are distinctions of excellence and inferiority of quality, appropriateness or otherwise of position; therefore good and bad outlooks are distinguished.

The first yang represents strength correctly oriented, and is the master of *thunder,* which stands for stirring, movement, and action. The best people to take charge of things are those who are most developed; this is obviously auspicious.

■ *2 yin:* Thunder comes—dangerous. Remembering that you have lost your treasure, you climb nine hills. But do not pursue it; in seven days you will get it.

THE IMAGE: The danger of thunder coming is mounting the unyielding.

The second yin rides on the unyielding strength of the first yang, which represents a fearsome companion who awes and refines you. Because of this you become profoundly concerned, and use this to slough off your habitual weaknesses, and remember how you have carelessly lost your treasure of balanced and upright pure goodness. Then you climb right up onto the nine hills of high illumination. Do not concern yourself any further with seeking for it, for in "seven days," when you return to your original state, those qualities of balanced and upright pure goodness will be there as ever.

■ *3 yin:* The thunder is faint. Act vigorously, and there will be no trouble.

THE IMAGE: The thunder is faint—the position is not appropriate.

The third line is far from the first. This means that the stirring effect that was there at first has become faint and is no longer intense. In this state, you should stir yourself into action and not relax the effort to practice cautious introspection just because you are far from your awesome companion; then there will be no trouble.

- *4 yang:* Thunder gets bogged down.

THE IMAGE: Thunder getting bogged down is not illuminating.

The fourth yin is also a master of *thunder,* but it is yang on top of yin, and is also trapped in the midst of four yins, so even though it comes repeatedly, it has lost its awesome quality and has gone into the mud. How can it have the illumination that was characterized by alarm and laughter?

- *5 yin:* Thunder goes and comes—dangerous. On reflection, there is no loss; there is something to do.

THE IMAGE: Thunder goes and comes—dangerous. This is acting in peril.

What stirs the second yin is only the first yang, so it only says "thunder comes—dangerous"; what stirs the fifth yin is the first yang and the fourth yang—once the first thunder has gone, the fourth thunder then comes. Because of this, the fifth yin is wary of danger, which causes activity to progress daily toward high illumination; therefore it is called action in peril.

As this yin is in the fifth place, it is not too weak and attains centered balance, so its virtue is very great, without any loss. There is only the work of cautious practice of introspection.

- *Top yin:* Thunder is faint; the look is shifty. An expedition leads to misfortune. The thunder does not reach you, but is in the vicinity. There is no blame. Association involves criticism.

THE IMAGE: The thunder is faint—balance has not been attained. Though there is misfortune, there is no blame. Fear nearby is a warning.

The strength of the first yang certainly is unable to reach you here, and the thunder of the fourth yang is "bogged down," so its sound is faint and has no more power. Also, the weakness of the yin here is extreme, so "the look is shifty," fearful and uncertain. If you go on an expedition this way, there is no mastery at the core of the heart, and since the spirit is already in disarray, obviously there will be misfortune.

However, while the thunder does not reach you here, only reaching the vicinity, if you can practice cautious introspection because the thunder is in the vicinity, you can still be blameless. However, the intelligent way to preserve yourself is to prevent disaster before it occurs; if you flirt with it, this will surely be considered twisted, and there will be criticism.

52. *Mountain*

mountain below, *mountain* above

**Stilling the back, one does not find the body.
Walking in the garden, one does not see the person.
There is no fault.**

Although movement and stillness are opposites, they are also interconnected, and they also have no real identity; ultimately they are nondual. Not moving is called stillness, not being still is called moving; this is said in reference to their opposition. Because of movement there is stillness, because of stillness there is movement; this is said in terms of their interconnectedness. Stilling movement is quiescence, stopping quiescence is movement; moving what is stilled is movement, shifting movement is stillness; this is said in terms of their lack of real identity. Stillness is itself movement, so while tranquil one always senses; movement is itself stillness, so while sensing one is always tranquil: this is said in terms of their nonduality. It is only possible to speak of stillness to those who know the nonduality of movement and stillness.

In the human body, the senses are in the front and are governed by internal organs. The internal organs are in the body cavities, which are joined by the back. When confronted with colors, people's emotions are aroused; if those colors are behind them, people are not aware of them. Therefore people ordinarily construe the back as stillness. So when the back is still, one remains in a state of tranquillity even though the senses are excited with emotions and desires. When emotions stir, even if the back discerns nothing, after all it goes along. Therefore, when the front follows the back, then when the back is still the front also is accordingly still; when the back follows the front, when the front is active the back is also accordingly active. Ultimately the front and back are fundamentally not two and cannot be divided.

This hexagram has the trigram *mountain* above and below; this stands for stopping and stilling: this is "stilling the back." How can stilling the back allow one to be faultless? Because it means "not finding the body, walking in the garden, not seeing the person." This is faultless.

The body is fundamentally not really substantial; only by binding it together by emotional desires do we erroneously perceive that there is a body. If we examine it calmly, we see that what is solid in it belongs to earth, what is moist in it belongs to water, what is warm in it belongs to fire, and what is motile in it belongs to air. The eyes, ears, nose, and tongue have different functions; the four limbs, head, and feet have different names; there are three hundred and sixty joints and eighty-four thousand pores—ultimately what is the body?

Since the body cannot be grasped, then as it goes through myriad changes, how can there be a graspable "person"? Therefore, walking through the garden, one does not see the person. So stillness does not interfere with action; action itself is stillness. Therefore there is no fault.

THE OVERALL JUDGMENT: Mountain stands for stillness. When it is time to stop, then stop; when it is time to go, then go. When action and repose are timely, then one's path is illumined. The stillness of the mountain means stopping in the right place. Above and below are opposed, and have nothing to do with each other. Therefore one does not find the body; walking in the garden, one does not see the person. There is no fault.

Stopping action is repose; stopping stillness is action. When action and repose are timely, they are both subtle stillness; therefore one's path is illumined.

Stillness does not mean the stillness of "facing a wall." The "right place" does not mean a specific location.

As phenomena fundamentally do not know each other and do not reach each other, just as the upper and lower trigrams of this hexagram are opposite and do not form a pair, therefore when one seeks the body, one ultimately cannot grasp it, and though one "walks in the garden" there is no definite "person" to be seen. Merging with the path of light, there is no fault.

THE IMAGE: The mountains are still. Thus the thoughts of developed people are not out of place.

Two mountains stand next to each other, each resting in its place. Therefore plants and trees grow on them, animals and birds live on them, lodes of precious stones develop in them. Each place is so because of the laws governing the universe.

It is not that developed people do not think about this; but they know that nothing can be grasped outside the place of present manifestation, so their thoughts are "not out of place." While not out of place, they are always thinking, so this is not dead quietism; though they think, it is not out of place, so this is not chasing around in confusion. Always thinking, they can fulfill the function of their place, so all the works that make the world go around flow from this realm of realities. Not being out of place, they can accord with the capacity of their position, so all capabilities that nurture beings return to this realm of realities.

- *First yin:* Stopping the feet, there is no blame.
  It is beneficial to be always correct.

THE IMAGE: Stop the feet before losing correctness.

Stopping the feet means stopping at the outset, not allowing oneself to indulge in impulses. Then one will certainly not lose correctness and will be blameless. However, it is beneficial when always correct. Stop when it is time to stop, go when it is time to go, and you will gain the good fortune of careful stopping.

- *2 yin:* Stopping the calves, they don't rise to follow.
  The mind is not happy.

THE IMAGE: Not rising to follow means not retreating to listen.

The feet, calves, and thighs all go or stop following the mind. But the feet have no power and cannot act on their own; and when walking, the feet are basically themselves still. Now, the position of this second yin is that of the calves, and it is yin in a yin position. When stopping, they can forcibly stop on their own and not follow the mind's movement, so this "not rising to follow." This is the path where timing is not missed but by movement or stillness. It is by not retreating humbly to listen to orders from the mind that one causes the mind to be unhappy.

- *3 yang:* Stopping at the waist breaks the spine.
  Danger affects the heart.

THE IMAGE: Stopping at the waist, danger affects the heart.

The third place is at the boundary, or the "waist." Here yang is in a yang position; this is the master of stillness. This is where the waist is stiff and inflexible. Above and below originally connect, like a spine. Now, because of "breaking the spine" they no longer interconnect, so the danger cannot but affect the heart.

■ *4 yin:* Stopping the torso, there is no fault.

THE IMAGE: Stopping the torso stills the body.

The fourth place is at the torso. The overall judgment speaks of "stopping the back," but here it just speaks of "stopping the torso." If the torso is stopped, so is the back. Countless faults and errors arise from the body; when flexibility is correct and one can stop them in the body, what faults can there be?

■ *5 yin:* Stopping the jaws, there is order in speech, and regret vanishes.

THE IMAGE: Stopping the jaws is done with balance and uprightness.

The fifth place is in the heart; the voice of the heart is expressed through the jaws. Here the recessive takes the place of the aggressive, and one is in balance; so one is able to assess the balance of one's words before speaking them. Thus one does not speak at random and there is order in one's speech, so that one can avoid making mistakes through speech.

■ *Top yang:* Careful stopping is auspicious.

THE IMAGE: The good outcome of careful stopping is a rich conclusion.

Being the master of stopping, and at the end of the hexagram, can be called resting in the highest good; that culmination is useful for everything. Essential virtue is fundamentally rich, and cultivating virtue can accord with essential nature and restore it. Therefore the commentary says there is a rich conclusion.

53. *Gradual Progress*

mountain below, *wind* above

**Gradual progress in a woman's marriage is auspicious.
It is beneficial to be chaste.**

In Buddhist terms, essence is realized all of a sudden; then you use this realization to clear your mind and make it fluid. Phenomena are not cleared away all at once; this is done through a gradual process, just as the procedure for a woman's marriage is a gradual one.

Also, the gradual method of meditation is called a "woman"; arriving at reality right in meditation on phenomena is called "marriage." Comprehensive cultivation of meditation on phenomena with complete understanding is called "chastity."

THE OVERALL JUDGMENT: **When it proceeds gradually, a woman's marriage is auspicious. When the procedure leads to the proper state, the process is successful. By correct progress it is possible to rectify the country. The proper state is when strength attains balance. When calm and flexible, action does not reach an impasse.**

Progress may be sudden or gradual. Here, gradual progress is being illustrated, so it is said to be like a woman's marriage being auspicious when it proceeds gradually. Achieving the right state, the process is successful. If the procedure does not lead to the right state, obviously it will not do to go through with it.

By correctness it is possible to rectify the country. Clearly, if progress is not right, it cannot make the country right.

But how does this hexagram illustrate a procedure leading to the proper state? By the fifth yang, where strength attains balance. How does it illustrate the success of the process? By action being calm and flexible, hence not coming to an impasse. Calm is the wellspring of action. Without calm, action comes to an impasse, like a gully that is temporarily filled by rain but dries up right away.

THE IMAGE: **There are trees on a mountain, gradually growing. Developed people improve customs by living wisely and virtuously.**

Trees on a mountain grow gradually, their growth unnoticed by those who gaze on them. So it is also with developed people who live wisely and virtuously. When there are huge trees on a mountain, the mountain increases in height. When there are developed people living wisely and virtuously in an area, the local way of life improves.

■ *First yin:* **Geese gradually proceed to the shoreline. If humble people are diligent and speak up, there is no blame.**

THE IMAGE: **The diligence of humble people is dutiful and blameless.**

Geese fly south in the fall and north in the spring; they go at specific times and nest in an orderly fashion. In human terms, they are like humble people, who should work hard, be wary of danger, and speak up to seek people who can help refine and develop them, just as geese on a shoreline call for mates. Then they will be blameless.

■ *2 yin:* Geese gradually proceed onto a boulder; they eat and drink happily. This is auspicious.

THE IMAGE: Eating and drinking happily, they don't just stuff themselves idly.

The second yin is in correspondence with the fifth yang. This is like gradually proceeding onto a boulder, eating and drinking with harmonious delight. Cultivating the Tao and awaiting the right time to act, one does not eat without working.

■ *3 yang:* Geese gradually proceed onto high ground. The husband goes on an expedition and does not return; the wife gets pregnant but does not raise the child. This is not good. It is beneficial to defend against enemies.

THE IMAGE: The husband goes on an expedition and does not return—leaving the group is disgraceful. The wife who gets pregnant but does not raise the child loses the way. It is beneficial to defend against enemies, harmoniously protecting one another.

The third yang is like geese gradually proceeding onto high ground; there is no corresponding partner above, so there is no water. Geese do not mate at random, but the fourth yin also has no corresponding partner and is next to the third yang. If the third yang "goes on an expedition" to follow the fourth yin, this is leaving the group of geese and is disgraceful. If the fourth yin goes down to the third yang, this is losing the way, and though she gets pregnant, she does not dare to raise the child. Obviously this is not good. When those who are not appropriate partners form a private liaison, in reality they are enemies. If the third yang remains upright and defends against this, then for him there is no disgrace of leaving the group, and for her there is no misfortune of losing the way—then they can harmoniously protect one another.

■ *4 yin:* Geese proceed gradually into the trees and may reach a level roost without trouble.

THE IMAGE: Reaching a level roost means following docilely.

The fourth yin is on top of the third yang, where it cannot really rest; this is like gradually proceeding into the trees, which is not a place where geese can rest, since they have webbed feet and cannot grasp the branches. They may, however, find a large, flat branch, where they would have no trouble. The meaning intended here is cleaving to the fifth yang above. By following docilely, it may be possible to be free from trouble.

■ *5 yang:* **Geese proceed gradually onto a mountaintop.**
The wife does not conceive for three years; after all, no one
could overcome her. This is auspicious.

THE IMAGE: **What is auspicious about no one being able to**
overcome her after all is getting what was wished for.

The fifth yang is in the honored position, which is like a high mountaintop. Below he corresponds with his wife, the second yin, who is eating and drinking happily, taking care of herself. As she is untouched by the third yang, she "does not conceive for three years; after all no one could overcome her," and "this is auspicious." This is like when an enlightened ruler finds excellent administrators, thus fulfilling the dream of finding wise people. Is this not delightful?

■ *Top yang:* **Geese gradually proceed onto high ground.**
Their feathers can be used for ceremonies. Good fortune.

THE IMAGE: **What is fortunate about their feathers being**
suitable for use in ceremonies is that they cannot be put in
disarray.

The top yang is also on high ground, like the third yang. But the high ground of the third yang is the south, where the geese fly in the fall; they go in among humans, so they are unfortunate. On the other hand, the high ground of the top yang is the north, where the geese go in spring; they rise beyond the skies, so they are fortunate. As it is said, when the geese fly out of sight, how can hunters shoot them? All that can be done is to look afar for their feathers and use them as ornaments for highly accomplished people.

Also, when geese fly, those in pairs are ranged behind, while only one with no partner is in the lead. This top yang is beyond things and has no corresponding partner below. This is like a just and dutiful man in society who is fortunate because his will cannot be deranged. "Using feathers for ceremonies" is a traditional expression for exemplary behavior; in such a person, the function is great indeed. So it is said, "A sage is the teacher of a hundred generations."

54. *Marrying a Young Girl*

lake below, *thunder* above

Marrying a young girl. To go on an expedition leads to misfortune, with nothing gained.

In Buddhist terms, this means practicing gradual meditation. Here "marriage" means that one takes concentration on worldly phenomena and "weds" it to true insight into the way to enlightenment. If one just uses this concentration on phenomena to set up a teaching method, one will surely fall into the web of sentimental views, which leads to misfortune. If one indulges in this concentration obsessively, then one will be partial to a temporary byway and will gain nothing.

THE OVERALL JUDGMENT: **Marrying a young girl is an important duty of heaven and earth. If heaven and earth do not commune, beings do not flourish. Marrying a young girl is a start toward an end for human society. If she acts out of attraction, the bride is an immature girl. She will be unfortunate if she goes on, because it is not her place to do so. Nothing is gained, because weakness prevails over strength.**

Contemplating mind uses subtle concentration to unite with subtle insight, but may also use gradual meditations to foster spiritual powers. If what the contemplating mind considers assistance on the way is in fact addictive meditation, then the "bride" is immature. If concentration leaves insight behind and goes on alone, misfortune is sure to result. If concentration is practiced habitually for a long time and becomes an obsession, nothing is gained.

THE IMAGE: **Thunder over a lake—marrying a young girl. Developed people consider lasting results and know what is wrong.**

When thunder peals, it reverberates over a lake, but the thunder soon dies out, while the lake remains the same. This is not the way of permanent marriage, nor is it the way of equilibrium of concentration and insight. The way developed people handle things is that before they take the time to ask how to start something, they first consider lasting results. If they think of lasting results, they know what is wrong with acting prematurely, like marrying an immature girl. If you understand the meaning of this, you can apply it to government and to contemplating mind as well.

- *First yang:* Marrying a young girl, taking junior wives.
The lame can walk. To go on leads to good fortune.

THE IMAGE: "Marrying a young girl, taking junior wives" is
because of constancy. The lame can walk to good fortune
because of service.

In this hexagram, the bottom trigram, *lake,* represents the young girls; the
top trigram, *thunder,* is the husband. Among the three lines of *lake,* the third
yin is the young bride, and the first and second yangs are the junior wives.
Among the three lines of *thunder,* the fourth yang is the husband, the fifth
yin is like the master of ceremonies, and the top yin is like the ancestral
shrine where the ceremony is held.

The yang, with the virtue of firmness and uprightness, follows the third
yin in marriage to the fourth yang and becomes his junior wife. The third
yin is as though lame, but can walk with the help of the first yang; therefore
"to go on leads to good fortune." In a junior wife, constancy is an important
virtue, serving the bride; thus both are fortunate.

- *2 yang:* The one-eyed can see. It is beneficial to be chaste as a
hermit.

THE IMAGE: The benefit of the chastity of a hermit is not
changing the norm.

The second yang, by virtue of strength in balance, also follows the third yin
as a junior wife. The third yin is as though one-eyed but can see with the
help of the second yang. If you do not have clarity of vision yourself, and
have another see for you, who can do this without the chastity of a hermit?
But this is also just a normal virtue for a junior wife.

- *3 yin:* When the bride-to-be seeks, it will be the little sister
who is married instead.

THE IMAGE: The bride-to-be who seeks is not right.

This line is the focus of the trigram *lake,* which stands for delight and attraction. For fear that the bride-to-be might be easily moved by attraction, here
she is warned that she must await the directive of the fifth yin and not let
people take her lightly, lest the little sister be preferred for marriage. She is
warned because she is out of place.

- *4 yang:* When it is the wrong time for a girl to marry,
she delays the marriage until the proper time.

THE IMAGE: **The purpose of putting off the marriage is to go at the right time.**

Since the third needs the order of the fifth to marry, here one must put off the wedding. But though the marriage is delayed, there will be a time of union.

■ *5 yin:* **The emperor marries off his younger sister. The attire of the lady is not as good as that of the junior wives. The moon is almost full. This is auspicious.**

THE IMAGE: **When the emperor marries off his younger sister, she is not dressed as well as the junior wives. The position is one of balance, behaving in a noble manner.**

The fifth yin is the emperor. The third yin is his younger sister, who is also called the lady. The first and second yangs are the junior wives. In terms of their attire, the third is not as good as the first and second; in terms of womanhood, she is like the moon nearly full, coming into blossom. She is a noblewoman, of the imperial family, yet she can marry beneath her station, not being arrogant or conceited. Is this not an auspicious path?

■ *Top yin:* **The woman receives a chest, but there is nothing in it. The man sacrifices a goat, but there is no blood. Nothing is gained.**

THE IMAGE: **The top yin has no fulfillment. This is receiving an empty chest.**

When one does not accumulate virtue in life, then one has no spirit after death and cannot cause one's descendants to flourish. When a man marries simply because he must, this is not the fault of the woman, but the fault of the insubstantiality of one who is weak-minded. Developed people, knowing what is wrong by thinking of the lasting results, see this at the outset.

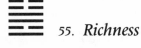

55. *Richness*

fire below, *thunder* above

Richness is success; a king attains this. Do not worry. Take advantage of the sun at noon.

When a family has a wife and concubines, it is rich. When a country has many citizens, it is rich. When contemplating mind has meditation on phenomena to assist the path, it is rich. Richness is surely success, but only a "king" can bring about richness. Richness thus is something to be concerned about, but do not worry fruitlessly. One should just be like the light of the sun illumining all beings.

THE OVERALL JUDGMENT: **Richness is greatness. Action with understanding results in richness. A king attaining this adds greatness. Do not worry—take advantage of the sun at noon; it is good to illumine the world. After noon, the sun goes down; after becoming full, the moon wanes. The filling and emptying of heaven and earth wax and wane with time; how much more so in the case of human beings, and how much more so in the case of ghosts and spirits?**

Understanding without action, action without understanding—neither of these is the way of kings, and neither can bring richness. Therefore only a king can add greatness.

When the text says to take advantage of the sun at noon, it does not mean to stop it and prevent it from setting; it means to take advantage of the light to illumine the world, thus not being shrouded by richness. When it comes to setting, waning, and emptying, even heaven and earth cannot avoid those when the time comes—so what is the benefit of useless worry?

THE IMAGE: **Thunder and lightning both come in richness. Thus do leaders pass judgments and execute punishments.**

Passing judgments is like the light of lightning. Executing punishments is like the awesomeness of thunder. Thunder and lightning in nature both come once in a while; if they came all the time, things would be destroyed. Similarly, punishments are meted out by true leaders only when unavoidable; if they were handed out casually, the people would be injured. And just as thunder and lightning come in summertime, true leaders use punishments in times of prosperity and ease.

■ *First yang:* Meeting your partner, even though you are equals, there is no problem. If you go on, there will be exaltation.

THE IMAGE: Though you are equals, there is no problem, but if you carry equality too far, there will be disaster.

In the lines of the other hexagrams, the correspondence of yin and yang is considered right, as in ancient political science when the weak govern firmly and the enlightened govern gently. Only in the lines of *richness* is the pairing of yang with yang and yin with yin considered right, as in ancient political science when powerful enemies are overcome by strength and weak allies are governed gently.

The first yang here is strong and upright; meeting the fourth yang, they become partners and refine each other through their interaction. Therefore, even though you are equals there is no problem, and if you go on there will be exaltation. If you do not go on quickly, and come to carry equality too far, you will not avoid "the sun setting after noon," and there will be disaster.

■ *2 yin:* With abundant shade, you see stars at midday. If you go, you will be afflicted by doubt. If sincerity is expressed, there will be good fortune.

THE IMAGE: Expressing sincerity means expressing intention truthfully.

The second yin is the focus of *fire*, representing one who is most illumined. Uniting with the flexible balance of the fifth yin allows mutual benefit, but the fifth yin is blocked by the fourth yang, so this is like seeing stars at midday because of the abundant shade. Now, the fifth yin is a gentle friend, and can be moved by sincerity, not to be answered in haste—therefore, if you go, you will be doubted. Only if sincerity is expressed will there be good fortune, because truthfulness can get rid of doubt, and its expression gets rid of the shadows. The shade is basically not real; it only exists because of doubt. When the intention is expressed, doubt is removed, and when doubt is removed, the shade is gone and the "sun" can be seen.

■ *3 yang:* With abundant rain, you see the drops in the sunlight. You break your right arm but are not to blame.

THE IMAGE: When the rain is abundant, you cannot do great works. When you break your right arm, it cannot be used.

One who is strong and upright, and also has understanding, can thereby observe the world. But because the third yang corresponds with the top yin,

yin and yang combine and shower a downpour of rain. Therefore you only see the raindrops flying in the sunlight and lose the attainment of the king adding greatness; after all, you cannot do anything thereby. For understanding, the left is best; for action, the right is best. The top yin is at the extreme of action, being hurt through arbitrary action; in terms of the third yang, this is like breaking the right arm. This is the fault of the top yin, not the fault of the third yang.

■ *4 yang:* With abundant shade, you see stars at midday. Meeting the hidden master is auspicious.

THE IMAGE: With abundant shade, the position is not appropriate. Seeing the stars at midday means it is dark and dim. Meeting the hidden master is auspicious in terms of action.

As positive strength is the master of action, producing clouds that block the sun, so the shade is abundant and you see stars at midday. Luckily you meet the first yang, which is firm and upright, like the sun just rising, so there is value in proceeding. Its power can be your "hidden master," dispersing the dark mist, illumining the world as it goes, not losing the meaning of rich success—therefore it is auspicious.

For the second yin, the abundant shade in which you see stars points to the fifth yin being obscured by the fourth yang. Here the fourth yang makes its own shade abundant, causing the stars to be visible in the daytime, so it is criticized for being out of place, dark and dim.

■ *5 yin:* Bringing brilliance, there is celebration and praise. This is auspicious.

THE IMAGE: What is auspicious about the fifth yin is that there is joyful celebration.

Here flexible balance is in the place of honor, while the second yin brings it to light with sincerity. Although this totally depends on the latter's quality of illumination, it is also due to one's ability to bring it out. This represents ruler and administrators combining their good qualities, so that all the world benefits.

■ *Top yin:* Making the house rich, shading the home. A peek in the door finds quiet, no one there, unseen for three years. Inauspicious.

THE IMAGE: **Making the house rich is pride. A peek in the door finds quiet, no one there, for one has hidden oneself.**

This is weakness in a negative position, at the culmination of action, at the top of richness. Here one rejects illumination, for fear that if the light were allowed in, it would reveal oneself. So one makes the house rich, with high walls and great overhanging eaves, like someone with enormous pride. Shading the home means putting up a lot of screens to hide oneself, so that even if someone peeked in the door, it would seem as if no one were there. This is going from darkness into darkness, unseen for as long as three years, incomparably inauspicious. There "three years" means a long time, and it also refers to the fact that the top yin is separated from the third yang by three lines.

 56. *Travel*

mountain below, *fire* above

Travel has a little success. Travel is auspicious if correct.

After midday, the sun begins to set; after the moon becomes full, it begins to wane: therefore, after richness, travel is explained. Richness adds greatness, travel has a little success; but there is no great or small in correctness—it is great in the great, small in the small. The essential point is not to lose correctness; then it is auspicious wherever one goes.

THE OVERALL JUDGMENT: **Travel has a little success. Flexibility attains balance on the outside and harmonizes with power. Calmly cleaving to understanding, therefore there is a little success, and travel is auspicious if correct. The significance of the time of travel is great indeed.**

Because of being outside, a journey is called travel. When on a journey, it is best to be flexible, and in applying flexibility it is best to be balanced. When balanced, one can harmonize with power, so that there is nowhere in the world where it is difficult to be. By being calm, one can be at peace wherever one is. By cleaving to understanding, one can see opportunities and act.

The correctness of this travel is the correctness of creativity, the correctness of receptivity, the correctness of the whole process. The great sages of all times, from emperors down to commoners, have all dealt with travel completely in terms of correctness of creativity, receptivity, and the whole process, so when they travel they fully perceive the correctness of creativity, receptivity, and the whole process. How can anyone be so careless as to disregard the great significance of the timing involved?

In Buddhist terms, the three lower worlds—the world of common presence, the world of expedient release, and the world of true reward—are all journeys. Performing great enlightening works in these worlds, the significance of time is therefore great. But from the point of view of the spiritual being in the world of silent light, this is still "a little success."

THE IMAGE: Fire on a mountain—traveling. True leaders apply punishments with understanding and prudence, and do not keep people imprisoned.

A mountain is like an inn, fire is like a passing traveler; this is a leader's inspection of the provinces on patrol, based on the understanding represented by the light of fire and the prudence represented by the steadiness of a mountain. Therefore punishments can be applied, but people are not to be kept in prison. If people are kept imprisoned without judgment, this means losing not only understanding but prudence as well.

In terms of contemplating mind, when thoughts arise, notice them. On noticing them, break through them by reflection, without becoming excited or rueful.

■ *First yin:* Petty fussing on a journey brings misfortune.

THE IMAGE: Petty fussing on a journey results in the misfortune of frustration.

Here negative weakness is in a low position, not balanced, not correctly oriented. This is one who gets worn out with petty fussing on a journey. Lacking lofty intelligence and great aspiration, one brings misfortune on oneself.

■ *2 yin:* Coming to an inn on a journey with supplies in hand, one gains the loyalty of a servant.

THE IMAGE: Gaining the loyalty of a servant, after all there is no complaint.

When traveling, for each line the next line above it is an inn, a resting place. Yin should stick with yang, and yang should stick with yin. Now the second yin is flexible, balanced, and correct, harmonizing with the strength of the third yang; therefore it "comes to an inn." Being yin in a yin place, and also in the body of *mountain*, this is having "supplies in hand." Below is the first yin, who fusses pettily but has no disloyalty to the one in the second place, so this is "gaining the loyalty of a servant." Now "coming to an inn with supplies in hand" relates to external conditions, while "gaining the loyalty of a servant" derives from inner qualities. When one has qualities like this, it can be said that travel is correct and auspicious, so "after all there is no complaint."

■ *3 yang:* Burning the inn on a journey, losing the servants, is dangerous even if one is upright.

THE IMAGE: Burning the inn on a journey, one will also be injured. In one's dealings with inferiors on a journey, duty is lost.

For the third line, the fourth is the inn; but here yang meets yang, and this one is in the body of *fire*, so one "burns the inn" and also is injured. Furthermore, one is too adamant and not balanced; when on this journey, one still does not know how to treat inferiors well, thus causing one's servants to become disaffected and leave, through no fault of their own.

■ *4 yang:* Traveling to a place, one gets resources and tools, but one's heart is not happy.

THE IMAGE: Traveling to a place, one has not gotten a position. Getting resources and tools, one's heart is not yet happy.

When developed people perform their duties, their aim is not in the resources and tools. This line represents those who come to a place to work and have the resources and tools, but still are not in a position to really exercise their abilities to the fullest. Therefore, even though they have the wherewithal, their desire to do what is right is still not fulfilled, so they are not happy.

■ *5 yin:* Shooting pheasant, one arrow is lost. Ultimately one is lauded and given a mandate.

THE IMAGE: Ultimately being lauded and given a mandate is reaching the highest.

This is just what is referred to as "flexibility attaining balance on the outside and harmonizing with power." Opening one's mind to invite the wise from all over the world to help one on one's journey is like shooting pheasant;

though one may lose an arrow, after all one will get pheasant. Therefore people laud one, and heaven gives one a mandate. This is because when people harmonize with heaven, heaven will help them; this is called reaching the highest.

■ *Top yang:* A bird burns its nest. The traveler first laughs, afterward cries. Losing the cow while at ease is unfortunate.

THE IMAGE: Because the travel is in a high place, it is just to be destroyed. Losing the cow while at ease, after all one does not listen.

When traveling, it is best to be flexible. Here firmness is not balanced or correct, and is at the culmination of *fire*, where there is nothing covering or protecting one; so it is like a bird burning its nest.

First one laughs because of the pleasure of being in a high place; later one cries because of having burnt the nest and having no place of refuge.

Fire originally has the docility of a cow, but by arrogance and laziness from presuming upon strength, one loses this unawares. What can compare to that misfortune?

So the burning of the nest is due to the travel being in a high place; this is treating people with hauteur, so it is only justice that one has brought this destruction about—it cannot be attributed to fate. The loss of the cow is due to not knowing how to examine oneself within, to being arrogant and self-righteous; therefore the disaster arises from carelessness and heedlessness—one cannot blame another.

57. *Wind*

wind below, *wind* above

The small comes through successfully. It is beneficial to have a place to go. It is beneficial to see great people.

Those who manage travel well are at home wherever they enter; without adaptability, there is no way to fit oneself in. *Wind* has one yin entering in under two yangs. The yin has ability and follows the yangs to effect its function; therefore "the small comes through successfully" and benefits from having a place to go, benefits from seeing great people.

In terms of contemplating mind, when learning concentration, it is best to follow true insight to see essential truth.

THE OVERALL JUDGMENT: **Double wind expresses directions. Strength follows balance and rectitude, so the aim is carried out. The weak all follow the strong, so the small come through successfully, benefiting from having a place to go, benefiting from seeing great people.**

When people with leadership qualities are on a journey, if they get a following they become leaders. When the people have ability and follow the leaders, the leaders are then considerate and respectful, expressing their directions in such a way as to comfort the people and make them secure.

It is because strength follows the virtues of balance and rectitude that the aim can be carried out; therefore the weak all follow it. If the strong are not balanced and upright, they cannot win over the weak; if the weak do not follow the strong, they cannot even attain a little success. The benefit they get from having a place to go and seeing great people is just how the small come through successfully; if they do not go and see the great, how can they succeed?

THE IMAGE: **Wind following wind—thus do leaders articulate directions and carry out tasks.**

Only when the wind comes continuously can it sway things; only when leaders articulate their directions clearly and carry out their tasks earnestly can they move the people. Therefore the virtue of true leaders is likened to wind.

■ *First yin:* **Advancing and retreating, it is beneficial to be as steadfast as a soldier.**

THE IMAGE: **Advancing and retreating means the mind is wavering. The benefit of the steadfastness of a soldier is that the mind is under control.**

The first yin is the subject of *Wind*. *Wind* focuses on entering, but being recessive and weak, it suffers from many doubts; therefore it may advance, but then retreats after a while. Now there is nothing in the world to doubt; it is only that one's mind itself wavers. Resolve this with the steadfastness of a soldier, and the mind will be under control; then there is nothing in the world that is hard to manage. The steadfastness of a soldier spoken of here is what the judgment calls having a place to go and seeing great people.

■ *2 yang:* **Obedience below the platform, using scribes and mediums frequently, is auspicious, without blame.**

THE IMAGE: What is auspicious about this frequency is the attainment of balance.

The positive strength of the fifth yang is balanced and correct; it is the master of *Wind* and is as though sitting on a platform. The second yang then stands for the administrator with the virtue of obedience, who should be below the platform. However, since here one has gotten the obedience of the first yin because of one's strength and central position, one cannot avoid suspicion of plotting to take power. Therefore it is necessary to use scribes to record one's actions and use mediums to convey one's sincerity, doing so frequently, not daring to be remiss. Then balance is attained, and there is good fortune, no blame.

■ *3 yang:* Repeatedly attempting obedience is humiliating.

THE IMAGE: The humiliation of repeatedly attempting obedience is that the aim is frustrated.

One who is strong and in a position of strength is not one who can be obedient; trying to learn obedience, time and again one fails. When the aim is frustrated, it is not merely that the mind wavers; the wavering can be overcome, but the frustration is humiliating.

■ *4 yin:* Regret vanishes. The hunt yields three catches.

THE IMAGE: The hunt yields three catches—there is success.

Flexibility that is correct is the main point in obedience. Following a leader who is strong and balanced, this line represents an easygoing, magnanimous high official, whom all the wise and talented people in the world would be glad to work for. Therefore it is like making three catches on a hunt; the three catches are the other three yangs besides the fifth, which is in the position of leader.

■ *5 yang:* Correctness leads to good fortune; regret vanishes, none do not benefit. There is no beginning, but there is an end. The three days before a change and the three days after a change are auspicious.

THE IMAGE: What is auspicious about the fifth yang is that its position is correctly balanced.

Though one may have the qualities, if one does not have the position, one dare not presume to make changes. If one has the position but does not have the qualities, one cannot make changes. The fifth yang represents one whose qualities and position are in mutual accord; therefore, attaining correctness of following, there is good fortune, regret vanishes, and none do not benefit.

But once things have changed, there is no beginning; when the change is right, therefore there is an end. Also, it is necessary to be careful "three days" before a change, and it is also necessary to first assess "three days" after a change; then it will be auspicious.

■ *Top yang:* The obedient are below the platform. Losing resources and tools, it is right that there be misfortune.

THE IMAGE: The obedient are below the platform; above there is an impasse. Losing resources and tools, it is proper that there be misfortune.

With positive strength at the top of the hexagram, one places the obedient in the positions of the fifth and second yangs below one's platform, while one is at an impasse above yet doesn't know it. Therefore the resources and tools of the first and fourth yin are employed by the second and fifth yangs, and do not work for one in the top position. That misfortune is proper and cannot be avoided.

To interpret the six lines in terms of Buddhism, the first represents meditation on worldly phenomena. There is progress, and there is also regression. The second represents insight into emptiness. Here one should use "scribes and mediums" to get in touch with the manifestations of reality. The third represents infertile intellectual insight, which cannot be kept securely. The fourth represents transmundane meditation, which has many virtues. The fifth represents accurate insight into the center of all things, which takes differentiating understanding into complete understanding, so it has no beginning but has an end. The top represents aberrant insight, which destroys good qualities.

 *58. Delight*

lake below, *lake* above

Delight comes through, beneficial if correct.

When one gets through, one is fulfilled; when one is fulfilled, one is delighted. When one is fulfilled, others find satisfaction in this; when others find satisfaction in this, they too are delighted. How can joy not come through?

However, developed people do not enjoy attempts to delight them with what is not right, so delight is only beneficial if correct. As the classics say, do not destroy people to follow your own desires; do not deviate from the right path to win people's praise.

THE OVERALL JUDGMENT: The lake stands for delight. Strength in balance, flexible outside, delight is beneficial if correct; this is how to obey heaven and respond to humanity. When the people are led with delight, the people forget their toil; when difficulty is entered into with delight, the people forget their death. The greatness of delight is how it inspires the people.

When strength is balanced, there is no biased selfishness of emotional desires; when flexible outside, there is no belligerence or violence. This is the most correct delight, the virtue shared by heaven and earth. If the people are led with this virtue, the people will naturally forget their toil. If difficulty is entered into with this virtue, the people will naturally forget their death. This is the greatness of delight; the people inspire themselves and transform each other for the better. It does not mean someone else urges them on.

THE IMAGE: Joined lakes are joyful. Thus do developed people study and practice with companions.

When lakes are joined, they do not dry up; when learning is done with associates, it is not isolated and narrow. Associating with companions in cultural pursuits is study; fostering humanity through association is practice. Study without practice leads to nothing; practice without study leads to danger. Study, and what is said does not go against the unsaid; practice, and the unsaid proves to tally with what is said. Also, when you study, the unsaid is said; when you practice, what is said becomes the unsaid.

■ *First yang:* **Harmonious delight is auspicious.**

THE IMAGE: What is auspicious about harmonious delight is that action is not doubted.

Strong and upright, without a correspondent, one harmonizes without imitating. This is correct delight. Because there is no selfishness, there is no doubt.

■ *2 yang:* **Sincere delight is auspicious. Regret vanishes.**

THE IMAGE: **What is auspicious about sincere delight is confidence in the aim.**

When strong and balanced, sincerity within shows outwardly. One has confidence in one's aim, and can also win the confidence of the world.

■ *3 yin:* **Coming for delight is inauspicious.**

THE IMAGE: **What is inauspicious about coming for delight is being out of place.**

If one has no inner substance, but vainly desires to act outwardly as if one did, thereby coming on to people to get their pleasure, this is sure to put relationships in disarray. This is why good people dislike the crafty.

■ *4 yang:* **Deliberating about delight, one is uneasy. If one is firm and swift, there will be happiness.**

THE IMAGE: **The happiness of the fourth yang is celebration.**

Delight is only beneficial if correct. The delight gotten from coming on to people is not worth caring about; if you cannot bear to give it up, then your mind will surely be uneasy. Only if you are firm and independently decisive, swift and unhesitating, will you have happiness. If high officials are not influenced by flatterers, then everyone in the country will have reason to celebrate; it won't be the happiness of one person alone.

■ *5 yang:* **There is inspiration in sincerity toward the fallen.**

THE IMAGE: **Being sincere toward the fallen, the position is indeed appropriate.**

This represents one with positive strength balanced and correct, whose sincerity within shows outside, developed to the highest degree. Thus one can exercise sincerity not only toward good people, but even toward people who have fallen from the right way, getting them to change their evil ways and follow what is good, to turn away from error and return to rectitude; so there is inspiration therein. Once one has the qualities and also has the position, one's influence can be this great.

■ *Top yin:* **Induced delight.**

THE IMAGE: **Induced delight is not enlightened.**

This represents being insubstantial and only hoping to draw people in by pleasing them. Thus the mental state is not clear.

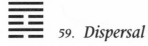

59. *Dispersal*

water below, *wind* above

Dispersal is successful. The king goes to his ancestral shrine. The benefit crosses great rivers. It is beneficial if correct.

To be joyful and then disperse the joy means to share the joy impartially with the world and not enjoy the happiness alone; therefore this dispersal is successful. Once the ruler can share happiness with the people, he can thereby please his ancestors, so "the king goes to his ancestral shrine," and he can thereby please the people of the surrounding nations, so "the benefit crosses great rivers." But joy must be in what is right; hence the warning that "it is beneficial if correct."

THE OVERALL JUDGMENT: **Dispersal is successful. Strength comes and does not become exhausted. Flexibility is in its place outwardly and assimilates above. The king goes to his ancestral shrine; the king is then in the center. The benefit crosses great rivers—riding on wood has success.**

The strength of the second yang "comes and does not become exhausted." The flexibility of the fourth yin "is in its place outwardly" and follows the fifth yang above. This is expanding the "firmness in the center and flexibility outside" indicated in the *Joy* hexagram, to disperse the joy throughout the world. How can it not be successful?

Also, the fifth yang is in the center of the upper trigram; this symbolizes the king going to his ancestral shrine and pleasing his ancestors. Riding on the wood of the *wind* trigram over the water of the *water* trigram symbolizes the certain success of pleasing the surrounding nations; correctness lies therein.

THE IMAGE: **Wind travels over the water, dispersing. Ancient kings honored God and set up shrines.**

When wind travels over water, there are waves everywhere, without exerting force. Ancient kings honored God to serve heaven and set up shrines to serve their ancestors. Their utter sincerity and devotion were able to move the world, and the waves of their gratitude reached everywhere. This is why Confucius said that one who understood the right way to honor heaven and earth, and the meaning of the ceremony in honor of the ancestors, could rule a country with the greatest of ease.

■ *First yin:* **For rescue, it is fortunate that the horse is strong.**

THE IMAGE: **The fortune of the first yin is in following.**

The first line is at the bottom of water; sensing the wind of the fourth line, it uses it for rescue. Being rescued, it emerges from water up onto land. The word for the name of the trigram *water* also means concavity; on a horse, a slightly concave back is considered beautiful. Now the first yin follows the second yang, so "the horse is strong," which is fortunate.

■ *2 yang:* **Running to support on dispersal, regret vanishes.**

THE IMAGE: **Running to support on dispersal is attaining what is wished.**

This is precisely what the judgment calls strength coming without getting exhausted. At the time of dispersal, one comes running to reliable support, resting unaffected in midstream, and attains the wish to please oneself and please others, so regret vanishes.

■ *3 yin:* **Dispersing the self, there is no regret.**

THE IMAGE: **Dispersing the self, the aim is outside.**

Here yin is on top of the body of water; the wind of the fourth yin in concert with the top yang "disperses" it in the sense that its whole being is scattered into waves to bring nourishing moisture to living beings. The aim is outside, not in oneself, so there is no regret.

■ *4 yin:* **Dispersing the group is very auspicious. On dispersal, there is assembly, inconceivable to the ordinary.**

THE IMAGE: **Dispersing the group is very auspicious—the illumination is great.**

This is what the judgment calls flexibility finding its place outside and assimilating above. Flexibility in the proper place is the main element of obedience; the fourth yin assimilates to the fifth yang above and has no corresponding partner below—it completely disperses its group to unite with the total community, so that the whole world is one family and all beings are one body. So even though there is dispersal, in reality there is assembly. Sages have no self, but there is nothing that is not their self. This is the path of illumination and true greatness, inconceivable to ordinary thought.

- *5 yang:* **Scattering sweat; the great call scatters. The king abides. There is no fault.**

THE IMAGE: **The king abides without fault; this is the right position.**

Giving out a great call to share joy with the people is like sweat coming from the center of the body and dripping over the four limbs. The point of this is that the fourth yin disperses its group because the fifth yang is the king and abides in the right position; the fourth then can assimilate and therefore gives a great call like sweat scattering outward. The king abiding in the right position is always in the center, so there is no fault.

- *Top yang:* **Scattering the blood, going far away, there is no fault.**

THE IMAGE: **Scattering the blood means avoiding harm.**

Blood here is an image of *water.* People have great afflictions because they have bodies, which they are always emotionally attached to and guard as their selves. But if we examine the body sanely, we see that it is a mass of lymph and blood, a source of harm.

The top yang uses the wind of the fourth yin to disperse the self of the third yin; the third yin can be called forgetting oneself for the sake of the country—therefore the aim is outside, and there is no regret. However, if not for the top yang putting harm at a distance, how could the third yin bring about any benefit?

To give a combined explanation of the six lines, the second yang is like a wise and good overseer who receives the current of civilizing influence and spreads it. The fourth yin is like an illustrious high official who is completely fair and impartial. The fifth yang is like a sage king who pacifies the age, sharing happiness with the populace. The top yang is like a minister of education who educates the people and removes what is harmful. The first yin thereby gets out of danger and, having gotten rid of suffering, will surely experience happiness, and so is fortunate. The third yin thereby forgets personal selfishness and, having avoided harm, will surely promote benefit, so has no regret.

60. *Regulation*

lake below, *water* above

Regulation is successful, but painful regulation is not to be held to.

Water is dispersed by wind, regulated by a lake. When it is regulated, it does not overflow and does not dry up, so it can always provide moisture; therefore regulation is successful. If dispersal is excessive, it results in exhaustion, so it is taken up with regulation; but too much regulation results in suffering, so it is not to be held to permanently.

THE OVERALL JUDGMENT: Regulation is successful. Firmness and flexibility divide, and firmness gains balance. Painful regulation is not to be held to, because that would lead to an impasse. Work through danger joyfully, take charge of the situation with discipline, get through with balance and rectitude. As heaven and earth are regulated, the four seasons take place. When laws are established with regulation, they do not damage property or injure people.

When one attains balance, one does not suffer pain. When one suffers pain, one comes to an impasse, and when one is at an impasse, one cannot deal with ordinary life. If one does not suffer pain, one is joyful, and so can also work through danger. Only by taking charge of the situation with discipline is balance and rectitude achieved; only by balance and rectitude can one get through and not come to an impasse. Nature has four seasons, kings have laws; both of these are what is referred to as getting through by balance and rectitude.

THE IMAGE: Water over a lake, regulated. Leaders establish numbers and measures, and consider virtuous conduct.

In matters of dress, architecture, music and dance, hierarchies, salary scales, and so on, there are appropriate numbers and measures, which are established to regularize them, so that there may be neither excess nor lack, neither extravagance nor restriction. Customary social relations are conducted based on virtues, considered so as to regularize them, so there is neither excess nor lack, and they can be inherited and transmitted. This is like a lake regulating water, according to the amount and depth. It is only essential to make sure that the water does not spill over or dry up.

■ *First yang:* Not leaving home, there is no fault.

THE IMAGE: Not leaving home is knowing passage and obstruction.

Regulation has many meanings, depending on the context in which it is applied.

Here, if we are talking about regulation in the sense of timing, one is strong and upright but is in a low place, and the second yang blocks one's advance; so one adapts to the time and stops, "not leaving home."

■ *2 yang:* Not going outside bodes ill.

THE IMAGE: Not going outside bodes ill, in that one misses the timing in the extreme.

In terms of timing, here one is in a position to act, and also has the qualities of strength and balance. The third yin has already opened the gate, but there is no corresponding partner above. Consequently, holding fast to petty regulation is a great loss.

■ *3 yin:* Without regulation there will be lament, but you cannot blame anyone.

THE IMAGE: Whose fault is the lament that comes from lack of regulation?

In terms of timing, this means first indulging in feelings and doing what you please, without knowing how to regulate yourself; afterward troubles come and you lament in vain. You bring fault upon yourself and cannot blame anyone else.

■ *4 yin:* Peaceful regulation is successful.

THE IMAGE: The success of peaceful regulation is in taking up the higher path.

In terms of timing, here flexibility gains correct orientation, being in the position of a high official and taking up the directives of the leader; therefore it is peaceful regulation. This is what is known as a prime minister of peace.

■ *5 yang:* Contented regulation is auspicious. To go on will result in exaltation.

THE IMAGE: **What is auspicious about contented regulation is that the position one is in is balanced.**

Here positive strength is balanced and correct, in the position of honor. This is one who manages the situation with discipline. There is neither excess nor lack, so there is contentment and a good outlook. This is carried out without anything wrong, so to go on will result in exaltation. Because one's position is balanced, one cannot be obstructed by the missed timing of others.

■ *Top yin:* **Painful regulation bodes ill if persisted in. By repenting, it is eliminated.**

THE IMAGE: **Painful regulation bodes ill if persisted in, because that path comes to an impasse.**

In terms of timing, this is weakness in a situation of extreme regulation, holding fast and not adapting. That path therefore comes to an impasse. Even if correct, it still bodes ill; one clings to it as correct, but really that is not correct. Only if one repents and changes can one avoid coming to an impasse. Since one does not come to an impasse, the bad outlook can be eliminated.

61. *Sincerity in the Center*

lake below, *wind* above

Sincerity in the center is auspicious when simple-minded. It is beneficial to cross great rivers. It is beneficial to be upright.

Because the four seasons have regularity, all beings trust them, and each attains its growth and development. Because measures and virtuous conduct have regularity, everyone in the land trusts them, and this makes them sensitively responsive.

Sincerity means sensitive response and integration; the center is the source of sensitive response and integration. Because of sensing from the center, there is response from the center, like the simple-minded, who do not set up arrangements or make deliberate calculations. When sincerity in the center can be simple-minded, it is auspicious.

But in order to reach this path, it is beneficial to cross great rivers, and it is also beneficial to be upright. Unless one crosses great rivers, one cannot achieve the ultimate fluidity to go anywhere. Unless one is upright, one cannot master ultimate constancy wherever one may be. If one does not cross great rivers, one cannot refine the mind by experience and effectively function. If one is not beneficially upright, one cannot integrate phenomena through the design of reality and establish a basis.

THE OVERALL JUDGMENT: With sincerity in the center, flexibility is within and firmness is in the center. Joyful and docile, sincerity then transforms the nation. The simple-minded are fortunate in that sincerity affects the simple-minded. It is beneficial to cross great rivers, riding on a wooden boat that is empty. Sincerity in the center with beneficial uprightness responds naturally.

If we look at the whole hexagram, the two flexible lines are inside: this stands for true obedience with an open mind, without the slightest bit of belligerent selfishness.

If we look at the hexagram divided into upper and lower parts, two firm lines are in the center: this stands for truthfulness and genuine sincerity, unadulterated by emotional desires.

The joy symbolized by the *lake* trigram moves people harmoniously; the docility symbolized by the *wind* trigram integrates with people harmoniously. Therefore the nation will be spontaneously transformed.

To say that sincerity affects the simple-minded is the same as saying that sincerity is like being simple-minded. That is because when people are clever and crafty, they mostly lose the sensitive response that comes from the subconscious, and are not as good in this respect as the simple-minded. Therefore it is necessary to be sincere in a simple-minded way before one can attain sincerity in the center.

The *wind* trigram is associated with wood and here forms a boat floating on *lake*, a body of water. The boat is empty inside, and the wood is strong; therefore it can carry anything and travel any distance. When people are flexible inside, they are like an empty boat; when their strength is in balance, they are like strong wood: then they can go through myriad ups and downs without being defeated.

Sincerity in the center is the ultimate righteousness in the world. Only by being beneficially upright can one attain sincerity in the center. This cannot be forced; it is just response to natural inherent qualities.

Observe how dolphins leap in the waves when a strong wind is about to arise. The dolphins have no intention of sensing the wind, and the wind has no intention of responding to the dolphins. It is because their minds are empty that their patterns are fulfilled.

So it is with the essence of the human mind in the immediate present: it is not inside, not outside, not in between, not in the past, not in the present, not in the future. When we look for it, we cannot grasp it—this can be called utterly empty. But for this, the sky has no way to cover; but for this, the earth has no way to support; but for this, the sun and moon have no way to shine; but for this, beings have no way to grow; but for this, sages have no way to proceed.

Comprehending things without missing anything can be called ultimate fulfillment. Emotional attachments are fundamentally empty, while the substance of mind is truly real and certainly cannot be called empty. The substance of the pattern of nature and being is fundamentally real, while appearances are the same as illusions and dreams; they cannot be called real.

Therefore flexibility and firmness are not two things, the inside and the center are not two places. Only those who know this can be called upright, can cross rivers, and can reach simplicity in sincerity, thus leading to good fortune.

THE IMAGE: **There is wind over a lake, with sincerity in the center. True leaders consider judgments and postpone execution.**

True leaders know that when people do wrong, sometimes it arises from circumstances beyond their control; if they know how the people feel, they are sympathetic and sad for them, so they consider their judgments, giving weight to the people's merits and trying to minimize their faults. When it comes to execution, they would prefer to let the wayward slip by than to kill the innocent. In this way, if one person is executed, everyone will submit and, even if executed, will not hate the executioner.

■ *First yang:* **Preparedness leads to a good outcome. If there is something else, one is not at rest.**

THE IMAGE: **The good outcome of the first yang's preparedness is because the mind is not changed.**

Developed people are wary of what they may not notice. This is setting to work before the arising of a single thought. The fundamental essence is itself the work, the work is itself the fundamental essence. Therefore one can go unrecognized and not regret it. This is what is called being obscure yet daily becoming more illustrious.

As soon as a thought arises, this is called "something else." Then the mind changes, and one is not at rest. The shameless adventurism of undeveloped people seeking a stroke of luck starts from a single thought; so it is best to be prepared at the outset.

■ *2 yang:* The calling crane is in the shade; the fledgling joins it. I have a good cup, which I will quaff with you.

THE IMAGE: The fledgling joining it is the heart's desire.

Here strength attains balance but is below two yins. This represents one who is obscure but daily becomes more illustrious. The crane calls, the fledgling joins in; the sensitive response comes from nature and involves no arrangement or forced effort. Therefore it is called the heart's desire. Here "the fledgling" does not have a specific reference; it just means someone of similar qualities in a relationship of mutual trust and sincerity.

■ *3 yin:* Finding a mate, one sometimes drums, sometimes stops, sometimes cries, sometimes sings.

THE IMAGE: Sometimes drumming, sometimes stopping, the position is not appropriate.

If we look at the whole hexagram, the third and fourth lines are what is referred to as flexibility being within. But now we are talking about each of the lines individually, in which case the third yin is not balanced or upright; originally it should correspond with the top yang, but the latter has ascended to the skies and calls alone, not paying any attention to the former. Nearby, the third yin finds the fourth yin, which is a mate of the same kind; therefore there is sometimes delight in what one has found, so "one sometimes drums," but sometimes there is resentment in the relationship, so one "sometimes stops." Sometimes one thinks of the top yang afar, so one "sometimes cries," and sometimes one temporarily enjoys the fourth yin, so one "sometimes sings." All of this is due to lack of virtuous qualities and being out of place.

■ *4 yin:* The moon is almost full. When the horse's mate disappears, there is no fault.

THE IMAGE: The horse's mate disappearing means breaking with peers to go higher.

Here flexibility is correctly oriented. This is one in whom hidden virtues are well developed, who is therefore like the moon approaching fullness. The third yin wrongly wants to be one's mate, but one must get rid of that association and rise higher to unite with universally impartial sincerity in the center, in order to be without fault.

■ *5 yang:* With sincerity that is firm, there is no fault.

THE IMAGE: With sincerity that is firm, the position is correct.

Here positive strength is balanced and correct, and is in the position of honor. With inner qualities and position in mutual accord, all the world trusts one, firm and unshakable.

However, this is just consummating the path of sincerity in the center, that is all; nothing more is added. That is why it only says there is no fault. This seems to be like the teaching that with complete fulfillment of enlightenment ultimately nothing is attained.

■ *Top yang:* A rooster ascends to the skies. Self-righteousness leads to misfortune.

THE IMAGE: How can the rooster who ascends to the skies last?

Here strength is not balanced correctly. This is one who believes in his own good name, lofty status, and intellectual views, and does not know the way of inner flexibility and balance. This is like a rooster abandoning his hen and climbing up to crow on the roof. This is already inauspicious; how much the more so if he wants to ascend to the skies, because a rooster cannot fly to the sky—people will surely think it strange and kill him, so he cannot last.

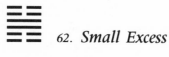

62. *Small Excess*

mountain below, *thunder* above

Small excess turns out all right. It is beneficial to be correct. It is all right for small matters, not for great matters. A flying bird leaves its cry; it should not ascend but descend— then there will be great good fortune.

When true leaders establish measures and consider virtuous conduct, they make them as regular as the four seasons, so that even ignorant people trust them. How can there be any excess in that? Only those who cannot "respond to nature" and "are uneasy because there is something else" may therefore give rise to excess.

However, when excess arises from seeking confidence, the excess is then small. When excess arises, the wise act so as to make up for imbalance and remedy defects.

In cases such as excessive deference in conduct, excessive grief in mourning, and excessive abstemiousness in consumption, there is still a need for correction. These are also examples of small excess.

When the search for confidence produces small excess, that excess can be corrected, so it turns out all right. When correcting deviations turns into small excess, that excess is wothwhile, so it turns out all right.

But it is essential to be correct. When one is correct, small excess then becomes no excess. If one is not correct, then small excess turns into great excess. Therefore, when there is small excess, one can only do small things, hoping to return to the state where there is no excess. One cannot do great things, lest unexpected problems develop.

It is like when a bird flies by, leaving its cry. It should not ascend, but rather descend: if it ascends, its cry becomes inaudible, while if it descends, its cry becomes audible. Hearing the bird's cry symbolizes hearing about one's own excesses and quickly changing; then one can return to the state where there is no excess. The excess is small, and the good fortune is then great.

THE OVERALL JUDGMENT: **Small excess is excess in small things, which turns out all right. When there is excess, it is beneficial to be correct, which means to act in accord with the time. Flexibility is in balance, so small matters have a good outcome. Firmness is out of place and not balanced, so it is not suitable for great matters. There is the image of a flying bird therein: the cry left by the flying bird should not rise but descend—then there will be great good fortune. Rising meets opposition, descending meets accord.**

Small things are small matters; when there is excess in small matters, they still do not fail to succeed. If there is excess in great things, then it is only beneficial if there is a place to go in order to succeed. Only by acting in accord with the time can one avoid losing correctness in spite of excess.

The main statement of the hexagram only speaks of correctness, while the judgment particularly points out acting in accord with the time. What this shows is that in a time when there is excess, that excess becomes the reason for correction. If one does not act in accord with the time, even if one insists on hiding oneself in the state where there is no excess, that would not be considered correct.

People have two qualities, firmness and flexibility. If they are in charge of great matters, it is appropriate to use firmness. In dealing with small matters, it is appropriate to use flexibility. Now in this hexagram, flexibility is in its proper balance. Being in balance, it can act in accord with the time; therefore, small matters turn out well. Firmness is out of place and unbalanced. Being unbalanced, it cannot act in accord with the time, so it won't do for great matters.

The two yang lines in the center of the hexagram resemble the back of a bird; on both sides are two yin lines, which resemble two unfolded wings: hence the image of a flying bird. If the bird flies upward, the wind opposes it and its cry becomes inaudible; if it flies downward, the wind goes along with it and its cry becomes audible.

THE IMAGE: **Thunder over a mountain—small excess. Genteel people are exceedingly deferential in conduct, exceedingly sad in mourning, and exceedingly abstemious in consumption.**

Deference is a remedy for arrogance; pity is a remedy for disregard; abstemiousness is a remedy for extravagance. The remedy uses excess to make up for lack, seeking only to attain equilibrium.

■ *First yin:* **The flying bird brings misfortune.**

THE IMAGE: **The flying bird brings misfortune. Nothing can be done about it.**

Here yin is not balanced correctly. It responds to the fourth yang, going upward when it should go downward. Misfortune cannot be helped.

■ *2 yin:* **Going past the grandfather, you meet the mother. Not reaching the ruler, you meet the administrator. There is no blame.**

THE IMAGE: **Not reaching the ruler—the administrator is not to be surpassed.**

If one here wants to progress upward, one must pass the "grandfather" of the fourth yin, to meet the "mother" of the fifth yin. But the two yins do not correspond, and the second yin is flexible, balanced, and upright, and is also in a state of calm, so it does not go further up to the "ruler" of the fifth yin, only meeting the "administrator" of the fourth yin. Thus we know that even though the fourth yin is an administrator, it really has virtue and certainly cannot be surpassed. The second and fourth have the same merit but different positions, so it is reasonable that they should meet.

■ *3 yang:* **One does not take precautions in excess, so pursuers attack one. This is unfortunate.**

THE IMAGE: **Pursuers attack one. How unfortunate!**

Here one is doubly strong but unbalanced, and responds to weakness above, like a bird that cannot take the lead and so instead flies off on high. Since one does not take precautions in excess, there will be pursuers attacking one—how unfortunate!

■ *4 yang:* No fault, meeting here without excess.
To go is dangerous; it is necessary to be cautious and not do it.
Always be correct.

THE IMAGE: Meeting here without excess, the position is not right. It is dangerous to go, requiring caution; after all, it cannot last.

The third yang represents people who believe that their strength is correct and consider themselves faultless; thus they do not take precautions and bring on attack. The fourth yang represents those whose position is not right and who know themselves to be at fault. The fourth corresponds with the first, thus "meeting here without excess." But only if the first comes and obeys the fourth, so that the fourth is the leader, is there then no fault. If the fourth goes and obeys the first, so that the first becomes the leader, liking to go upward and not liking to go downward, then the first is unfortunate and the fourth is in great danger too. Therefore it is necessary to be cautious and not do it. It is imperative always to maintain the correctness according to which it is not appropriate to go up but is appropriate to go down—then one can last.

■ *5 yin:* Dense clouds do not rain, coming from one's western province. The prince shoots, catching the quarry in the den.

THE IMAGE: Dense clouds do not rain—they have already risen.

Here one is weak and aberrant, with no partner below. Though one may be ruler of the land, no benefit extends to the populace. This is like clouds coming from one's western province, not raining even though they are dense. So this allows the "prince" symbolized by the fourth yin to preside over the wise people below, like one who shoots the quarry in the den, which does not require much effort. This is all because the fifth yin has already risen, violating the correctness of descending when it is inappropriate to ascend.

■ *Top yin:* Passing by without meeting—the flying birds leave.
This is unfortunate. This is called calamity.

THE IMAGE: **Passing by without meeting is because of arrogance.**

This line corresponds with the third yang below, but it is weak, and at the culmination of action, just when the bird of the first yin has taken off in flight; therefore it doesn't meet the third yang, and after all passes by. All the birds have left; leaving the group and rising alone, one eventually dies. This misfortune is because of being shot down by heaven; that is why it is called calamity. In reality, one has called the calamity down upon oneself, so it is said to be because of arrogance.

When ancient tyrants lost their countries, this was also simply because they tried to go higher when they should have lowered themselves. If they have been willing to be "exceedingly deferential in conduct, exceedingly sad in mourning, exceedingly abstemious in consumption," how would they have turned out as they did?

 63. Settled

fire below, *water* above

Settlement is successful, even in small matters. It is beneficial to be correct; otherwise there is good fortune at first but confusion in the end.

Developed people deal with things by using deference to settle arrogance, pity to settle disregard, frugality to settle extravagance. In all matters, when balance is attained, then everything is settled.

Because everything is settled, there is success, not only in great matters, but also in small matters. That is to say that everything turns out all right.

But when secure, do not forget danger; while you are alive, do not forget death; in times of order, do not forget confusion—this is a true principle that applies to all times.

Observe how a boat that does not capsize in rapids will turn over in a canal, how a horse that does not stumble on a winding mountain trail will stumble on level ground: it is not because the canal and the level ground are more dangerous than the rapids and the mountain trail; calamity always comes from failure to anticipate it. There is no greater problem than lack of preparedness.

Therefore it is always beneficial to be correct, in order to sustain success. Otherwise, on first attaining settlement, everyone considers it auspicious and thereby winds up by bringing on hopeless confusion.

This is like water being boiled to make it drinkable; if you are not careful to prevent it, the fire will get too hot and the water will all evaporate, or the water will boil over and put out the fire.

THE OVERALL JUDGMENT: **Settlement is successful; small matters succeed. It is beneficial to be correct; firmness and flexibility are correct and in their places. At first it is auspicious; flexibility gains balance. Stop in the end and there is confusion; the path reaches an impasse.**

If even small matters are successful, obviously great matters are also successful. Among the sixty-four hexagrams, only in this hexagram are the firm and flexible lines all in place; hence it is correct.

The second yin's flexibility is in proper balance, as the main element of *fire*. When this is used to treat water, the water becomes usable. Therefore at first it is auspicious. However, if you think that once everything is settled you can finally stop, you will surely bring on the "confusion" of the water boiling over to extinguish the fire, or the fire getting too hot and evaporating the water. You let either the fire go out or the water evaporate—therefore the path reaches an impasse.

THE IMAGE: **Water over fire—settled. Developed people consider problems and prevent them.**

When settlement has taken place, it seems as if there were no problems, but problems will surely come along; so developed people consider them seriously and prevent them. This is what the statement on the hexagram calls beneficial correctness.

■ *First yang:* **Dragging the wheels—it is right that there be no problem.**

All six lines indicate considering problems and preventing them. Since the hexagram stands for settlement, in the first line the settlement has already taken place. The wheels are still skidding, yet you are ready to go; the tail is still wet, yet you are ready to cross the river—this stands for not forgetting that there will be something to do, even in times when there is nothing to do, preparing for it beforehand so as not to wind up in confusion. Therefore it is right that there be no error.

■ *2 yin:* **A woman loses her protection. Let her not give chase: she will find it in seven days.**

THE IMAGE: **She will find it in seven days because of her balanced course.**

The fifth yang has positive strength balanced correctly and is in the position of the leader. The second yin responds to this with flexibility that is balanced and correct. There are sure to be petty people who will try to come between them and steal her protection, but the second yin is on a balanced course and therefore remains calm and does not give chase. Only by not giving chase does she spontaneously find it in seven days; if she gave chase, she would lose balance and not find it. The words "let her not give chase" indicate a subtle way of considering problems and preventing them.

■ *3 yang:* **The emperor attacks barbarians and conquers them after three years. Do not employ inferior people.**

THE IMAGE: **Conquering them after three years, he is weary.**

This is firm strength at the peak of clarity, the image of the emperor attacking barbarians. However, it takes three years to conquer them; it is very fatiguing, and even more so for those who are not so strong and clear-minded. It is even worse if inferior people are employed, ruining the military, destroying the people, and plundering the nation. How can one but consider these problems so as to prevent them?

■ *4 yin:* **There are rags in fine cloth—be alert all the time.**

THE IMAGE: **Being alert all the time, there is doubt.**

Fine cloth eventually turns into rags; can we afford not to be alert? "Doubt" means the thought taken to consider problems and prevent them.

■ *5 yang:* **The slaughtering of the ox in the neighborhood to the east is not as good as the ceremony in the neighborhood to the west. The genuine get the blessings.**

THE IMAGE: **The slaughtering of the ox in the neighborhood to the east is not as good as the timing of the neighborhood to the west. The genuine get the blessings—good fortune comes in great measure.**

Fire is east, *water* is west. The lower trigram fully exerts the function of the illumination of *fire* to achieve settlement; this is like slaughtering an ox. The fifth yang, with the strong and upright genuine virtue in the center of *water*, receives it as an offering, without expending any effort, like performing a ceremony.

Even if one has the virtue, without the proper timing it is impossible to accomplish this; even if one has the timing, if one does not have genuine virtue, it is still not possible to accomplish this. The meaning of considering problems and preventing them here lies in sincerity, and is not seen in material things.

■ *Top yin:* **Getting the head wet is dangerous.**

THE IMAGE: **Getting the head wet, how can one last long?**

This is weakness in extreme danger, at the end of settlement. This is what was referred to as final stopping leading to confusion; this is one who is unable to consider problems and prevent them. It is like crossing a river and getting in over one's head—is it not dangerous?

64. Unsettled

water below, *fire* above

Being unsettled leads to success. A little fox, almost crossing, gets its tail wet. Nothing is gained.

Since there is settlement, there must be a condition of being unsettled, because there is basically no end to things. Since there is a state of being unsettled, there must be settlement, because settlement originally derives from settling what was unsettled. Therefore there is a path to success therein.

But if one wants to settle what is unsettled, this requires maturity, decisiveness, and consistency from beginning to end. If one is like a little fox about to cross a river holding back when it gets its tail wet, then nothing is gained.

THE OVERALL JUDGMENT: **Being unsettled leads to success, insofar as flexibility is in balance. The little fox about to cross has not yet gotten out. Getting its tail wet, it gains nothing, in that it does not continue to the end. Although out of place, the firm and the flexible correspond.**

The flexibility indicated by the fifth yin is in balance; this represents one who is mature and decisive, consistent from beginning to end. "Not yet gotten out" means not yet out of danger. At this time, properly relying on mature and decisive ability and perceptivity, this spirit of continuity from start to finish, one will not be like the little fox who does not continue to the end. Although they are not in their proper places, firmness and flexibility correspond; this is why a state of being unsettled can lead to success.

THE IMAGE: Fire over water—unsettled. Developed people carefully discern things and keep them in their places.

The natures of things must be discerned, and they must be put in their appropriate places; therefore developed people are careful about this. For example, the nature of fire is to flame upward, and the nature of water is to flow downward; these are things that must be distinguished. When fire flames up, it rises, whereas it should be below water to balance it. When water flows down, it descends, whereas it should rise to balance fire. This is an example of how things should be put in their places.

Water can control fire, and it can also extinguish fire; fire can balance water, and it can also evaporate water. Also, water and fire can nurture people, and they can also kill people. This one example can stand for all things, showing how it is necessary to distinguish with precision and clarity, to assess their proper places.

- *First yin:* Getting the tail wet is humiliating.

THE IMAGE: Getting the tail wet, one still does not know the limit.

Here one is weak and in a low position, with nothing to balance worldly cleverness, about to end up in an unsettled condition; this is shameful. Would one who knows that the momentum of the time is at an end be so stubborn and contemptuous as to pretend to power?

- *2 yang:* Dragging the wheels, rectitude is auspicious.

THE IMAGE: The good outlook of the rectitude of the second yang is because its activity is balanced.

Being strong but not excessive, thereby proceeding while dragging the wheels, is the right way to go on attaining settlement. Because of being centered, one can act correctly and see that balance and rectitude are not two principles.

- *3 yin:* While unsettled, it bodes ill to go on an expedition, but it is beneficial to cross great rivers.

THE IMAGE: It bodes ill to go on an expedition while unsettled, because the position is inappropriate.

Here yin is not balanced correctly; both ability and virtue are inferior, so it bodes ill to proceed. However, it is about time to get out of danger; if one can ride a boat across great rivers, not vainly relying on one's own power, then danger can be resolved.

■ *4 yang:* **Correctness brings good results; regret vanishes.**
Vigorously acting to conquer barbarians, in three years one
has the reward of a great country.

THE IMAGE: Correctness brings good results; regret vanishes.
The aim is carried out.

When strong but not excessive, one is like the sun rising, attaining the virtue, ability, and position appropriate to the time of settlement. Therefore correctness brings good results and regret vanishes. When one activates the function of great illumination and conquers the "barbarians" of ignorance, in "three years" the work is accomplished, so there will be the reward of a great country. At the time of settlement, the aim one cherished in seclusion can be carried out.

■ *5 yin:* **Correctness brings good results; regret vanishes.**
The illumination of developed people has truthfulness and
leads to good results.

THE IMAGE: **The radiance of the illumination of developed**
people leads to good results.

Here flexibility in balance, the main element of illumination, is in the position of leadership; this is fundamentally correct, fundamentally without regret. This is the illumination of developed people. This also stands for opening oneself to be honest with the second yang, so that the illumination of both mutually reflects; the whole world looks up to this, and it surely leads to good results.

■ *Top yang:* **There is sincerity in drinking wine, without fault.**
But if one becomes totally immersed, having faith ceases to be
right.

THE IMAGE: **Becoming totally immersed in drinking wine is**
also not knowing proper measure.

The truthfulness leading to good results in the fifth yin is the settlement of the world; therefore the top yang preserves what has been accomplished, and has sincerity in drinking wine—this is sharing pleasure with the people, a course of action that is blameless.

But the way developed people relate to the world is that they do not forget danger when secure, they do not forget death while alive, and they do not forget disorder in times of order; if they gave themselves up entirely to enjoying the pleasures of peace, and had no sense of striving and caution, that would be like becoming immersed in drinking wine. I am sure they would certainly lose the happiness of the present, because they did not know proper measure.

Proper measure is like the four seasons of nature, which cannot exceed their bounds. This is also called the limit. The weakness of the first yin is that doubt is excessive; so it is referred to as still not knowing the limit. The adamancy of the top yang is that faith is excessive; so it is referred to as not knowing proper measure.

Knowing limits and knowing proper measure, the unsettled can be settled, and having attained settlement, the settled can be preserved.

Key for Identifying the Hexagrams

TRIGRAMS UPPER ▶ / LOWER ◀	Ch'ien ☰	Chên ☳	K'an ☵	Kên ☶	K'un ☷	Sun ☴	Li ☲	Tui ☱
Chi'en ☰	1	34	5	26	11	9	14	43
Chên ☳	25	51	3	27	24	42	21	17
K'an ☵	6	40	29	4	7	59	64	47
Kên ☶	33	62	39	52	15	53	56	31
K'un ☷	12	16	8	23	2	20	35	45
Sun ☴	44	32	48	18	46	57	50	28
Li ☲	13	55	63	22	36	37	30	49
Tui ☱	10	54	60	41	19	61	38	58

The Shambhala Dictionary of Buddhism and Zen. Translated by Michael H. Kohn.

The Spiritual Teaching of Ramana Maharshi, by Ramana Maharshi. Foreword by C. G. Jung.

Start Where You Are: A Guide to Compassionate Living, by Pema Chödrön.

The Sutra of Hui-neng, Grand Master of Zen: With Hui-neng's Commentary on the Diamond Sutra. Translated by Thomas Cleary.

Tao Teh Ching, by Lao Tzu. Translated by John C. H. Wu.

Teachings of the Buddha, revised and expanded edition. Edited by Jack Kornfield.

Vitality, Energy, Spirit: A Taoist Sourcebook. Translated and edited by Thomas Cleary.

The Way of the Bodhisattva: A Translation of the Bodhicharyavatara. Translated by the Padmakara Translation Group.

Wen-tzu: Understanding the Mysteries, by Lao-tzu. Translated by Thomas Cleary.

Zen Essence: The Science of Freedom. Translated and edited by Thomas Cleary.